Please renew/return this item by the last date shown.

So that your telephone call is charged at local rate, please call the numbers as set out below:

	From Area codes 01923 or 0208:	From the rest of Herts:
Renewals:	01923 471373	01438 737373
Enquiries:	01923 471333	01438 737333
Minicom:	01923 471599	01438 737599

L32b

FOOD WITH THE FAMOUS

Also by Jane Grigson

CHARCUTERIE AND FRENCH PORK COOKERY

GOOD THINGS

FISH COOKERY

ENGLISH FOOD

THE MUSHROOM FEAST

JANE GRIGSON'S VEGETABLE BOOK

JANE GRIGSON

FOOD
WITH THE
FAMOUS

MICHAEL JOSEPH: LONDON

First published in Great Britain by
Michael Joseph Limited
44 Bedford Square
London W.C.1.

©1979 by Jane Grigson

ISBN 07181 1855 3

Printed in Great Britain by
Hollen Street Press Ltd at Slough, Berkshire

For Anthony Ellis
who thought of the idea

CONTENTS

ILLUSTRATIONS

Introduction & acknowledgements

When we were talking about a new subject for cookery articles in the *Observer Magazine* in 1978, Anthony Ellis suggested that I take a number of famous people who liked eating for their favourite dishes. That week a reader Nottinghamshire, had written to me asking w meant, in *Pride and Prejudice,* by white soup. T few days, I had an absorbing subject *and* the sta first article. From a selfish point of view this has have most enjoyed writing, in eleven years at t excuse to re-read favourite novels, look again at f visit places associated with them, spend hours in collections of letters and in journals, study early cookery books in the Bodleian Library and buy more than I could really afford, gave me a chance of relating cookery to life beyond the kitchen. Which is what, in the end, I think cookery should do.

To start with, I was surprised all over again at the realisation of how puritan the English, in particular, have always been about food. Dickens apart, who is allowed his cowheel and tripe and Christmas goose, writers and painters should, we feel, be above such things. High artistry = plain living. Though if you think about it further, such talents should be more sensitive to the pleasures of life than most. When I looked in economic and social histories, purporting to deal with daily life, I found that food occupied a very tiny section of the index. When I looked at paintings, confidently expecting to turn up banquets and abundantly provided kitchens and markets, still life paintings of fruit and vegetables, I came up with little more than John Gay and his sisters drinking tea, and a Rowlandson kitchen that was stronger on personalities than provisions. With the French, the joys of food and cooking and dining are so wonderfully attended to, that it was difficult to know who to choose, where to begin.

In saying this, I do not mean to imply that the English have never enjoyed cooking and eating. They have – and they do – but they are not prepared to concede how important a place they occupy in our lives and affections. It seems almost gross to acknowledge that Jane Austen fancied herself as a housekeeper, that she enjoyed experimenting with new things, and that she attributed her success to the fact that she always took care to provide what she liked eating best. But once her earthy competence and concern are acknowledged, her novels, *Emma* in particular, become richer in enjoyment. In her delicate, witty way, she uses supper at Hartfield, strawberry picking at Donnithorne Abbey, a conducted tour round the model kitchens at Northanger Abbey to make subtle comments, amusing comments, about the main characters.

In this I do not think she was as emphatic as Zola, who wrote scenes in some of his novels as if his nose were twitching at the smells creeping down the corridor from the kitchen into the study. For him, food and feasts have much to say about the plot and settings: he uses them to give the tone of a scene, to emphasize qualities in his characters, or to indicate what their destiny might be.

Once I began to read diaries, letters, novels, journals, biographies, memoirs, and – in the case of the French – look at paintings, I was surprised at how much material there was. Occasionally there were extra bits of luck. For instance the publication of extracts from a manuscript receipt book kept by Jane Austen's friend, Martha Lloyd; she lived with the family for years and recorded their dishes, wrote down recipes from relations and friends, and eventually married one of the Austen brothers. For the Jefferson and Sydney Smith material, I found that both men had bought copies of famous cookery books of the day so that they could enjoy at home in America and in England some of the delicious things they had eaten in France, Holland or Italy.

With Zola, it was not difficult from the grouping and choice of dishes to see what contemporary cookery books he had been reading. And with Proust, it was easier still. In the early books of *A la recherche de temps perdu*, there is much loving description of the food provided by Françoise at Combray and then in Paris. Now Combray is really the town of Illiers, near Chartres. It lies on the Loir, in those parts a narrow if vigorous stream: we know it well further down, in our small village of Trôo. On re-reading Proust's novel, I recognized instantly the atmosphere of cooking and sociable meals in that favoured part of France. The gentle atmosphere of good things, tables spread out of doors under lime trees in the summer weeks, the geniality and homely grace of life in that river valley. When Proust imprisoned himself to write his great novel, he barely ate at all, subsisting on milk in the main; he almost seemed to live on his memories of the meals prepared by Françoise when she showered the visiting family with the riches of the Loir.

My one failure, a great disappointment, was with Monet. A receipt book was kept by his second wife and step-daughters, and it survives. But it has not been published, nor will his wife's descendants permit anyone to see it. So the Monet chapter is based on descriptions of visits to his house by friends and family, on his paintings, and known preferences. At Giverny, his hospitality at midday was famous, the food superb. Above all things, I should like to have sat in the yellow dining-room, waiting for the next course to come through from the blue and white-tiled kitchen, watching the roses outside move in the light, contemplating a saunter down to the water-lily garden after coffee had been served, and listening to Monet's vigorous and good-humoured conversation.

John Evelyn had to be there in the book, as one of the founding fathers of the English garden, and the man who more than any other was responsible for the greening of England with trees, to clothe its bare countryside. In practical terms he enlarged our vegetable gardens by promoting new and improved food plants from abroad, he drew up a scheme of planting so that a green salad could be put on the table every day of the year. In his book on salads, *Acetaria*, he gives a good number of vegetable recipes, and writes rhapsodic paragraphs on olive oil and the picking and dressing of salads. From his journal, too, there were hints to be found of the dishes he liked.

The most hospitable of my subjects were Jefferson and Dumas. Jefferson was a great gardener in the Evelyn tradition, trying every new vegetable he could, and a great civiliser. Dumas was a splendid cook, and loved food enough to devote his last years to a huge food dictionary, which is more of an anthology of the things he loved and knew about and had experienced on his travels. Both men spent fortunes on the table. Often they did not even know the

names of all their guests, so any of us might have wandered into
Monticello at dinner-time, or joined a party at Dumas's house
without any difficulty.

Like Jefferson, Sydney Smith once remarked that he was more
of an inn-keeper than anything else, but he would certainly have
known exactly who was sitting round his table. The particular
pleasure of dining with Sydney Smith, whether at his own home or
at somebody else's house, was that he had the gift of turning the
whole evening into a delight. People did remember what he said,
and took trouble to write it down sometimes, but even more they
remembered the happiness of his company and the way everyone
seemed to sparkle in his kindness and wit. Now that Saint George
has been removed from credibility, I would propose Sydney Smith
as the secular patron saint of England. He had the best qualities
that a human being can have – including an appreciation of good
food and wine.

Parson Woodforde was not so distinguished a cleric as Sydney
Smith, but he kept a record of almost everything he ate over a
period of more than twenty-five years. He kept a record of much
else, too, so that the fuller version of extracts from his diary reads
at times like a novel. Unfortunately this meticulous listing of
dinners and family meals has led many people, especially the more
puritan English, to dismiss him as a greedy pig and little else. They
speak of him with disgust, instead of falling on their knees with
gratitude. I wonder if anywhere else in Europe, anyone has kept so
lively and detailed an account of what they ate day by day? Or
anywhere else in the world? A superior tone of distaste comes
partly from ignorance – in the eighteenth century, as in the past,
company to dinner meant a fine display of dishes. A lot of dishes.
This did not mean that everyone ate everything. Ten people to
dinner did not expect every item to provide a helping for them all.
We are used to dinners of three dishes, i.e. ten avocado halves, ten
steaks, ten trifles, and judge Parson Woodforde's dinner parties on
that kind of scale.

Oddly enough, I have noticed in French restaurants these days,
especially those that go in for the nouvelle cuisine, a tendency to
offer the clients small helpings of three or four dishes from each
course. When the whole table of four people chooses to do this, you
have the chance of tasting almost everything on the menu. But at

the end of the meal, you have not eaten very much – probably you have eaten less than you do in a three- or four-course meal establishment, where they pile food on to your plate. This new style of serving dinner depends on a large kitchen staff, cooking for a fair number of people – something in the style of a comfortable rectory or manor house in Parson Woodforde's day, but quite impossible for most of us at home, in present conditions.

The only ones in the book who may seem a little out of my general scheme are the Shaftesburys. I was given Lady Shaftesbury's household receipt book, and found it so interesting to study, vis-à-vis their remarkable lives, that they had to be included. And it is cheering to find out that a great evangelical and social reformer at least had a wife who appreciated delicious things, and made sure that he enjoyed his meals even if they had little money to spend on the major luxuries of nineteenth-century eating.

One thing I had not expected was to find that the dishes my eleven people liked so much, would be thoroughly enjoyable today – just as their novels or wit or paintings or achievements give us pleasure still. I had thought that quite a high proportion would not appeal to modern tastes; I should have known better. The recipes have been altered as little as possible. No major liberties have been taken. This seemed essential. After all, the difference in my lifetime between the realities behind *chicken* or *celery* is marked enough; though perhaps the maize-fed farmyard chicken, the winter garden celery, of the days before the mass production of so much of our food, is closer to Evelyn's experience three centuries ago, than it is to frozen battery chicken and tasteless summer celery. To have made greater changes would not have been an improvement; moreover, it would have invalidated the whole basis of the book, which is to give people a chance to share the meals that some famous men and women of the past have found delightful.

The book is arranged in chronological order of birth – giving the advantage of a progress and development in the style of cookery – except for Jane Austen, whom I have taken back to follow Parson Woodforde. Their rectory lives had much in common, although they were a generation apart; Jane Austen's desire for unusual dishes and experiment was necessarily limited by the foods available to her, so that in the end she and her family ate things that would not have shocked Parson Woodforde with his more limited view of what was properly English.

Jefferson, Sydney Smith and the Shaftesburys had the chance to travel and live abroad; they were all delighted with many of the dishes they ate in France, Germany, Holland and Switzerland. And said so. They make a natural progression to the last four people in the book, who all enjoyed different aspects of the marvellous food that was to be found in France, their own country, during the nineteenth and early twentieth centuries.

Acknowledgements

Debts of assistance from colleagues and their books have been acknowledged in the main text of the book. Geoffrey Grigson went on journeys, helped me particularly with gardening and botanical information, flagged references, and ate his way through the book. Robert Gordon and Jean Sébastien Stehli shared their time and knowledge with me generously on a visit to Monet's Giverny. Mr and Mrs A. R. Read, who are restoring Sydney Smith's rectory at Combe Florey, showed the house from front door to attic, to two complete strangers, and answered many questions. Others who helped include: Miss G. Allix Joan Bailey of the London Library; Alan Bell whose biography of Sydney Smith will be published by Oxford University Press; Paul Bailey; Sue and Paul de Brantes; Anne and Mark Cherniavsky; Caroline Davidson; Mimi Errington; Richard Hatchwell; Sarah Howell; Elizabeth Jenkins and the Jane Austen Society; John Murray; A. R. Paske; Patricia Payne; W. J. Stallings, jnr, of Bethesda, Maryland, provided me with much information on the early history of ices; William Tullberg; Dr and Madame Vettier.

Quantities

Most of the dishes in this book are for 6 to 8 people. Ingredients are given in metric and imperial weights: follow one or the other consistently in each recipe.

John Evelyn (1620–1706)

John Evelyn was a Royalist who was abroad for the early years of the Commonwealth. In 1652 he took over Sayes Court in Deptford from his father-in-law, and lived quietly there until the Restoration, and for many years afterwards until he returned to the family home at Wotton, in Surrey where he died in 1706. He liked food, gardening, trees, pictures and science (he was a founder member of the Royal Society, with Kenelm Digby, Christopher Wren, Robert Boyle, Isaac Newton among others). During his years of travel, then of exile, he spent much time in Holland, Italy and above all France, visiting gardens and learning about all the vegetables and fruit which were newly grown or more skilfully cultivated in other countries.

He gave a great fillip to English gardening by translating the best French books of the day. First Bonnefons' *The French Gardener*, and later *The Compleat Gardener* by de la Quintinie, who worked for the Sun King, and who was the greatest expert in France on fruit growing and gardens (he visited England, and corresponded with some of the best gardeners here). From Evelyn, less distinguished people – country squires, parsons and rectors, housewives – acquired knowledge of new vegetables and kinds of vegetables.

He helped to alter the whole look of England by encouraging the planting of its then rather bare landscape with trees of every kind. Avenues of trees are something we owe to him. If England looks like a park, Evelyn was the first man responsible. He had a vision of translating England into an Earthly Paradise. Everything that people could do by way of gardening and forestry elsewhere, could, he felt, be done even better in this country. To his great scheme that he was never able to complete he gave the name of *Elysium Britanicum*.

This noticing, innovating man with a long sad face and sober mind has left us the first account of coffee drinking in England, having met a fellow student at Oxford, a Greek from Crete, brew-

ing coffee in Balliol in 1637. Coffee houses started in London twenty years and more later. In Italy, he described in his journal the smell of Parmesan, salami and botargo (compacted grey mullet roe, much appreciated as a stimulus to thirst) in the hot streets of Bologna. That still seems to me a characteristic smell of Italy, its midday smell in summer.

Evelyn was also much concerned with two major innovations in the preparation of food. First the ice-house, then the pressure-cooker. Charles II seems to have been the initiator, with an ice-house in St James's Park like the ones he had seen in exile abroad. It was celebrated in verse by Evelyn's friend and early travelling companion, the poet Edmund Waller:

> Yonder the harvest of cold months laid up,
> Gives a fresh coolness to the royal cup,
> There ice, like crystal, firm and never lost,
> Tempers hot July with December's frost.

And Evelyn himself was among the first to mention ice-houses – in print, at any rate, in one of the headings for the intended chapters of his *Elysium*:

> Of rocks, grots, cryptae, mounts, precipices,
> ventiducts, conservatories of ice and snow, and other
> hortulan refreshments.

The pressure-cooker was invented by Denis Papin, a refugee from French Huguenot persecution. He was a member of the Royal Society and described his new machine and demonstrated it at their meetings. Evelyn has left a fine account of the meal that they all ate, entirely cooked with the Digester as it was called until modern times. 'This Philosophical Supper raised much mirth amongst us, and exceedingly pleased all the company.' Obviously a more light-hearted occasion than the meetings at which Boyle or Newton or Wren spoke of their great discoveries.

CHILLED MELON SOUP

Why choose melon soup? My excuse is that Evelyn had a partiality for melons. He commented on their unsuccessful cultivation in England 'so as to bring them to maturity, until Sir Geo. Gardner came out of Spain. I myself remembering, when an ordinary melon would have been sold for five or six shillings.' He was proud too, when translating Jean de la Quintinie, to have been able to include in *The Compleat Gardener* a section on raising melons which was not in French editions. In the earlier Bonnefons' translation of *The French Gardener*, there was a description of a hedged and locked enclosure for growing melons; this was 'particularly to keep out women-kind at certain times, for reasons you may imagine'. A superstition that lingered on in France until the 1960s, though – in my experience at least – confined to elderly mushroom growers in the caves of the Loir. The idea that menstruating women can damage certain crops goes right back to the Romans and Pliny.

You may use any kind of melon, so long as it is ripe. I have the feeling that honeydews are the least successful, as they have less taste than the others.

> 750 ml (1¼ pt) water
> 250 g (8 oz) sugar
> ¾–1 kilo (1½–2 lb) melon pulp, minus seeds, peel, etc.
> 300 ml (10 fl oz) dry white wine
> 200 ml (7 fl oz) soured cream
> juice of a lemon
> nutmeg or cinnamon

Bring water and sugar to the boil, stirring to dissolve the sugar. Leave to simmer for 5 minutes. Cool. Liquidise or sieve melon pulp, mix in the wine and then syrup to taste – if the melon is very sweet, use less syrup and add extra water. The flavour should be natural and refreshing. Stir in the cream, then the lemon juice to taste. Just before serving sprinkle the top of the well-chilled soup with nutmeg or cinnamon. If you have used one very large melon, and removed the pulp carefully from the shell, it can serve as a soup dish; cut the top into Van Dyck points, and stand it in a bowl of bay leaves.

Note Slices of melon served early in the meal, after the soup for instance, did not come in until the 1860s. Until then, it had been either a dessert fruit, or a main-course fruit vegetable, perhaps with a forcemeat and chicken stuffing.

THE GRAND SALAD

The perfect first course for a dinner in honour of Evelyn, or as the main course for a summer meal. It goes far beyond the green salad. Best to keep in your mind the better Scandinavian cold tables (not those encountered on Channel ferries to France) or an elaborated *mezze* in Greece and Cyprus.

Sometimes the different ingredients were layered up into a pyramid or cone on a large serving dish: if the cook had little skill, a larder full of left-overs and no eye for colour, this version must have been disgusting. Few people these days like their food messed up together in this way, and I would advise following the second version – the major items would be piled on a central dish with a low pedestal, surrounded by small bowls full of extra delights for people to choose what they liked.

The essential thing, for Evelyn at any rate, is a fine head of celery. It was a new vegetable from Italy via France (boring chauvinists classed it with other 'French kickshaws' such as champagne, ragoûts, fricassés, cultivated mushrooms and frogs' legs), which 'for its high and grateful taste is ever placed in the middle of the Grand Salad . . . as the grace of the whole board.' You will have to stand the stalks in a pot in the centre of the dish, so that you can mound up slices of chicken, tongue and salami, on a bed of shredded lettuce, to conceal it.

Choose from among the following for the little bowls, dressing items as appropriate with vinaigrette and herbs, hard-boiled egg etc (p. 23): sliced raw fennel, watercress, mustard and cress, cooked beetroot, sliced sweet onion or spring onion, orange and lemon seedlings or seed and bean sprouts, cooked peas, diced cooked new potatoes, tiny artichokes (p. 29), olives, capers, gherkins, cucumber, raisins, almonds, fresh figs, melon dice. Parma ham, cooked ham, various French and German and Italian sausages, pickled fish and cured fish (smoked salmon to sweet pickled herring), anchovies, sardines or brisling, fish roes from botargo, caviar, taramasalata or creamed cod's roe, to fried soft roes or cod's roe and bacon dressed while still warm with vinaigrette. Pickled walnuts would be an especially English detail, so would spiced quinces or pears, or the fruitier chutneys (some cooks tried to imitate mango chutney with melon), as well as pickled mushrooms and cauliflower.

There is such a choice to be made from store-cupboard, refrigerator, garden and delicatessen, that I would only say one thing – be discreet. If you are feeling extravagant, put your money into quality rather than quantity.

EVELYN ON VEGETABLES

Asparagus – 'Speedily boiled, as not to lose the verdure and agreeable tenderness; which is done by letting the water boil before you put them in. I do not esteem the Dutch great and larger sort . . . so sweet and agreeable as those of a moderate size.'

Beetroot – 'Martial . . . names it indeed – *Fabrorum prandia* for its being so vulgar. But eaten with oil and vinegar, as usually, it is no despicable salad . . . pared into thin slices and circles, are by the French and Italians contrived into curious figures to adorn their salads.'

Purple sprouting broccoli etc – 'Sprouts rather of the cole' are 'very delicate, so boiled as to retain their verdure and green colour.'

Root chervil – 'Boiled and eaten cold . . . This (as likewise spinach) is used in tarts, and serves alone for divers sauces.' See recipe for spinach tart later on.

Corn salad or lamb's salad – 'The French call them *salade de preter,* for their being generally eaten in Lent.' Corn salad is indeed useful in the New Year, its soft green leaves blending well with beetroot, hard-boiled egg crumbled, and little cubes of fat bacon fried and added while hot; in Paris in January and February, corn salad is used as an edible green garnish for many meat and fish dishes.

Fennel – 'The stalks are to be peeled when young and then dressed like celery. The tender tufts and leaves emerging, being minced, are eaten alone with vinegar, or oil, and pepper' – in other words, fennel could be eaten as part of the Grand Salad, or at the dessert stage, along with fruit and nuts.

Leeks – 'The Welsh, who eat them much, are observed to be very fruitful: they are also friendly to the lungs and stomach, being sod' – i.e. stewed – 'in milk: a few therefore of the slender and green summities, a little shred, do not come amiss in composition' of salads.

Mustard, in the mustard and cress sense – "So necessary an ingredient to all cold and raw salading, that it is very rarely, if at all, to be left out.'

Onions – The best 'are brought out of Spain, whence they of St Omer had them, and some that have weighed eight pounds'. Use raw in salads, they are not so hot as garlic. 'An honest laborious countryman, with good bread, salt, and a little parsley, will make a contented meal with a roasted onion.'

Orange seedlings – 'Impart an aromatic exceedingly grateful to the stomach'. Sow orange – or lemon, – pips a centimetre down in good potting soil. Put a tall plastic bag over the pot, with a rubber band. Leave in a dark warm place, and keep the soil moist. Shoots appear 7–14 days later, and can be cut and scattered over salads like mustard and cress or other seed sprouts.

Parsnip – Cook and dress while still warm with oil and vinegar. Robert May, who published his popular *Accomplisht Cook* in 1665, recommends putting some 'small salad or watercresses and lettuce' with the parsnips.
– Evelyn's recipe for hot parsnip: 'There is made a mash or pomade of this root, being boiled very tender, with a little fresh cream; and being heated again, put to it some butter, a little sugar, and juice of lemon; dish it upon sippets; sometimes a few currants are added.'
– another delicious way, was to boil and cut the parsnips in slices across, then to finish them slowly in butter, scattering on a little cinnamon sugar, and serving a bowl of it for people to help themselves to more: cinnamon sugar is made by mixing a teaspoon of cinnamon with a tablespoon of sugar.

Salad burnet, or *pimprinelle* to the French, *Poterium sanguisorba* – Once a common salad plant. Evelyn quotes an Italian tag:

> *L'insalata non è buon, ne bella*
> *Ove non è la Pimpinella.*

Salsify – 'Excellent even in salad, and very nutritive.' Peel and drop it into acidulated water (2 tablespoons malt vinegar to a litre of water), then simmer in salted water with a squeeze of lemon juice until cooked. Finish in butter with a little cream and parsley, or dress while warm with an olive oil vinaigrette and herbs and leave to cool.

Scorzonera – 'A more excellent root there is hardly growing.' Yes, indeed. Treat like salsify.

EVELYN'S GREEN SALAD

The garden at Sayes Court was organised so that a mixed green salad could be put on the table every day of the year. A calendar was drawn up for the gardener's benefit, which was published in 1664 and went into ten editions. Special 'light and neatly made withy-Dutch-baskets, divided into several partitions' were provided for the salad-gatherers. The greenery was to be rinsed with spring water, drained in a colander and finally swung 'altogether gently in a clean coarse napkin'.

The different elements of greenery should 'fall into their places, like the notes in music, in which there should be nothing harsh or grating'. He had read Milton's description of Eve making a salad for her angelical guest:

> What choice to choose, for delicacy best,
> What order so contriv'd, as not to mix
> Tastes not well join'd, inelegant, but bring
> Taste after taste, upheld by kindliest change.

The dressing was to be made from the best oil 'of a pallid olive green . . . smooth, light and pleasant upon the tongue; such as the geniune omphacine and native Lucca olives afford', the 'best of the best wine vinegar' perhaps impregnated with herbs or flowers, with lemon or orange juice (Seville) as alternatives. Salt must be dry, 'the brightest Bay grey-salt', the pepper 'not bruised to too small a dust'. Extras might include sugar – 'if perfectly refined', the best Tewkesbury mustard, a little grated horseradish and the yolks of hard-boiled eggs (additions typical of French corn-salad mixtures).

JOHN EVELYN

(left margin, vertical) IX. Blanched.

SPECIES	ORDERING AND CULTURE
1. *Endive*	Tied up to blanch
2. *Chicory*	
3. *Celery*	Earthed-up
4. *Sweet Fennel*	
5. *Rampions*	
6. *Roman** ⎫	Tied up to blanch
7. *Cos* ⎬ Lettuce	
8. *Silesian** ⎭	Tied close up
9. *Cabbage*	Pome and blanch themselves
10. *Lob-lettuce**	Leaves, all of a middling size
11. *Corn-Sallet*	
12. *Purslane*	
13. *Cresses,* broad	Seed-leaves, and the next to them.
14. *Spinach,* curled	
15. *Sorrel,* French	The fine young leaves only, with the first shoots
16. *Sorrel,* Greenland	
17. *Radish*	Only the tender young leaves
18. *Cresses*	The seed-leaves, and those only next to them
19. *Turnip*	
20. *Mustard*	
21. *Scurvy-grass*	The seed-leaves only
22. *Chervil*	
23. *Burnet*	The young leaves immediately after the seedlings
24. *Rocket,* Spanish	
25. *Parsley*	
26. *Tarragon*	The tender shoots and tops
27. *Mints*	
28. *Sampier*†	
29. *Balm*	The young tender leaves and shoots
30. *Sage,* Red	
31. *Shallots*	
32. *Chives* and *Onion*	The tender young leaves
33. *Nasturtium,* Indian	The flowers and flower-buds
34. *Rampion,* Belgrade	The seed-leaves and young tops
35. *Trip-Madame*‡	

MONTH	ORDERING AND CULTURE	SPECIES
January	Blanched as before	*Rampions*, *Endive*, *Succory*, *Fennel*, sweet, *Celery*
February and *March*	Green and unblanched	*Lamb-Lettuce*, *Lob-Lettuce**, *Radish*, *Cresses*, *Turnips*, *Mustard* seedlings, *Scurvy-grass*, *Spinach*, *Sorrel*, Greenland, *Sorrel*, French, *Chervil*, sweet, *Burnet*, *Rocket*, *Tarragon*, *Balm*, *Mint*, *Sampier*, *Shallots*, *Chives*, *Cabbage*-Winter
April *May*	Blanched	*Lop**, *Silesian** Winter, *Roman**Winter ⎬ Lettuce; *Radishes*
	Green herbs unblanched	*Cresses*, *Purselan*, *Sorrel*, French, *Sampier*

* Lop or Lob, Silesian, Roman are varieties of Cos lettuce.
† Sampier is probably marsh samphire, q.v.
‡ Trip-Madame is Yellow Stonecrop, *Sedum reflexum*, used in the 16th and 17th century as a salad.
'Note that by parts is to be understood a pugil; which is no more than one does usually take up between the thumb and the two next fingers, by fascicule a reasonable full grip, or handful.'

LAD CALENDAR

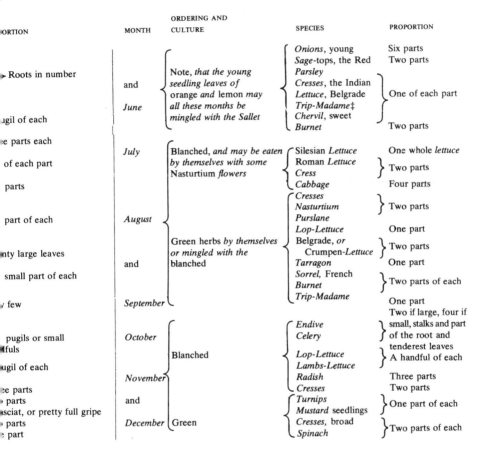

ORTION	MONTH	ORDERING AND CULTURE	SPECIES	PROPORTION
			Onions, young	Six parts
			Sage-tops, the Red	Two parts
► Roots in number	*and*	Note, *that the young*	*Parsley*	
		seedling leaves of	*Cresses*, the Indian	
	June	*orange and* lemon *may*	*Lettuce,* Belgrade	One of each part
⅃gil of each		*all these months be*	*Trip-Madame*‡	
		mingled with the Sallet	*Chervil,* sweet	
ⅇe parts each			*Burnet*	Two parts
	July	Blanched, *and may be eaten*	Silesian *Lettuce*	One whole *lettuce*
of each part		*by themselves with some*	Roman *Lettuce*	Two parts
		Nasturtium *flowers*	*Cress*	
parts			*Cabbage*	Four parts
			Cresses	Two parts
part of each	*August*		*Nasturtium*	
			Purslane	
			Lop-Lettuce	One part
ⅇnty large leaves		Green herbs *by themselves*	Belgrade, *or*	Two parts
	and	*or mingled with the*	Crumpen-*Lettuce*	
small part of each		blanched	*Tarragon*	One part
			Sorrel, French	Two parts of each
			Burnet	
⅍ few	*September*		*Trip-Madame*	One part
				Two if large, four if
			Endive	small, stalks and part
pugils or small	*October*		*Celery*	of the root and
⅃fuls		Blanched		tenderest leaves
			Lop-Lettuce	A handful of each
⅃gil of each	*November*		*Lambs-Lettuce*	
			Radish	Three parts
ⅇe parts	*and*		*Cresses*	Two parts
ⅉ parts			*Turnips*	One part of each
⅃sciat, or pretty full gripe	*December*	Green	Mustard seedlings	
ⅉ parts			*Cresses,* broad	Two parts of each
ⅇ part			*Spinach*	

Eighty-five years before *Acetaria* was published, an Italian had castigated the dripping wet, over-vinegared salads of the English table. Obviously Evelyn had read his pamphlet, as he emphasises the need for generosity with oil, meanness with vinegar.

You will notice from the salad calendar that the English were eating a far wider choice of greenery and herbs than we do today, although there is no reason why gardeners should not return to some of the plants we have so unwisely given up.

TURNIP, PUMPKIN AND POTATO BREADS

Evelyn recorded that he had eaten turnip bread 'at the greatest person's tables, hardly to be distinguished from the best of wheat'. When translating a famous French book on gardening, he passed on the idea of adding boiled and drained pumpkin to bread, too. Potatoes he did not mention, though the idea was about at the time – in one gardening book, potatoes are commended as 'they will make very good bread, cakes, paste and pies'.

Surprising perhaps that potato bread should be so light. Turnip and pumpkin give a softer, moister texture; however efficiently you dry out the purée, the dough does not cohere into a close ball, but remains slightly like batter. As a bonus, such breads keep well. All three of them are good with salads and vegetable dishes, and for salad or chicken sandwiches. It would be impossible for someone not in the know to guess at the flavouring.

Some recipes for potato bread after Evelyn's time, give quantities of half and half with flour. It reminds us that the finest wheat flour was a great luxury, from the Midlands north a rare treat. In some years of bad harvest, it had to be eked out by the poor, and potatoes, turnip or pumpkin do this far more lightly and satisfactorily than beans and pulses. In the proportions given below, these breads make pleasant eating, without any hint of being a second-best. Although you could increase the amount of potato, I would not recommend it with turnip and pumpkin.

The first thing to do is to cook enough of the chosen vegetable to give you about 200 g (7 oz) drained, mashed weight – say half a kilo of turnip, nearly a kilo of pumpkin and 375 g (12 oz) potatoes. Put it into a heavy, lightly greased pan, and stir over a low heat to evaporate as much moisture as possible. You should end up with 150–175 g (5–6 oz) of purée. Mix it while still warm with the warmed flour to make a total weight of ¾ kilo (1½ lb).

I find an electric dough hook and dried yeast simplify bread-making so well that I can keep the family in bread without any trouble at all. If you have only your hands, you can still use the recipe; just extend the kneading period slightly once the dough is mixed.

> *2 rounded teaspoons dried yeast*
> *150 ml (5 fl oz) water at blood heat*
> *2 rounded teaspoons sugar*
> *200 ml (7 fl oz) milk and water mixed, at blood heat*
> *30 g (1 oz) butter, or 2 tablespoons olive oil*
> *3 level teaspoons salt*
> *¾ kilo (1½ lb) strong plain flour and vegetable purée*

Dissolve yeast in the water with one teaspoon sugar, in the big bowl of an electric mixer. Leave in a warm place for about 10 minutes until it looks like a creamy cushion. To the milk and water, add the other teaspoon of sugar, the fat and salt, stirring until everything is dissolved.

Tip the flour and purée on to the creamy yeast, then most of the milk mixture. Switch on the dough hook at lowest speed, then raise through 1 and 2 to speed 3, as the mixture coheres and finally sticks in a close muff to the hook leaving the sides of the bowl clean (potato), or is thoroughly mixed into a damp very thick batter (turnip and pumpkin). Should the mixture be too dry to cohere, add the rest of the milk mixture. If it is on the sloppy side, add 60 g (2 oz) more flour, but no more.

Place the bowl in a plastic carrier bag secured at the top with a metal tie, and put in a warm place; alternatively, stretch plastic film tightly across the top – this has the advantage that you can easily see how the dough is rising. Leave for 1–2 hours until doubled in size. Break down with your hand, or with a ladle. No need for working the dough any further if you use a dough hook: hand kneaders may like to give it a minute or two. Divide between warmed buttered or oiled loaf tins filling them half to two-thirds full. If the destiny of your bread is sandwiches, use one very large loaf tin, and remember to increase the cooking time by 15 minutes.

Put back in the carrier bag, or drape the film lightly over the tins; in both cases, balloon them up so that there is no risk of them sticking to the dough. After half an hour in a warm place, or slightly longer, the dough should be at the top of the tins more or less.

Bake at mark 7, 220° (425°) for 30 minutes. Remove from the oven. Bang the tins sharply on a hard surface (potato) to dislodge the loaves, or run a knife round the edge and treat them more gingerly if they seem soft (turnip and pumpkin). Turn the loaves upside down in their tins, and return to the oven for 5 minutes for bottom and sides to crisp. Take them out of the oven, turn them right way up and stand across their tins to cool. Quickly brush them over with milk to give the tops a shine.

Remember that bread stores well in the freezer for at least a month. When it is cool, wrap it in cling film and put into the freezer. On removing it, leave for 30–40 minutes in the oven at mark 4–5, 180–190° (350–375°) or at a higher temperature for a slightly shorter time. Unwrap it first, of course. This gives the bread an even better crust, although if you want to keep the bread for two or three days eating, you should allow it to thaw out on its own. Take off any wrappings and stand on a rack; after 5 hours, you should be able to eat it.

GLOBE ARTICHOKES

''Tis not very long since this noble thistle came first into Italy, improved to this magnitude by culture; and so rare in England that they were commonly sold for crowns a piece.' Not very long? An odd remark, because it was at least two and a quarter centuries, as Sir Thomas Browne, a correspondent of Evelyn's, knew from his reading. He noted that in the time of Hermolaus Barbarus, the commentator and translator of Pliny's *Natural History*, there had been only one garden growing artichokes in Venice, which means a date of c. 1479.

And it must have been some time before, that more southerly

Italians had taken to the artichoke which Arab gardeners were growing in North Africa (they called it al-kharsūf, which gives us our European names). Once established in Italy, it travelled fast. Artichokes were familiar enough to be carved on misericords in Tréguier Cathedral in 1508 (in the same part of Brittany that grows such splendid artichokes still, and ships them to us from Roscoff). Henry VIII and his court enjoyed them, just as Catherine de'Medici, Rabelais and Ronsard did in Touraine.

By Evelyn's time they were much grown in large private gardens, and he gives several cooking suggestions, the first two are based, I would say, on his experience of them in Italy, the third one certainly is:

1) Cut tiny tender artichokes in quarters and eat them raw with an olive oil vinaigrette (at this stage the choke has not formed, so the whole thing can be eaten without fuss).

2) Fry the same young artichokes whole until they are crisp, with parsley, in butter.

3) 'In Italy they sometimes broil' – i.e. grill – 'them, and as the scaly leaves open, baste them with care extraordinary, for if a drop fall upon the coals, all is marred; that hazard escaped they eat them with juice of orange and sugar.' Seville oranges most likely.

4) Parboil the bottoms, and pot them in clarified butter, 'like small game birds'.

5) String the bottoms on pack thread, with bits of paper in between to prevent them touching each other, and hang them up to dry for winter use. When you want to cook them, soak them in hot water until they regain their original size, more or less, then simmer them in the normal way.

6) Pickle them.

So enthusiastically were they grown, that most seventeenth-century cookery books include at least one recipe for artichoke pie, or a pie of mixed delights that included artichokes. Here is one example:

shortcrust pastry
6 cooked artichoke bottoms
15 g (½ oz) cinnamon
125 g (4 oz) sugar
about 3 tablespoons of beef marrow
4 hard-boiled eggs, quartered
12 fresh dates, stoned and quartered
175 g (6 oz) candied eringo root or candied peel
6 blades mace
1 lemon, sliced
250 g (8 oz) butter
3 tablespoons of white wine
1 teaspoon vinegar
1 large egg yolk
1 teaspoon sugar

Line a pie dish with pastry, keeping back enough for the lid. Quarter the artichokes and put them on a plate; mix cinnamon and sugar and scatter it over the artichokes. Turn the artichoke pieces over so that they are well seasoned with the cinnamon sugar. Place them in the pie dish with the beef marrow evenly distributed in the gaps. Turn the egg pieces in any cinnamon sugar left on the plate, and put them on top of the artichokes with the dates, candied eringo (sea holly) root – you will have to substitute candied peel as I do not think this ancient aphrodisiac sweetmeat is made any more. Over all this put the mace, pushing it down a little, and the lemon slices. Melt the butter and pour it over the lot. Cover with pastry, brush with a little of the egg yolk and bake at mark 5, 190° (375°) for about an hour until the pastry is cooked and the contents bubbling long enough for the flavours to blend. Beat the remaining ingredients into the egg yok. Take the pie out of the oven and pour this liquid – or caudle as it used to be called – into the pie through a funnel inserted in the centre hole. Return to the oven for 5 minutes.

This recipe certainly belongs to the time when vegetables were regarded almost as a substitute for, or an extension of fruit – see the spinach and carrot pies later on in this chapter. The less brave might prefer a simple artichoke and egg gratin, without any ambiguities of flavour. To make this, put quartered, cooked artichoke bottoms in a well-buttered gratin dish. Scatter 4 hard-boiled, crumbled eggs over the top, then pour on a cheese sauce. Put crumbs and melted butter over the whole thing if you like. Bake at mark 5, 190° (375°) until the gratin is nicely browned and bubbling vigorously at the sides.

This makes a good first course – though you would also be in perfect seventeenth-century order to serve artichokes plainly boiled, with a vinaigrette, or with clotted cream sharpened with lemon juice.

As another alternative, artichokes could accompany the main course, as in the next recipe.

ROAST VENISON

On 3 July 1679, 'sending a piece of venison to Mr Pepys Secretary of the Admiralty, still a prisoner, I went and dined with him'. For recipe, *see* p. 121.

Pepys was in the Tower awaiting trial on a trumped-up charge of selling naval information to the French and trying to overthrow the Protestant church in favour of Roman Catholicism. He had been a friend of Evelyn's for many years.

DIGESTER PIGEONS

After dining with Pepys on venison, in the Tower, Evelyn went on to a Royal Society meeting. First they heard about 'innumerable worms or insects in the sperm of a horse' to be seen through a microscope, then Dr Denis Papin gave the first lecture about his new invention, the Digester – or pressure cooker, as we now call it. Three years later, on 12 April 1682, he demonstrated the machine more fully when the Royal Society met for a 'philosophical supper'.

Everyone enjoyed the occasion so much that Evelyn wrote a long piece about it in his diary. Monsieur Papin had taken refuge in England, being a Huguenot. He was a native of Blois, and you may see a statue of him with his Digester at his feet, half way up the splendid flight of steps in the centre of the town.

The effect of the invention was astonishing. 'The hardest bones

of beef itself, and mutton, were without water, or other liquor, and
with less than eight ounces of coals made as soft as cheese, produced an incredible quantity of gravy, and for close, a jelly made of
the bones of beef, the best for clearness and good relish, the most
delicious that I had ever seen or tasted; so as I sent my wife a glass
of it, to the reproach of all that the lady's ever made of the best
hartshorn.' Moreover the bones themselves, 'breaking as it were
into crumbs, one may strew on bread and eat without harm'. (The
bones of canned salmon which is processed under high pressure are
reduced to the same texture.)

The success of the pressure cooker was delayed until this century
when aluminium and sealing rings made it light and safe enough to
use at home. Sometimes earlier pressure cookers, labelled diges-
ters very often, turn up in antique shops; they are black and heavy
compared with ours. There is no need these days to worry about
the Sunday joint disintegrating to a superior mush: the pressure of
a modern cooker is 15 lb to the inch, whereas Monsieur Papin
raised pressure to 35 and even 50 lb.

Another point, the pigeons – 'Nothing exceeded the pigeons,
which tasted just as if baked in a pie, all these being stewed in their
own juice, without any addition of water, save what swam about in
the digester' – were tender squabs from the dovecot. These you can
only find at Harrods and one or two London butcher's. I made the
dish with casserole wood pigeons – they required 45 minutes.
Guineafowl could be used instead, and would take a shorter time.
So would a really well brought up farm chicken.

6 globe artichokes, boiled
butter
3 hard-boiled eggs
12 tablespoons long grain rice
lump pork or bacon fat
6 pigeons
lard
300 ml (10 fl oz) beef stock
150 ml (5 fl oz) dry white wine
10 cm (4 inches) celery stalk
generous pinch thyme

¼ teaspoon sugar
level teaspoon salt
nutmeg, lemon juice

Deal first with the artichokes. Strip off the leaves and scrape the edible part into a bowl. Remove chokes carefully. Mash artichoke in the bowl with a large knob of butter and two chopped eggs. Slice the third egg and set it aside. Fill the artichoke mash into the saucer-shaped bottoms, mounding it up. Set aside, too, until you come to boil the rice: then they can be reheated on top of the rice pan in a covered plate or steamer.

Chill the pork or bacon fat and cut it into strips so that you can lard the pigeons (unnecessary with guineafowl or chicken). Halve them and cut away the breast bone. Brown on both sides in lard. Put into the cooker with the next six items, and sand them lightly with nutmeg. Bring to the boil, put on the lid and pressure cook for 35 minutes. Check the birds – they may be tender enough by now. If not cook for a further 10 minutes.

Meanwhile boil and butter the rice, and put it on a serving dish. Arrange the pieces of bird around it, with the artichoke saucers and the sliced egg in between. Season them and keep warm. Degrease, then taste the cooking juices. Boil them down to a concentrated syrupy liquid, adding a little lemon juice to accentuate the flavour, and extra salt if necessary. Pour over the whole thing and serve.

VEAL OLIVES

A dish that has remained unchanged for centuries, like salmi of duck or poor knights' pudding. It was especially popular with seventeenth-century cooks. Six thin veal escalopes of the right size should weigh something in the region of half a kilo or a little more (1 lb upwards). If veal is out of the question, use the larger fillet of chicken breast, or the turkey 'escalopes' that some supermarkets sell. Slices of pork tenderloin would do, but however carefully you cut the slices on the bias, you would have to fiddle with a large number of small olives. With any of these meats the cooking time is not long, but for poultry and pork you would need slightly less time than for veal.

6 veal escalopes
1 beaten egg, salt, pepper
6 long rashers streaky bacon
100 g (3–4 oz) breadcrumbs
small bunch parsley, chopped
¼ teaspoon thyme
grated peel of a lemon
½ litre (17–18 fl oz) beef stock
2 tablespoons lemon juice
2 teaspoons anchovy essence
tablespoon each butter and flour
60–100 g (2–3½ oz) mushrooms, fried
clarified butter

Trim escalopes, beat them out and brush with egg. Then season them. Stretch and cut each rasher in half across; lay two pieces on each escalope lengthwise. Mix breadcrumbs with parsley. Set half aside. Season the other half with thyme and lemon peel, and spread over the 6 escalopes. Roll them up, starting with a long side, so that the bacon runs right through parallel to the edge. Press firmly together. According to length, cut each roll across into two or three shorter rolls – these are the 'olives'. Dip them in the remaining egg, then in the other lot of breadcrumbs and parsley. Keep the flap side down. Chill in the refrigerator, to firm them up.

Meanwhile make the sauce. Bring stock, lemon and anchovy to the boil. Mash butter and flour together (*beurre manié*) and add in small pieces to the stock to thicken it; keep the sauce just under boiling point. Set aside a few mushrooms for garnish, chop the rest and add to the sauce. Taste for seasoning.

Cook 'olives' in clarified butter. Start flap side down. After 4 minutes, turn them and give them 3 minutes on the other 3 sides. Serve with some of the sauce poured round (the rest in a boat), and garnished with the mushrooms.

SPINACH TART

In Evelyn's day, cooks treated vegetables without prejudice, as I have remarked, putting them into sweet or savoury dishes as they thought appropriate. Winter vegetables in particular were seen as alternatives to fruit which was difficult to store successfully and which did not always grow as abundantly here as it did further south in Europe (hence, too, our addiction to dried fruit). The next recipe, for carrot pudding, is a fine example of this, a dish that remained popular until after Mrs Beeton's day; Evelyn says that it can be adapted to other roots, potatoes for instance, and I would think to salsify and scorzonera.

Vegetables do have a natural sweetness of their own. Elizabeth David has recommended a slightly sweet white wine to go with them. And in his *Cuisine Minceur*, Michel Guérard revives an old idea in his spinach and pear purée (for six–600 g (1½ lb) boiled spinach, reduced in a blender with 150 g (5 oz) peeled, cored, quartered and boiled pears).

In England this spinach tart has not been as popular as carrot pudding, perhaps because it is not so easy to buy spinach as carrots. It lingers on in Provence, as part of the *Grand Dessert* of Christmas Eve dinner, with almost the same flavourings. A good pudding that is worth bringing back.

> *1 kilo (2 lb) spinach*
> *300 ml (10 fl oz) single cream*
> *30 g (1 oz) white breadcrumbs*
> *30–60 g (1–2 oz) macaroons*
> *60 g (2 oz) butter*
> *4 egg yolks*
> *2 egg whites*
> *2–3 tablespoons sugar*
> *60 g (2 oz) currants or raisins or candied peel*
> *grated nutmeg*
> *puff pastry*

Cook the cleaned spinach in plenty of boiling salted water, very rapidly. Drain and run it under the cold tap, drain again and chop. Bring cream to the boil with the breadcrumbs, and stir over a low heat until thickened. Mix with cooked, chopped spinach. Add 30 g (1 oz) of crumbled macaroons, the butter, egg yolks and whites, and 2 tablespoons sugar. Plump the dried fruit in a little hot water, then drain and add it to the spinach mixture; alternatively cut up the peel and stir that in, instead. Stir gently over a low heat until the whole thing is well mixed. Add grated nutmeg to taste, the last tablespoon of sugar and extra macaroon crumbs if you think it needs it.

Line a 22–25 cm (9–10 inch) tart tin with puff pastry. Pour in the filling. Bake at mark 7, 220° (425°) for about 15 minutes, until the pastry edges start to colour, then lower the heat to mark 4, 180° (350°), and leave for a further 30 minutes, or until the filling is just set. Eat hot or warm with cream.

Note Evelyn recommends a blend of greenery, and calls it a 'Tart of herbs' – 'chervil, spinach, beet (or what other herb you please)'. By beet he meant beet greens or chard greens, not beetroot. This may be an easier option for gardeners than all spinach.

CARROT PUDDING

Evelyn's recipe gives too many breadcrumbs in proportion to the carrot, so I always use quantities from later recipes, as follows:

125 g (4 oz) trimmed, peeled carrots
60 g (2 oz) breadcrumbs
125 ml (4 fl oz) whipping cream
1 large egg
2 yolks of medium eggs
125 g (4 oz) melted butter
sugar, nutmeg and pudding spice
dry sherry or orange-flower water (optional)
shortcrust or puff pastry

Grate the carrots finely. Mix with breadcrumbs, cream, egg and yolks, butter and sugar, nutmeg and spice to taste. Sherry or orange-flower water were common seventeenth- and eighteenth-century flavourings for carrot puddings: use a tablespoonful.

Line a 22–25 cm (9–10 inch) tart tin with the pastry. Pour in the filling and bake at mark 4, 180° (350°) until risen and nicely crusted with golden brown – if you use puff pastry, it is a good idea to give the pudding 10 minutes at a higher temperature, say mark 7 as in the spinach tart recipe, but the longer cooking at a moderate temperature is best when raw carrot is used.

BUTTER'D ORANGES

De la Quintinie – *see* chilled melon soup, p. 19 – was also an authority on growing oranges (his instructions were included in the Evelyn translation). This was nothing new for aristocratic English gardeners, who had planted oranges from Tudor times. The first one was, it seems, Sir Francis Carew, at Beddington. Evelyn visited the gardens as a boy of twelve, and was enchanted with 'the curiosities there, as they then appeared to me'. Years later when he was a much-travelled gardener who had seen it all, he went there again in the September of 1658, the year his translation, *The French Gardener*, appeared. 'To Beddington that ancient seat of the Carews . . . famous for the first orange garden of England, being now over-grown trees, and planted in the ground, and secured in winter with a wooden tabernacle and stoves.' This is rather the system used in Italy to protect citrus orchards. It is not altogether adequate for our climate, though the Beddington trees did last until the winter of 1739–40, so they did not do too badly – a shame that the Carew estate with its 'curiosities' and orange trees is now swallowed up in Croydon.

The later system was to plant the trees in tubs, so that they could be wheeled into the heated orangery in winter. In the summer now in some gardens in England, and in many gardens of northern France, the day the orange tubs are wheeled out in early but established summer is a small family festival. I remember Stendhal's definition of the true south, as the place where orange trees remain safely in the *ground* all year. He was brought up at Grenoble, and hated the day in autumn when orange trees were put under cover.

Early oranges in Europe were all of the bitter, Seville type. Sweet oranges came to London from Portugal in the 1660s. Orange-women, such as Nell Gwynne, sold them at the theatres, and Pepys cautiously tried a drink of orange juice – delicious, but he was not quite sure whether it would be good for him, or whether it would be too cold for his stomach. Odd to think that the great golden globes in the dark leaves of Botticelli's *Birth of Venus* and *Primavera*, were too sour for the goddesses to peel and eat if they felt thirsty.

Sometimes in cookery books of Evelyn's day, and into the

eighteenth century, it is difficult to decide which kind is required. Occasionally a writer stipulates Portugals or China oranges – the sweet kind – sometimes Seville orange, but mainly you have to guess. In many orange puddings, both can be used with advantage, the bitter juice enforcing the flavour of the sweet. This version of a popular seventeenth-century recipe comes from Michael Smith's *Fine English Cookery* (Faber). Mr Smith wisely plumps for sweet oranges and uses the double-boiler cooking method; I admit to jiggering with his recipe, using Seville or even lemon juice to bring out the flavour, as well as a pinch of salt.

This kind of mixture was sometimes baked between layers of pastry in a double-crust pie. It is not nearly so good, or so attractive.

> *8 sweet oranges*
> *5 egg yolks*
> *60 g (2 oz) caster sugar*
> *teaspoon triple-distilled rosewater, from an oriental*
>   *delicatessen, not the chemist whose rosewater has been*
>   *diluted usually with glycerine*
> *125 g (4 oz) unsalted butter*
> *150 ml (5 fl oz) double cream*
> *large piece candied orange peel*

Turn six oranges on to their stalk ends. Using a zig-zag Van Dyck cut, remove lids, starting about 2 cm (¾ inch) down. Scoop out the pulp with a pointed teaspoon, and keep it for other dishes. Grate the peel of the two remaining oranges, and squeeze their juice into the top of a double boiler (or basin set over simmering water). Beat in yolks and sugar, and the grated peel; stir until very thick.

Remove top part of boiler, or the basin, to a bowl of iced water, to cool the mixture rapidly to tepid. Take out of the water, stir in rosewater, then the butter in small bits: it should soften into the mixture, rather than melt. When mixture is smooth and quite cold, fold in the half-whipped cream.* Chill until very thick, add the

---

* Add the Seville or lemon juice to taste, at this stage, if you think the flavour needs a little encouragement. The pinch of salt, too. Another alternative is to use lightly salted Danish butter rather than unsalted, but it must be Danish Lurpak; other 'lightly' salted butters can be on the strong side.

shredded candied orange peel and divide between the orange shells. Replace the lids.

Michael Smith decorates his butter'd oranges with crystallised rose petals and extra whipped cream, but you can use 'any other notion that takes your fancy'. The paper jacket of the original hardback edition of his book, showed these oranges piled up on a stemmed cake or fruit dish, decorated with baubles and butterflies, as well as the rose petals.

FRUIT ICE-CREAMS

Edward and Lorna Bunyard have observed, in their *Epicure's Companion* of 1937, that strawberries, cherries and ice-cream were served at a Garter Banquet in 1671. I have not been able to get at the source, but it seems sensible. Ice-cream was first eaten at the French court in 1660, and – it is said – a limonadier from Sicily, Procopio, was supplying it to Parisians about the same time. Which ties in neatly with the Restoration and the St James's ice-house. The first mention of making ices, water ice in this case, comes in a translation of D'Emery's *Nouveau Receuil de Curiosités*, of 1685. Cookery books are silent until 1718 it seems. Ices remained a grand treat for the rich and aristocratic – such as Evelyn – for a long time. Only with Hannah Glasse, the illegitimate but cherished daughter of a country gentleman who ran off with a subaltern on half-pay, do you get the feeling that ices were beginning to be a possibility for prosperous middle-class families. In the 1751 edition of her book, *The Art of Cookery*, she gives a raspberry ice cream, and tells readers that they can buy the necessary equipment from a pewterer, consisting of a large basin to hold ice and salt, and a smaller basin to go inside (for the ice cream mixture, with a fitting lid).

Early recipes consist mainly of frozen fools. To bring out the flavour of the fruit, in these days of bland pasteurised cream, it is necessary to add some lemon or orange juice; another dodge is to use half soured cream and half double cream (I suspect that earlier on our cream was much closer in taste to *crème fraiche* which is deliberately 'ripened' to give it a faintly acid flavour).

*½ kilo (1 lb) apricots, raspberries, strawberries, peaches
    or cherries*
175 g (6 oz) sugar
500 ml (17 fl oz) double cream
lemon or orange juice

Stone or hull the fruit. Liquidise and then sieve it to remove seeds
or tough skin. Stir in sugar. Whip the cream and fold it in. Taste and
flavour with citrus juice. Add more sugar, if the mixture needs it.
Freeze at as low a temperature as possible, stirring sides to middle
when they set firm. At this stage you can beat the mixture electrically, or add 2 stiffly whipped egg whites, to lighten the
texture.

SPANISH EGGS

As you might expect from the history of the times, dishes from
Spain and Portugal became familiar to English people in the sixteenth and seventeenth centuries. Evelyn's friend, Sir Kenelm
Digby describes Portuguese eggs*, as made by the Countess of
Penalva for Henrietta Maria (12 yolks stirred with a spoon of
rosewater and 1 lb of sugar over a low fire); and Robert May, who
dedicated his *Accomplisht Cook* to several noble patrons, including Digby, has this delicious version of Spanish eggs:

5 large eggs
3 tablespoons sherry, claret or white wine
30 g (1 oz) sugar
juice from quarter of an orange
pinch salt, nutmeg
*3 baps, halved and toasted, or 6 slices of brioche or milk
    bread, toasted*
extra orange juice, claret or wine as above
*crushed sugar lumps, or sugared cumin seeds or
    almonds*

---

* In *The Closet of the Eminently Learned Sir Kenelme Digby Kt. Opened*, which was
published posthumously in 1669.

Whisk eggs, wine, sugar, orange juice, salt and a little nutmeg in a bowl over a pan of simmering water until very thick and foamy – like a zabaglione. Serve it on the baps, brioche or bread which has first been sprinkled with orange juice or claret. Scatter the tops with crushed sugar or sugared seeds or almonds.

Parson James Woodforde (1740–1803)

I opened the first volume of my Christmas present, the five-volume edition of Parson Woodforde's diary, edited by John Beresford and published from 1926 to 1931. And I read that on 22 May 1781, at a friend's house in Mattishall, halfway between their two Norfolk parishes, he met the Reverend William Grigson of Reymerston. It seems that dinner was more interesting than my great-great-grandfather-in-law – '. . . appears to be a sensible, good young man. We had for dinner a piece of boiled beef, a forequarter of lamb roasted, a pigeon pie, custards and tarts' – but the surprise of it set me thinking about the food that was so important to Parson Woodforde that he noted it daily.

At first, and especially in the abbreviated one-volume edition of the diary, Parson Woodforde sounds a sad glutton, greedy and gouty from over-indulgence. Then I came to feel that these entries represent skill and delight, rather than piggery. Like Jane Austen's father, or the Reverend Sydney Smith, he farmed his glebe himself. With help certainly, but without the housekeeper and head-gardener of the country house. In other words, there was no one to whom the parson and his wife – or in this case, niece – could hand over large areas of responsibility. They were thoroughly in charge. James Woodforde was sometimes caught by early visitors, still in his cotton nightshirt, working among the artichokes and cauli-flowers and cucumbers. Nancy Woodforde may have had her awkward moments, but she was good at little cakes, and knew how to put on a dinner.

This sort of intelligent energy is what makes the Parson's diary such lively reading. When anything happened, he was there to see it. 'Brewed a vessel of strong beer today. My two large pigs, by drinking some beer grounds taken out of one of my barrels today, got so amazingly drunk by it, that they were not able to stand and appeared like dead things almost, and so remained all night from dinner time today. I never saw pigs so drunk in my life, I slit their ears for them without feeling.' Next day, 'My two pigs are still unable to walk yet, but they are better than they were yesterday. They tumble about the yard and can by no means stand at all steady yet. In the afternoon my two pigs were tolerably sober.' He also had to deal with drunken man-servants and pregnant maids, which he did humanely, trying to get them married. We hear about Nancy's moods – it cannot have been an easy life for her – and the precarious sophistication of another clergyman's young wife. He records his own wounded feelings as well as his stomach pains (once from eating too many walnuts at a New College dinner, where he had been an undergraduate – Weston Longeville, his parish near Norwich, was a New College living). He notes with happy modesty that he has given fruit and vegetables to his neighbours for their dinner parties, or that they had had a successful party at his house.

One thing that has led to condemnation of Parson Woodforde's appetite is a misunderstanding of the way a dinner was organised in those days. The normal household meal, when nobody was invited, consisted of a couple of dishes with a pudding or some dessert to follow. Very much the sort of meal we still eat today. When friends came, it was another matter. The table was set with a large dish at each end, and four fairly large dishes in the centre. The corners were taken up with vegetables and sweet dishes. There were two courses like this, the second one with a higher proportion of sweet things, and 'made' dishes. Last of all, the third course, a dessert of fruit, nuts, sweetmeats and little cakes. The quantities, especially of the corner dishes, were often small – creamed spinach might only be topped with four eggs, even though upwards of ten people were sitting round the table. You were dependent for your meal on what was directly in front of you, and on the good manners of the people on either side, who were expected to carve if they were men, and to pass something from further down the table that you might prefer to eat. In other words a successful dinner depended not only on the cook's skill, but on the civilised behaviour of the company. The men especially prided themselves on their elegant concern and ability to lead an agreeable conversation. London dinner parties, say at Holland House, were often kept witty by such conversationalists as Sydney Smith (q.v.) and Tom Moore. In the country, the atmosphere was jolly. Parson Woodforde laughed so much one evening, that he choked on hot gooseberry pie.

What helped to keep parsonage food up to scratch in the provinces was the regular dining club, organised in turn by groups of neighbouring clergy. This was common all over the country, until cars changed social life. My father-in-law, vicar of Pelynt in Cornwall, belonged to a rotation club of this kind, as his clerical forbears had done right back at least to that earlier William Grigson whom Parson Woodforde had met at Mattishall. The same people, with the same resources, often met weekly for decades, with an occasional visitor to make a small change in the conversation or to introduce a new game. Perhaps a relative who had come to stay, perhaps a young clergyman from just outside the dining club area who wanted to meet his colleagues and didn't mind the extra long ride. In the Woodforde diary, one catches the note of criticism or self-congratulation that ensured an even better meal, a greater effort, next time the group met at the parsonage of Weston Longeville.

GIBLET SOUP

A staple dish of Rotation Club dinners. When chickens were roasted on the spit, it was a good way of making the most of the giblets and wing tips, as well as the heads (in France today poultry is usually sold with claws and head, which makes an important addition to any stock). The only advantage of the vast trade in battery chickens is the possibility of being able to buy giblets on their own. Sometimes you may also see turkey giblets, which are even better for this recipe as they have more flavour. Do not hesitate to ask your butcher if he has heads and claws to spare.

> *1 kilo (2 lb) poultry giblets, minus liver*
> *generous 2 litres (3½–4 pt) light beef or veal stock*
> *2 tablespoons butter, heaped*
> *2 rounded tablespoons flour*
> *small bunch parsley*
> *chives, marjoram*
> *pennyroyal (optional)*
> *glass Madeira or port*
> *salt, pepper, Cayenne*

Check over and clean the giblets if necessary. Put them into a pot with the stock, and stew until tender. This can be done in advance. Strain off the stock into a basin, and leave in the refrigerator overnight, then remove congealed fat next day: keep the best giblet meat and chop it.

To make the soup, cook the butter to a golden brown colour, then stir in the flour. When the roux is smooth, stir the giblet stock into it. Simmer 20–30 minutes. Add the chopped giblet meat 10 minutes before serving. Then 5 minutes before serving, add the chopped herbs – if you do grow pennyroyal, its minty flavour blends well into the soup – the wine, and extra seasonings as required.

Serve with a bowl of croûtons.

ARTICHOKES STUFFED WITH BROAD BEANS

Artichokes were a commonplace of kitchen gardens here in the seventeenth and eighteenth centuries. Parson Woodforde some-times had enough to give away to his friends. It is puzzling to know why they dropped out of our regular vegetable diet in the nineteenth century. They are now imported, mainly from Brittany, and people have to be told how to deal with them.

The most delightful way of eating artichokes is with a broad bean purée. And to make a good broad bean purée, you must skin the beans after they have been cooked. It sounds like a chore, but it's worth it and once you get used to slitting the skins with a pointed knife and popping out the beans, it doesn't take long. By the time artichokes drop to a reasonable price, broad beans are on the large side, so this business of removing the skins is even·more essential.

> *2½ kilos (5 lb) broad beans*
> *60–90 g (2–3 oz) butter*
> *4–6 tablespoons double cream*
> *salt, pepper, Cayenne*
> *lemon juice*
> *6 large artichokes of good appearance*
> *vinegar*

Shell, cook, skin and sieve the beans. Mix them while still warm –

or reheat them – with the butter and cream. Season to taste, and add a little lemon juice. Set aside.

Slice about 2 cm (¾ inch) from the tops of the artichokes, or less if they are very squat. Rub the cuts with some lemon juice to prevent discoloration. Cut off the stalks and rub the bases with lemon, too. Cook them in salted water, adding 2 tablespoons vinegar – malt will do – to every litre (1¾ pt). When tender, drain and remove centre leaves and the hairy choke, so that you are left with 6 cups. Fill them with reheated broad bean purée and serve.

To eat, pull off the outer leaves first, dipping them into the purée before you chew off the nugget of flesh at their base. Then tackle the rest with a knife and fork. One of the best of all artichoke dishes.

MACKEREL WITH GOOSEBERRIES

With May came a certain anxiety – would the gooseberries be ripe enough by the time the first mackerel arrived? '1789, May 11th. We had mackerel today for dinner, being the first we have seen anywhere this season, 5d apiece, but the spring is so very backward that there are no green gooseberries to eat with them.'

Gooseberries were also served with roast pork and young goose – 'a green goose roasted and gooseberries' – as well as in puddings. They provide an excellent sharpness with rich meats as with oily fish.

Slash the mackerel three times each side, and grill under a high heat until the skin is caught with brown crispness at the edges. Serve with a purée of slightly sweetened gooseberries, mixed with some béchamel sauce. If it grows in your garden, add a flavouring of chopped green fennel leaves. May gooseberries are acid and green-tasting; as the season goes on, they will need hardly any sugar at all for this kind of sauce.

If you wish to bake the mackerel, stuff them with breadcrumbs and herbs with a few gooseberries included. Serve with gooseberry sauce.

FRIED AND STEWED EEL

Mr Foster of Lenwade Bridge near Weston was Parson Wood-

forde's landlord on behalf of the New College lands that he cultivated. He was also a miller, and sometimes sent to the parsonage a
'fine string of eels' that had presumably been caught in traps by the
sluice gates of the mill leat.

Two ways of cooking eels were popular in Norfolk, and they are
both good. There is no need to skin the eels first for either recipe;
ask the fishmonger to kill them, cut off the heads and cut them into
15 cm lengths (3 inches). A kilo of eel (2 lb) is enough for 4 people,
just.

1) To fry the eels, roll the pieces in seasoned flour and cook them
in clarified butter. Do this slowly at first, turning the pieces; then
raise the heat so that the skins become a little crusty. Eel is ready to
eat when you can separate the fillets from the bones – push in a
sharp pointed knife, and you will soon see if they are ready. Serve
with lemon quarters. Eat the skiñ or not, as you please.

2) To stew eels, cover them with milk, add one or more sliced
onions according to taste, and a bay leaf. Put in salt and pepper.
Bring to simmering point, cover and leave for about half an hour. If
you feel especially tender towards your guests, take the trouble to
skin and fillet the pieces and lay them on slices of bread fried in
butter, with some of the onion. Reduce the liquor, thicken it with
beurre manié (a tablespoon of butter mashed with the same of
flour, added to the liquor in little bits), and season with lemon
juice. Add a little cream if you like. Some chopped parsley is
essential. Pour a little sauce over the eel, serve the rest separately.

Eel is under-rated these days by many English people. A great
mistake as it is one of the finest and most delicate of fish.

SALT FISH WITH PARSNIPS AND EGG SAUCE

If you live in an area with West Indian shops or markets, you may
be able to buy salt cod in neat packages, all the year round.
Elsewhere you may find that fishmongers stock it only in Lent, and
not in packages but in large flat greyish yellow kite-shaped boards
that do not look particularly appetising. Do not let appearances
put you off, salt cod is delicious and easy to deal with. Buy one of
the pieces, or two if necessary to make up a kilo (2 lb) weight, and
ask the fishmonger to cut it into four large sections, or more, so that
they can be fitted flat into a wide saucepan. Soak for 48 hours,

changing the water twice. Then put it into a pan with plenty of fresh cold water, bring it to just below boiling point and keep it there until the skin and bone can be easily removed. Put the pieces on a serving dish, and surround them with parsnips.

> *1 kilo (2 lb) parsnips*
> *125 g (4 oz) butter*
> *chopped parsley*

Peel and slice the parsnips. Parboil them in salted water. Cook them finally in butter in a sauté pan, but slowly so that they absorb the butter and end up a rich yellow colour, patched lightly with brown. Sprinkle them with parsley, and drain off surplus butter.

Pour a little egg sauce over the fish, and put the rest into a sauce boat:

> *175 g (6 oz) butter*
> *small onion, small carrot, small turnip, chopped*
> *30 g (1 oz) flour*
> *½ litre (17–18 fl oz) milk*
> *bouquet garni, salt, pepper, nutmeg*
> *2 good tablespoons double cream*
> *lemon juice*
> *2 hard-boiled eggs, shelled*

Melt a third of the butter and cook the vegetables in it until they begin to soften; neither butter nor vegetables should brown beyond a golden-brown tinge. Stir in the flour, leave 2 minutes, then add the milk, *bouquet* and seasonings. Simmer down to the consistency of double cream. Sieve into a clean pan but do not push through much of the vegetables: be guided by your own taste in this. Check the seasoning, add the cream, remaining butter and a little lemon juice to taste. Just before pouring the sauce over the fish, crush the eggs to crumbs and add to the sauce.

A very few new potatoes could be added to the dish, but cut down the parsnips slightly.

Haddock could be used instead of salt cod. Simmer it in milk, or half milk-half water, and use this liquor for the sauce.

If you want to make a small first-course dish, cook salt cod or haddock in half-quantity, and divide it between 6 or 8 ramekins, flaking it into smallish pieces first. Pour over some of the egg sauce and set in the oven to heat through. Scatter a little cheese over the top and brown under the grill. Omit the parsnip.

COTTAGE PIE

'1794, Oct. 27, Monday . . . Very dull wet melancholy day, but mild. Dinner today, Cottage Pie and a Neck of Mutton roasted. Betty, both the washerwomen as well as ourselves, say that our maid Molly is with child, but she persists in it that she is not.'

What a Monday! Grey skies and rain, cottage pie for dinner, and a pregnant girl who would not admit it.

I looked hard in eighteenth- and early nineteenth-century cookery books to find a recipe for cottage pie, but without success. I assume from its being eaten on Monday, and from the frequency of hashes in the Woodforde diet, that it was the same cottage pie that, because it is usually so badly made, has ruined our Mondays ever since.

As far as the Woodfordes were concerned, the mashed potato topping was a fairly novel charm. Although potatoes had conquered the north of England and the wealthier classes inLondon by the middle of the century, elsewhere they made astonishingly slow progress. In particular in such counties as Norfolk where the open field system of agriculture prevailed. When Arthur Young toured East Anglia in 1784, he recorded only one farmer growing potatoes, and saw none in cottage gardens. Vicarage and manor gardens he does not mention. Certainly in the 1790s, Parson Woodforde and his neighbours grew them habitually. One dinner was felt to be lacking because there were 'no potatoes, greens etc.'. On another occasion he noted that they had had mashed potatoes in three scallop shells 'browned over'. This does not seem a lavish provision for a party of ten people perhaps, but then special meals consisted of many dishes put on the table buffet style, so that everyone had a little of each or a lot of what was exactly in front of them.

That potatoes eventually conquered Norfolk during this decade and the beginning of the next century, is an indication of the high rise in food prices unaccompanied by a similar rise in wages. It took inflation and consequent poverty to break through the kind of prejudice that Jane Austen's mother encountered in Hampshire in 1770. She suggested to a tenant that she should grow potatoes, and was told that they were for the gentry, being too costly for anyone else to rear.

When at last potatoes became popular, not everyone approved. Cobbett realised that the 'lazy root', being in fact so easy to grow, was the last resort. The Irish famines proved him right in one way. And the poor choice of potato varieties on sale now, when such good ones are available, is proof that he was right in another way – though we are cushioned against the failure of the crop by other imported staple foods and cereals.

To make a decent cottage pie from leftovers, you need to use undercooked meat next to the bone, and potatoes cooked for the dish. Even better, use fresh lean beef or lamb. Include a proportion of fat, and some cured pork such as bacon or ham to give zest to the flavour.

1)   *½ kilo (1 lb) cooked meat*
      90 g (3 oz) bacon, gammon or ham
      1 heaped tablespoon butter
      125 g (4 oz) chopped onion
      1 large clove garlic, crushed
      1 heaped tablespoon flour
      about ½ litre (17–18 fl oz) appropriate stock
      tablespoon mushroom ketchup, or soy sauce
      ½ kilo (1 lb) potatoes, mashed with milk and butter
      egg to glaze

Chop the meats together (better than mincing). Melt butter and cook onion and garlic in it, slowly at first, then raise the heat to brown it lightly. Stir in flour, then the stock. Simmer down to a good consistency for 15 minutes. Add meat and heat through. Season well, adding mushroom ketchup if possible, soy sauce or perhaps some fortified liquor if not. Butter a dish and put in the meat. Spread potato on top and mark with a fork. Brush with beaten egg and put into a hot oven – mark 6–7, 200–220° (400–425°) – until browned and bubbling.

2) If you use fresh meat, chop it with bacon. Melt butter in a wide pan, brown onion and garlic, then add meat to brown. Put in flour, then just enough stock to bind the mixture. Simmer 5 minutes, then complete as above, pouring away any surplus fat that may have accumulated in the pan, before putting the meat hash into the dish.

'STAKES IN PASTE'

I had thought that steaks in pastry, *en croûte*, were a fairly modern introduction from France, and that the name of Beef Wellington was a recent invention to try and nationalise a foreign dish. It seems that in the first instance at least, I was quite wrong. Parson Woodforde ate 'Beef-stake tarts in turrets of paste' when dining with his grand neighbour, Charles Townshend, MP for Yarmouth, in 1791. The menu also included pig's ears, which shows that the Townshends did not despise good food wherever it might be found.

> 100 g (3–4 oz) butter
> 1 large chopped onion
> 375 g (12 oz) chopped mushrooms
> salt, pepper
> 8 trimmed fillet steaks, 2 cm (¾ inch) thick
> kilo weight (2 lb) puff pastry, or two large frozen
>   packages
> beaten egg to glaze
> 1 rounded tablespoon flour
> ½ litre (17–18 fl oz) beef stock
> 8 tablespoons Madeira

Stew two-thirds of the butter with onion and mushrooms. When they soften and their juices begin to run, raise the heat and evaporate to a moist purée. Season. Sear steaks quickly on both sides in a very hot, heavy, greased pan or a non-stick pan. Set aside one-third of the mushroom mixture, and spoon the rest on to the steaks.

Roll out the pastry and enclose the cooled steaks completely. The neat-fingered could emulate the raised-pie turret effect that Parson Woodforde noted; the less confident should be satisfied with a neat pasty shape and a few chaste decorative leaves, which will taste just as good. Slash the tops, brush with egg and bake 20 minutes at mark 8, 230° (450°).

To make the sauce, reheat the balance of mushroom mixture, stir in the flour, then the stock. Boil down to a pouring consistency. Add the Madeira and boil again for 5 minutes. Taste for seasoning. Just before serving, whisk in the remaining butter.

GRILLED PIG'S EARS

Also part of the Townshend dinner party, along with roast saddle of mutton, boiled chicken, tongue, veal cutlets, a brace of pheasant and a roasted rabbit, an omelette, macaroni, spinach and eggs (see p. 117), and tartlets.

You will have to go to a small butcher for pig's ears, and speak to him nicely if you want them without the head. You may even get them for nothing. Another way is to order them in advance, so that he can ask for them when next he goes to the abattoir. He will usually clean and singe them for you; but if he doesn't, it is quite a simple job to do yourself. (In France, you pay a high price for pig's ears, as they are rightly regarded as a delicacy – and they are sold ready boiled, in their own jelly, for re-heating at home.)

With eight people, you could serve pigs' ears as a first course and make four of them do. Alternatively you could keep your ears as a family treat, and allow one each. I doubt you will ever be able to acquire more than four at one time.

> *pig's ears, cleaned, hairs singed away*
> *stock*
> *aromatic vegetables and herbs,* see *p. 54*
> *salt, pepper*
> *melted butter*
> *white breadcrumbs*

Put pig's ears into a pot, add enough warm stock to cover with the vegetables and herbs, salt and pepper. Simmer until tender – about an hour. Drain and cut in two, being as fair as possible in your division of the fleshy base. Brush with melted butter and cover with breadcrumbs pressing them lightly into place. Sprinkle with more melted butter and grill until brown and crisp.

Serve with Dijon mustard and mashed potatoes. Some people eat everything and enjoy the contrast of jellied meat to crunchy cartilage (I do), others will prefer to scrape off the crumbed meat and leave the rest. Pigs' ears can also be included in a mixed stew of tails and trotters; if possible salt them all in brine overnight, before stewing them as above. Tail and trotters can be boned if you have the patience, crumbed and grilled. Serve with the *sauce tartare* on p. 121.

SMOTHERED RABBIT (OR DUCK)

On Tithe Audit day, in December, Parson Woodforde entertained the people who came to pay their dues, and softened the painfulness with plenty of drink. One year, twenty-two of them drank six bottles of rum, four bottles of port with plenty of strong beer – no wonder two of the party left 'rather full' when it broke up at midnight. Dinner was as usual substantial on this occasion: roast sirloin, marrow bone from the shin, a boiled leg of mutton and caper sauce, salt fish with parsnips and egg sauce (p. 49), two rabbits and onion sauce, 'plenty of plum puddings and plain ditto'.

For this kind of dish, you must have wild rabbit. Otherwise get duck, as tame rabbit is too insipid for boiling. Eight people will need two duck, and two rabbits if they are on the small side.

> *rabbit or duck, with giblets minus liver*
> *beef or poultry stock*
> bouquet garni
> *onion stuck with 2 cloves*
> *medium carrot, quartered*
> *½ stalk celery*
> *kilo (2 lb) large onions, sliced*
> *milk*
> *1 level tablespoon flour*
> *100 g (3–4 oz) butter*
> *200 g (6–7 fl oz) whipping cream*
> *lemon juice, salt, pepper, nutmeg*

Put rabbit or duck with giblets into a large pot, breast down, and cover with warm stock. Add *bouquet* and next three items. Bring to simmering point, cover and cook until tender, turning the rabbit or duck after half an hour or 45 minutes. They should be tender after 1½ hours simmering. Wiggle the legs to see if they move loosely: the meat should also be pulling away from the bone. Drain and quarter or carve. Put on a hot dish and season. The remaining stock should come in handy for soups and stews.

Have ready a thick onion sauce: simmer sliced onions in half milk/half water to cover. When tender, drain, chop and return to pan. Season and sprinkle with flour. Stir over a low heat for 2 minutes, then add butter in bits. When melted and boiling, mix in the cream. Check seasoning, adding a little lemon juice to give a slight sharpness, and a good grating of nutmeg. Smother duck or rabbit with the sauce. Surround with matchstick potatoes.

BOILED MUTTON AND CAPER SAUCE

Another dish served at Parson Woodforde's Tithe Audit party – otherwise known as a Frolic, which it certainly was – was boiled mutton and caper sauce (see previous recipe for the rest of the menu). If you cannot buy mutton, or do not care for it, use good home-produced lamb. Cook in light stock with vegetables as in the recipe for smothered rabbit. It will take longer, allow an hour per kilo (2 lb), and keep the liquid below boiling point at a burping simmer. Serve with caper sauce.

> *2 heaped tablespoons butter*
> *1 heaped tablespoon flour*
> *½ litre (17–18 fl oz) stock from the simmering mutton*
> *salt, pepper*
> *1 egg yolk*
> *2 tablespoons whipping cream*
> *at least 1 heaped tablespoon capers, with a little of their vinegar*
> *level tablespoon chopped parsley*

Melt half the butter, stir in the flour and moisten with the stock. Leave to simmer down to the consistency of whipping cream. Season with salt and pepper. About 5 minutes before serving, beat in the remaining butter, then the yolk beaten with the cream. Stir over a moderate heat so that the sauce thickens slightly without coming up to boiling point. Last of all add the capers, their vinegar to taste, and the parsley. If you know the tastes of your company, you can put in more capers; we like plenty.

Pickled nasturtium buds were sometimes used in place of capers in the past, but they do not have as good a flavour – they merely look the same.

BATTER AND NORFOLK PUDDINGS

A Yorkshire pudding batter boiled in a cloth or basin, or baked, was often served as a sweet dish with sugar scattered over the top, and warmed currant, raspberry or strawberry jelly as sauce. Norfolk pudding was a batter mixture poured over a layer of apples and dried fruit; the pie or pudding dish was greased not with butter, but with dripping. Parson Woodforde often ate 'batter pudding with currant jelly', and Norfolk pudding 'with drippings'. The apples should be firm eaters, not Bramleys which collapse to a foam when baked. You could use Cox's Orange Pippins or one of the varieties that the Parson had in his orchard: 'Gathered in my keeping apples this morn' had but very few Nonpareils or Pearmains but a good many large Russetts, and seven bushel-baskets of the old true Beefans, so peculiar to the county of Norfolk.'

BATTER PUDDING:
>   *3 eggs*
>   *3 heaped tablespoons (4 oz) flour*
>   *about 300 ml (10 fl oz) milk*
>   *sugar*

Separate the yolks and the whites if you want to make a very light pudding. Beat the yolks with the flour and a little of the milk to make a smooth batter; gradually add the rest of the milk. Alternatively put the yolks and milk into the blender, whizz at top speed for a few minutes, then tip in the flour. Just before you put the pudding into the oven, whisk the egg whites until stiff and fold into the batter. Butter a metal pie dish, tip in the batter, and bake at mark 8, 230° (450°) for about half an hour, or until risen and nicely browned. The time will depend on the depth of mixture in the tin.

Sprinkle thickly with sugar and serve with half a jar (8 oz) jelly, warmed to melting point.

NORFOLK PUDDING
> *batter as above*
> *½ kilo (1 lb) firm eating apples*
> *dripping*
> *60 g (2 oz) sugar*
> *60 g (2 oz) dried fruit*

Leave the batter to stand while you peel, core and halve or slice the apples. Grease the pie dish with dripping – about 15 g or ½ oz – put the apples as evenly on top. Sprinkle over the sugar. Bake at mark 6, 200° (400°) for about 5 minutes. Remove and raise the oven temperature to mark 8, 230° (450°). Scatter the dried fruit over the top, then whisk the egg whites, fold in the batter mixture and pour over the apples. By this time the oven should be up to the right temperature. Put in the pudding for half an hour, or until well-risen and brown. Serve sprinkled with sugar.

Note I am not very fond of apples and dried fruit mixed together in puddings, so I substitute candied peel for currants or raisins, or leave them out altogether.

NORFOLK BIFFINS (BEEFANS, BEEFINGS)

'The Norfolk biffin is a hard and very red apple, the flesh of the true kind being partly red as well as the skin. It is most excellent when carefully dried; and much finer we should say when left more juicy and but partly flattened, than it is when prepared for sale.' A description from Eliza Acton's *Modern Cookery* of 1845. You will notice from the previous recipe (p. 56) that even in the eighteenth century – in 1796 – the biffin was regarded as an old apple (see also the Jane Austen chapter p. 84). Mary Norwak in her *East Anglian Recipes* (1978) adds an important point for anyone living outside the county of Norfolk – Blenheims can be used instead. She also notes that apples for drying were placed on a rack between layers of clean wheat straw. Commercial enterprises put a metal baking tray on top with a 10 lb weight; I imagine that this energetic pressure is what Miss Acton objects to in the quotation above.

Wipe over the apples, which should all be perfect specimens, and arrange them on a rack (with straw if you can get hold of any). Put them into the cool oven of a solid-fuel or oil-fired stove – Aga, Esse, Rayburn are ideal – but be careful to check that the temperature is between 55° and 60°, 130° and 140°F, and no higher. By leaving the door slightly ajar, you can lower the temperature, but glance at the thermometer from time to time to make sure it is not too low.

After 5 hours, take out the apples and press them gently so that the skins do not burst. They should look like 'small cakes of less than an inch thick'. Return them to the oven for an hour. Cool and test one. If the oven temperature was variable, they may take longer – or if you have made use of an electric or gas cooker, and had to take the apples out to cook a family meal. Aim for a juicy dryness, rather than a leathery texture.

To finish off the apples, Mary Norwak suggests melting some sugar over a low heat – it must not caramelize – and coating the apples. They should be eaten cold, with cream.

LEMON CREAMS AND LEMON SOLIDS

Lemon creams are livelier than they sound, being a mixture of lemon juice, water and sugar, thickened with eggs. No cream, so the flavour remains clear and slightly sharp. Most early recipes use egg whites with perhaps one yolk, but I find that the most successful version is Elizabeth David's Lemon Solids, from her *Spices, Salt and Aromatics in the English Kitchen.*

> *4 leaves of gelatine, or 1 packet powdered gelatine*
> *2 large lemons*
> *90 g (3 oz) caster sugar*
> *4 egg yolks*
> *4 tablespoons sherry*

Cut leaf gelatine in strips into a saucepan, or tip in the powdered gelatine. Stir in slowly 600 ml (1 pt) hot – not boiling – water. Soak for at least 15 minutes to dissolve the gelatine.

Grate the peel from the lemons into this liquid. Use either a special lemon zester (too much is left behind in graters), or else 4 lumps of sugar rubbed against the peel one after the other (use correspondingly less caster sugar). Add the sugar to the gelatine liquid. Heat slowly without allowing it to boil.

Mix lemon juice, yolks and sherry in a blender if possible, or with a whisk. Pour on a little of the hot liquid. Blend or whisk again, then return to the saucepan. Stir over a low heat until you have a slightly thickened custard. Do not allow it to come near boiling point, or the yolks will curdle.

Strain into a jug or bowl, and stir until cool. Pour into 8 glasses or custard cups. Leave until next day in a cold larder or the refrigerator, by which time 'the little confections should be just set, not rock-like or rubbery'.

'SMALL RASPBERRY TARTLETS'

Pastry made with ground almonds instead of flour, and mixed to a dough with egg white and orange flower water, was popular in the eighteenth century for tarts, and pastry biscuits. This crackling crust is difficult to manage; by substituting ground almonds for part of the flour when making a sweet shortcrust, you can at least get something of the well-flavoured crispness without the dough being too brittle to manipulate.

200 g (7 oz) plain flour
100 g (3 oz) ground almonds
2 heaped tablespoons vanilla sugar
150 g (5 oz) unsalted butter, plus a pinch of salt or
* 150 g lightly salted butter*
1 large egg
sugared raspberries
redcurrant jelly (optional)
whipped cream

Mix the dry ingredients, rub in the butter and mix to a dough with the egg. No water is necessary if you use a large egg.

Chill for an hour, then roll out in batches, and cut circles to fit into your tart tins. This amount of pastry will be enough for at least 30 tartlet cases, 36 if you roll it really thinly.

Prick the base of the tarts with a fork – it is not necessary to put in foil and beans – and bake for 10 minutes at mark 6, 200° (400°). If the pastry is not as brown as you would like, lower the heat to mark 4, 180° (350°) and give them another 5 minutes.

Cool the cases. Just before the meal, fill with well-sugared ripe raspberries. Glaze them if you like with redcurrant jelly melted to a syrup with a little water; brush it over the fruit while just tepid. Top with a swirl of slightly sweetened whipped cream.

'1789, October 31, Saturday . . . Very high wind with much rain in the night . . . It blew down a great many apples and split a large weeping willow in the raspberry garden.'

GOOSEBERRY CREAM

Everyone has their favourite recipes for hot gooseberry tarts, pies, steamed puddings and fools, but gooseberry cream – and fruit creams in general – seem to have dropped out of our repertoire. A pity, as such dishes are easy to make and particularly good to eat. The recipe may be adapted to many other fruits, apricot, peaches, apples, pears, quinces etc. Make the purée a little more liquid than you would for a gooseberry fool, as it will be much thickened by the eggs.

> ¾ *kilo (1½ lb) gooseberries, topping and tailing*
>   *unnecessary*
> *60 g (2 oz) butter*
> *125 g (4 oz) sugar*
> *3 eggs (*see *recipe)*
> *extra knob butter*
> *orange-flower water, muscatel wine eg Frontignan, or a*
>   *head of elderflowers tied in muslin*

Put the gooseberries in a pan in which you have melted the butter. Stir in the sugar, and add a teacup of water. Should you be flavouring the cream with an elderflower head, put it into the pan as well, pushing it well down among the gooseberries. Cover the pan, and leave over a moderate heat until the gooseberries are soft.

Remove the elderflower head if used, and sieve the rest. Measure it. If there is over a pint, use 3 large eggs. If there is a pint or less, use 3 medium-sized eggs. Beat them first, before stirring them into the purée. Return to the pan and stir over a lowered heat until the mixture thickens and becomes opaque. Taste and add the extra butter and some more sugar if the gooseberries are sharp. Allow to cool to tepid, before putting in a tablespoon of orange-flower water or wine; taste again, and add more flavouring if you like.

Put into glasses or custard cups, and serve with thin home-made biscuits or *tuiles amandes*.

Note When preparing gooseberries for a pie, tart or pudding, turn them for a few minutes in melted butter and sugar as above, until they are coated. They will become warm, but they should not cook in any proper sense of the word.

FLOATING ISLAND

Mrs Jeanes, the young wife of the rector of Great Witchingham, came from London. When she arrived, their house was not ready, and she knew little of the skills required for comfortable living in the country. Then she proceeded to have three children in five years. None of this prevented Parson Woodforde and his niece from sharp judgements. Her house was 'filthy' and the servants difficult. Her manner was 'pretentious'. She 'talked high' (always an unforgivable sin in the country). Her cooking was unpredictable. She made unfortunate attempts to liven what must have seemed to her a dull and restricted social life, once with a picnic, another time with a fashionable pudding noted by Parson Woodforde in his diary – you can hear the sniff – as 'trifle alias floating island'. I suspect Mrs Jeanes had acquired a set of animals, specially made to adorn such frivolities, on one of her London visits. She may well have bought Mrs Raffald's *Experienced Housekeeper*, too, one of the most popular cookery books of the day; it goes into such novelties in great detail.

As well as the animals, you could also buy special moulds in fancy shapes, for instance to make Solomon's Temple in Flummery. Sydney Smith (*q.v.*) found such things a great joke: to one friend who was coming for dinner he wrote, 'The artiste (who is instructing our lady cook) is not despicable; but his forte seems to be culinary architecture. He has done Solomon's Temple in red sugar, and Somerset House with Powlett Thomson looking out of the window, in chocolate.' Powlett Thomson was a great geologist – conspicuous for his accurate study of volcanoes – and a keen reformer. In the year that Sydney Smith's artiste put him into chocolate, he was elected MP for Stroud, near his rich wife's village of Castle Combe.

The apotheosis of this kind of 'culinary architecture' was Carême's book of 120 designs, *Le Pâtissier Pittoresque*, published in Paris in 1815. It went into a number of editions, right up to 1856; the designs were far ahead of Solomon's Temple or Floating Island and included gothic ruins, the Tower of the Winds, a Chinese pavilion on a rock and a Gaulish hermitage. Let us be content with the simple provincial drama of a Floating Island.

> *3 large eggs*
> *100 g (3–4 oz) caster sugar*
> *100 g (3–4 oz) sifted flour*
> *jams and jellies of different colours*
> *syllabub (see p. 84)*
> *crystallized violets, cumin seeds, silver and gold balls,*
>   *toasted nuts etc*
> *sprigs of rosemary*

Whisk eggs and sugar over barely simmering water until thick. Cool slightly, fold in flour with a metal spoon. Line a swiss roll tin with bakewell paper, brush with melted butter. Spread out the mixture evenly. Bake 15 minutes at mark 5, 190° (375°). Cool. From this sheet of sponge cake, cut one large unevenly circular shape for the island base, then progressively smaller shapes to build up a craggy island. Stick them together with different jams and jellies. If you like, you can sprinkle the sponge with fortified wine – whatever you may have used to make the syllabub would be appropriate – do not overdo this as nobody likes boggy islands. From the trimmings of the sponge make standing rocks.

Put the whole thing on to a large shallow dish. Spread about two-thirds of the syllabub round the island in billowing waves. Drop more syllabub on the island to look like snow. Trail a few sprigs of rosemary in the remaining syllabub and stick them into the island as trees. Decorate with violets, sugared cumin seeds – sugared almonds if you like – silver balls and so on, but avoid glacé cherries which are too gaudy for eighteenth-century taste. Angelica is fine, and so are yellow and green cherries and bits of candied peel cut from the large pieces one can buy at good groceries.

Floating Island is certainly an excuse for culinary fantasy, so have fun with it.

The quantities above should be enough for 10 or even a dozen people.

GREEN TEA AND GENEVER

On 29 March 1777, 'Andrews the smuggler brought me this night about 11 o'clock a bag of Hyson Tea 6 pound weight. He frightened us a little by whistling under the parlour window just as we were going to bed. I gave him some Geneva and paid him for the tea at 10s 6d per pound.'

Hyson, which is unfermented green or gunpowder tea, comes from the Chinese name for it, *hsi chun*, meaning bright spring. It was popular with Charles Lamb who thought that roast goose followed by green tea made a perfect evening, and with Thackeray who liked green tea and muffins in the afternoon. Indeed it is delicious – and excellent, too, for flavouring creams, ices and soufflés – but people find it upsets their stomachs if they drink it regularly. The Parson and Nancy drove over 'one fine cheery morning' in October to the Jeanes's, for a confirmation breakfast with the Bishop of Norwich; they had 'chocolate, green and brown tea, hot rolls, dried toast, bread and butter, honey, tongue and ham grated very small'.

Smuggled gin or genever, from Holland, was another regular purchase. The Parson seems to have regarded it more as a medicine than a pleasure – he preferred to drink rum – and dosed himself and his servants with it when they fell ill or had colic.

Duties were so high until Pitt began to repeal them in the mid-1780s – tea tax came down from 119% to 12½% – that smuggling was a vast and respectable business. Smugglers took prudent measures to avoid being caught, and to remain unobtrusive, but Parson Woodforde did not seem to regard the trade as immoral, or bother at all about the illegality. As he was in no way a rebel against society, his matter-of-fact attitude may be taken as typical.

Jane Austen (1775–1817)

Not long ago I was asked what Mr Bingley meant – in *Pride and Prejudice* – when he declared the Netherfield ball a settled thing, then added, 'as soon as Nicholls has made white soup enough, I shall send round my cards'. Was white soup such a marathon?

In those days, yes – as Jane Austen knew. She was expert in the underpinnings of country sociability. For a start, a parson's family was likely to be almost self-supporting in the matter of food. The Reverend George Austen supplemented his small stipend by farming his glebe. At first Mrs Austen was the energetic housekeeper, then as she grew more frail her daughters took over the running of the house. Cassandra was the mainstay, but when she went away from home on a visit, Jane took over gladly. 'My mother desires me to tell you' – this was from a letter to Cassandra in 1798 – 'that I am a very good housekeeper, which I have no reluctance in doing, because I really think it is my peculiar excellence, and for this reason – I always take care to provide such things as please my own appetite, which I consider as the chief merit in housekeeping.' She thought they might have a dish of ox cheek, with little dumplings to make her think she was with her brother Edward in his grand house at Godmersham – 'I am very fond of experimental housekeeping.'

Cheese-making, ham-curing – her mother promised to cure six hams for one of the brothers, somewhat rashly, 'at first it was a distress, but now it is a pleasure' – and poultry-rearing, kitchen garden and fruit-growing, the making of wines, medicines and beer, soap, toothpowder, scented toilet waters and hand cream, were among the family enterprises. True they had a gardener and help in the house and kitchen, but in days before electricity and gas they managed a hard-working life with grace. They make modern self-sufficiency 'experts' seem amateur. And in between times, Jane Austen wrote novels, and they all wrote letters.

A pity the Austens lived before blenders and thermostat ovens, to judge by the way Jane Austen teases her romantic heroine,

Catherine Morland. She knew that every kind of modern invention was to be welcomed, and laughs gently at Catherine's disappointment when General Tilney shows her his splendid new kitchens. 'All that was venerable ceased here ... Catherine could have raved at the hand which had swept away what must have been beyond the value of all the rest, for the purpose of mere domestic economy.' The General quite misunderstood, 'he was convinced that, to a mind like Miss Morland's, a view of the accommodations and comforts by which the labours of her inferiors were softened, must always be gratifying.' And indeed 'the General's improving hand had not loitered here: every modern invention to facilitate the labour of the cooks had been adopted ... and, when the genius of others had failed, his own had often produced the perfection wanted.'

Even if you are unfamiliar with the letters and their talk of apple pies, gooseberry tarts, cheesecakes at Devizes and lobster, you will find it easy to choose a dinner that would have delighted Jane Austen from her novels. Moreover *A Jane Austen Household Book* was published in 1977, full of recipes from the collection made by Martha Lloyd, Jane's great friend, who lived with the family for many years and in the end, long after Jane's death, married one of her brothers. In the days before the endless publication of cookery books that we know today, the exchange of dishes was important to many families. All the friends contributed, and other members of the family. The book has been edited by Peggy Hickman, with a linking narrative and many quotations.

As to the novels, I would say that *Emma* is the most nourishing of them all. Many of the most important scenes occur against a background of meals and refreshments. Emma's father, hypochondriacal Mr Woodhouse, is perpetually diverting his guests from wedding cake, asparagus, roast pork, baked custard – all of which he declares 'unwholesome' – towards gruel and lightly-boiled eggs, or salt pork with a very little turnip. Emma circumvented these situations with tact, while furthering her own plans. Jane Fairfax suffers the pains of concealed love against a twitter of baked apples from her aunt, and over the pigeon pie and cold lamb of that thunderous picnic at Box Hill; in despair she seeks solitude from the strawberry pickers at Mr Knightley's house.

Unless you prefer a made dish like the sweetbread fricassée, or haricot of mutton, choose a main course from roast venison, partridge, pheasant, roast pork, or beef, boiled fowl with oyster sauce, roast goose or lamb. When planning the other courses, remember Aunt Norris's soft curd cheese that had to be cradled so carefully to protect it from the jolting carriage, or the high-piled fruit of Mr Darcy's Pemberley, or the Northanger pineapples. As to drink, think how Dr Grant loved having guests because it gave him an excuse to drink claret every day, and how the unpleasant Mr Elton was under suspicion of having taken too much of 'Mr Weston's good wine' when he tried so clumsily in the carriage to propose to Emma.

WHITE SOUP

We know that this was a popular soup of country-house entertaining not only from Jane Austen, but also from Eliza Acton who published her *Modern Cookery* in 1845. One of the two recipes she gives is headed *Westerfield white soup*, and at the end she adds this note: 'We have given this receipt without any variation from the original, as the soup made by it – of which we have often partaken – seemed always much approved by the guests of the hospitable country gentleman from whose family it was derived, and at whose well-arranged table it was very commonly served.'

Miss Acton grew up in Ipswich – she was born in 1799, which makes her a generation younger than Jane Austen – and seems to have shared in the kind of country society described in *Emma* or *Pride and Prejudice*. Westerfield is to the north of Ipswich, and Westerfield Hall, built in the seventeenth century, is still standing – perhaps this is the house where everyone enjoyed the white soup.

White soup goes back to the Middle Ages when many dishes were thickened with almonds or made with almond milk. Few people make it now, and I wondered why, until I read this sentence in Mrs Beeton, at the end of her recipe: 'A more economical version may be made by using common veal stock, and thickening with rice, flour and milk.' Horrible. The decline in English food through meanness is summed up in that remark.

125 g (4 oz) lean gammon, or a small bacon hock
meaty veal knuckle bone, chopped in three
onion and carrot, quartered
4 large stalks celery, sliced
teaspoon lightly crushed peppercorns
2 blades mace
60 g (2 oz) blanched almonds
30 g (1 oz) white breadcrumbs
1 egg yolk
300 ml (10 fl oz) double or whipping cream
lemon juice, Cayenne, salt

First make the basic veal stock by putting the bacon and veal bone into a large pan, and covering them with at least 2 litres of cold water (3¾ pt). Bring to the boil, skim, add a ladle of cold water, then skim again until clear. Add the vegetables, pepper, mace and 2 level tablespoons of salt. Keep the pan at a bare simmer for 4 hours. Strain, chill overnight and remove any fat from the jellied stock (the soup debris can be boiled up again with more water for a secondary stock for other dishes).

Heat the first stock, and boil it down to 1½ litres (2½ pt). Put almonds and bread into a blender, adding some of the stock, so that you can liquidise them to a smooth paste. Strain into the remaining stock, pushing through as much as you can – this is quite easy after liquidising the almonds and bread, but it helps to make the soup smoother. Beat the egg yolk with the cream and add that to the soup. If possible leave for 2–3 hours, as the flavour develops better with a rest of this kind. Reheat, keeping the soup well below boiling point. Add lemon and Cayenne to enhance the flavour.

Serve with small croûtons of bread fried in butter. Or with 30 g (1 oz) blanched almonds cut into strips – this was the garnish of Miss Acton's Westerfield soup, but writing twenty-five years later she added that almond spikes could be suppressed, as they were 'unsuited to the preparation, and also to the taste of the present day'.

Boiled vermicelli or macaroni was also added on occasion, but this I think is unsuited to our modern tastes. We should prefer almonds or croûtons.

PEA SOUPS

Soup made with fresh peas in the summer and dried peas in winter was a standby of middle-class households in the past. When Jane Austen wrote that she was not ashamed to ask an unexpected visitor – their doctor – to sit down with them and share the dinner, the menu was pease soup, a spare-rib of pork and a pudding. Incidentally, this shows that the huge meals recorded by Parson Woodforde (p. 44) and drawn in diagrams in the cookery books of the time, were for dinner parties; when families ate on their own, the meals were very much like our own today.

With frozen peas, we can make a fresh-flavoured soup all winter long, but I am giving both recipes as dried pea soup, pease soup, is now neglected.

1) *generous ½ litre (¾–1 pt) shelled mature peas*
    ½ large cucumber, unpeeled, sliced
    heart of a crisp lettuce, preferably Cos, shredded
    small handful of spinach, shredded (optional)
    175 g (6 oz) chopped onion
    3 sprigs mint
    60 g (2 oz) butter
    salt, pepper, Cayenne
    heaped tablespoon each chopped parsley and
      mint
    a teacupful young green peas

Cook the mature peas in plenty of water until tender. Meanwhile, in another pan, covered, stew the cucumber, lettuce, spinach, onion and mint sprigs in butter until they are cooked; do this slowly, so that the vegetables do not brown.

Liquidise the peas. Return them to their pan. Then liquidise the vegetables in butter, and add to the peas. Stir in more water to get the consistency you prefer. Season. Add the chopped herbs and the young peas which have been separately cooked. Reheat gently.

2)   *1 large chopped onion*
         1 medium carrot, diced
         1 small turnip, diced
         60 g (2 oz) butter
         250 g (8 oz) split green or yellow pease
         pepper
         heaped teaspoon curry powder (optional)
         1–1½ litres (1¾–2½ pt) stock or water
         salt

Soften vegetables in the butter, covered. Stir in the peas, pepper and curry powder. Pour in plenty of stock and simmer until the pease are done. Liquidise or sieve, and dilute further to taste. Add salt. Serve when reheated with tiny croûtons of fried bread or toast.

HARICOT OF MUTTON OR LAMB

A pedestrian sort of dish unless you are prepared to buy first-class, home-grown meat from a butcher who understands about the importance of hanging. The Austens had their own Leicestershire sheep, so they were well placed in this respect; they would sell to the local butcher who slaughtered and hung it, then a week to ten days later it would be ready for eating.

Mutton is not easy to come by these days, so you will most likely have to use lamb instead. For this kind of dish, mountain or hill lamb is best.

Ask the butcher to bone out a whole best end of neck – assuming you are cooking for 6–8 people. Then the two long pieces can each be cut into 6–8 slices. Use the bones to make a little stock for the dish. It is prudent to cook the haricot the day before it is required; this gives the fat a chance to solidify on top so that it can be removed before reheating. Fattiness can ruin mutton and lamb stews. Ketchups made from mushroom, walnut, anchovy, cockles, lemons and so on were the ready flavourings of eighteenth- and nineteenth-century cooks; they added a piquant zest to made dishes and ragoûts of this kind. Mushroom and walnut ketchup can occasionally be bought in good grocers' shops, but soya sauce can be used instead.

As well as the mutton or lamb, you will need:

seasoned flour
butter
light stock made from lamb bones, or veal or chicken
    stock
375 g (12 oz) turnips, peeled, diced
375 g (12 oz) carrots, peeled, diced
1 large onion, sliced
bouquet garni
pepper, salt, Cayenne
ketchup

Turn the meat in seasoned flour and brown it in a little butter. Transfer to a casserole or flame-proof pan. Stir 2 rounded table-spoons flour into the buttery juices, and when the mixture browns a little, pour in ½ litre (¾ pt) stock to make a sauce. When it is well mixed and simmering steadily, pour it on to the meat. Add the vegetables and *bouquet*. If the sauce is well below the surface of the solid ingredients, add a little extra stock, but the liquid should barely cover them. Put a lid on the pan, and leave to simmer on top of the stove or in the oven at mark 2, 150°, (300°), whichever suits you best. The slower this kind of dish cooks, the better. Allow an hour for lamb on top of the stove, longer for mutton. In the oven, allow approximately 1½ hours for lamb. Always test the meat and be guided by its feel; sticking to a rigid time is impossible as everything depends on the tenderness of the meat, the thickness of the slices, your interpretation of the word 'simmer'.

To finish the haricot, remove the *bouquet* and skim all fat from the sauce. Taste it, and add seasoning. Sitr in a teaspoon of ketchup, taste and continue to add a little more to bring out the flavours, but do not overdo it.

Serve with boiled potatoes, if you like. This kind of dish made in the summer with young turnips and carrots, and eaten with new potatoes, can be a delight; winter versions of these vegetables will be stronger in flavour.

MARTHA LLOYD'S CURRY IN THE INDIAN MANNER

Most eighteenth- and early nineteenth-century recipes start with instructions to brown the meat, as one does for any stew. Here the chicken is simmered first, in water, so that the sauce eventually benefits from the resulting stock. This means using a good, well-flavoured chicken, or a not too ancient boiling fowl.

It seems surprising to come across 'curry powder' at so early a date. In fact, curry powder blends were on sale from about 1780. These have now become so monotonous in flavour that people are returning to the idea of making their own blends; easily done in small electric mills – powdered and whole spices can be put in together, and whizzed to an even mixture. I went to Dr Kitchiner for the blend given below. In his *Cook's Oracle*, first published in 1817, the year of Jane Austen's death, he has this to say: 'This receipt was an attempt to imitate some of the best *India Curry Powder*, selected for me, by a friend at the India House – the flavour approximates to the Indian Powder so exactly, the most profound Palaticians have pronounced it a perfect copy of the original *Curry Stuff*.' Dr Kitchiner's tone is always self-confident, and his mixture is indeed a good one, because he had realised that 'the common fault of curry powder is the too great proportion of Cayenne (to the milder Aromatics from which its agreeable flavour is derived), preventing a sufficient quantity of the Curry Powder being used'. The fault these days is too much fenugreek, I think.

> *3 rounded teaspoons coriander seed*
> *3 level teaspoons ground turmeric*
> *1 rounded teaspoon black peppercorns*
> *1 rounded teaspoon black mustard seeds*
> *1 level teaspoon ground ginger*
> *½ teaspoon cardamon seeds (removed from their pods*
> *before measuring)*
> *¼ teaspoon Cayenne pepper*
> *¼ teaspoon cumin*

Whizz to a powder. There is more than you will need for this recipe; store the remainder in a tightly closed jar and it will stay good for a fortnight. Clean the mill out with paper, then with bread cubes whirled to crumbs. Try to have two mills, one for coffee, one for spices, to avoid cross-flavours.

1 chicken, jointed
salt
125 g (4 oz) butter, cut in 6 pieces
125 g (4 oz) chopped onion
1 large clove garlic, crushed
1 rounded tablespoon curry powder (see above)
juice of an orange and a lemon

Put the chicken pieces, with the giblets minus the liver, into a large sauté pan in a single layer. Pour on 300 ml ($\frac{1}{2}$ pt) hot water and add a teaspoon of salt. Cover and simmer until the pieces are just tender, turning them every 10 minutes; according to the rate of simmer, they will need 30–45 minutes (if you decide to use a good boiling fowl, you will need at least $1\frac{1}{4}$ hours). Check the breast pieces and remove them before the rest of the chicken is cooked and set it aside. Return the bones to the pan with liquor and giblets. Add a little extra water and simmer for a further hour to strengthen the broth. This can be omitted – it is not part of the Austen recipe – but it does improve the flavour. So far, the dish can be prepared well in advance of the meal.

Bring the butter to the boil in a small pan and strain into the clean sauté pan. Heat until it begins to smell nutty, then put in the onion and garlic. Cover and leave until they are golden brown; lower the heat if there seems any chance of the onions burning. Put in the chicken pieces, and sprinkle on the curry powder; this quantity is fairly mild, but highly aromatic in its effect. Cover again and leave for 10 minutes, turning the pieces after 5. The chicken should have browned slightly from the butter, and it will begin to look yellowish too from the turmeric in the curry powder. Strain in about 300 ml ($\frac{1}{2}$ pt) of the chicken broth and leave to simmer uncovered until the flavours have mellowed and the chicken is tenderly impregnated with the spices, about 20–30 minutes. Flavour to taste with the citrus juices, adding them slowly and giving them a chance to boil into the sauce.

Serve with the usual curry accompaniments, poppadums, mango chutney if you like it, diced cucumber, hard-boiled egg, thin onion slices and so on. You will find that Dr Kitchiner's curry mixture leaves a refreshed feeling in your mouth, and that the hot Cayenne does not drown the other spices.

PIGEON PIE

Cold ham, cold chicken and pigeon pie were the main items for a picnic on a day's expedition. Dovecot pigeons, tender and plump, were used; sometimes you can buy them in the best London shops under the name of squabs, but wood pigeons can be substituted if they are cooked first.

> *shortcrust or puff pastry*
> *beaten egg to glaze*
>
> FILLING:
> *4 cooked wood pigeons*
> *175 g (6 oz) piece rump steak*
> *4 hard-boiled egg yolks*
> *heaped tablespoon chopped onion*
> *250 g (8 oz) sliced mushrooms*
> *parsley, salt, pepper*
> *stock from cooking the pigeons*

Remove the breasts from the wood pigeons; boil up the carcasses with the cooking stock to strengthen its flavour.

Into a deep pie dish, rubbed with a butter paper, lay the rump steak. Season it and put the pigeon breasts on top. Fill in the gaps with crumbled egg yolk, onion and mushrooms. Add plenty of parsley, pepper and salt. Then strain over enough stock to cover the meat.

Roll out the pastry and use to cover the pie in the usual way. Make a hole in the centre, and decorate with pastry leaves and roses made from the trimmings. Knock up the edge. Brush over with beaten egg. Put into a hot oven to start with (mark 7–8, 220–230°, 425–450°) so that the pastry colours. Check after 20 minutes, then reduce the heat to mark 3, 160° (325°) and leave for a further 1 hour and 10 minutes. Protect the pastry when it takes on a good colour with thick brown paper, or several layers of butter paper or greaseproof paper. Once the pie is bubbling hot, the heat can be lowered still further.

Note If you do manage to buy squabs, put them whole into the pie dish, breast down – into the cavities put a ball of butter seasoned with cayenne and mace. Complete the pie as above, using veal stock. The cooking time will be the same, as you started off with uncooked but tender birds.

TOMATO SAUCE

As Elizabeth David has remarked, Mrs Rundell was one of the first cookery writers to give a recipe for tomato sauce – or for tomatoes at all. This seems odd as tomatoes were introduced into the country at the end of the sixteenth century. Suspicion centred around its supposed 'cold' effects, its possible aphrodisiac qualities. When Jane Austen was staying at her brother's grand house, Godmersham Park in Kent, one summer, she was delighted to tell Cassandra that she had 'regaled on them every day', and wondered how the tomatoes at home were doing.

Mrs Rundell's excellent system was to bake the tomatoes in an ovenproof pot – 1–1½ kilos (2–3 lb) at mark 2–3, 150–160° (300–325°) until they were quite soft. They were then sieved to get rid of the skins, and mixed with chilli vinegar, garlic, ginger and salt. White wine vinegar and Cayenne could be used if you had no chilli vinegar. The mixture was then bottled and served either with hot or with cold meats.

Elizabeth David's suggested seasonings are more to our taste these days: to each pound of tomatoes, add a teaspoon of salt, a teaspoon of sugar, and – if you like – ginger or cinnamon, dried or fresh basil or marjoram and some crushed garlic. 'A tablespoon of port per pound of tomatoes has a wonderfully mellowing effect on the sauce.' Reheat the tomato pulp before adding the seasonings, but cook it as little as possible to keep the fresh flavour. Serve with pasta and eggs as well as meat, or use as the basis for soup.

If you intend to use the sauce quickly, it can be stored in the fridge. Otherwise freeze it, in suitable quantities in small cartons.

Note This sauce is not worth making unless you use tomatoes grown out of doors in your garden, or the large craggy tomatoes one may sometimes buy in the shops. The small round supermarket tomato is too flavourless.

LAVERBREAD

One of Bath's most famous people, the poet Christopher Anstey, died while the Austen family were living in Bath. In 1766 his *New Bath Guide* had been published, a series of mocking letters in verse describing the fun and follies of the place, and the way some of the simple-minded visitors were gulled. It was an instant success and much praised, over-praised in fact. In one letter, Mr Simkin Blunderhead describes how enticing Bath is: even if you are just sitting at the window, so much is going on in the street below.

> What a number of turnspits and builders he'll find
> For relaxing his cares, and unbending his mind,
> While notes of sweet music contend with the cries
> Of *fine potted laver, fresh oysters, and pies!*

Laver was a great speciality of Bath, and as far as I have been able to find out the first cookery writer to mention it was Mrs Rundell, the widow of a jeweller who had been brought up in Bath and died there in 1795. Her book, *Domestic Cookery*, put the publishing firm of John Murray on its feet. It came out in 1806, perhaps earlier, and the Austen household would certainly have known it; everyone did, it was such a success and went into many editions. Moreover, John Murray was also interested in Jane Austen's novels and published *Emma* in 1816, so one way and another she could not have escaped knowledge of Mrs Rundell's book.

One of Mrs Rundell's complaints was that women in the old days knew how to run their establishments, just as Mrs Austen did, but that now 'ladies' were being brought up to know nothing of household matters. They were merely decorative. Lydia Bennett, for instance. The opening words of her introduction are a leaden version of one of Jane Austen's themes: 'In every rank, those deserve the greatest praise who best acquit themselves of the duties which their station requires. Indeed, this line of conduct is not a matter of choice but of necessity, if we would maintain the dignity of our character as rational beings.' The distance between these two sentences and, for instance, *Emma*, is a matter of wit and genius rather than philosophy.

Mrs Rundell's instructions for cooking and serving laver are as practical today as they were then.

'This is a plant that grows on the rocks near the sea in the West of England, and is sent in pots or casks boiled and prepared for dressing as follows:

'Set some of it on a dish over a lamp, with a bit of butter and the squeeze of a Seville orange: stir it till hot. It is eaten with roast meat, and is a great sweetener of the blood. It is seldom liked at first but people become extremely fond of it by habit.'

Indeed they do. Out of the Seville season, mix sweet orange and lemon juice together. Serve laver, or laverbread as it is usually called, with roast mutton and lamb. To Bath, in those days, the Welsh drove their mountain flocks, trading them in the main for Cheddar cheese. Few things are more delicious than a roasted rack of best end of neck of lamb, new potatoes and laverbread, with a few slices of orange.

If you do not live in the West of England or Wales, laverbread can be bought by post from James Howell Ltd, the large department store of Cardiff. It keeps well for a week in the fridge. Its dark green spinachy appearance makes it easy to recognise, so look out for it should you visit Marlborough where it is often on sale at the fishmonger's stall at the Wednesday and Saturday markets, or if you find yourself near a fishmonger's in Bristol. I am surprised it is not a standard item in health food stores all over the country. It makes a delicious soup and, if mixed with porridge oats or fine or medium oatmeal, can be fried in little cakes and served with bacon.

SCALLOPED OYSTERS OR MUSSELS

Owing I suspect to bad management or lack of enterprise rather than pollution, oysters in this country are in the high-luxury class. In France they are a sensible price still, though not as cheap as they were everywhere in Europe in Jane Austen's day, when scalloped oysters were a favourite dish at such houses as Hartfield. You may remember the small party there, when Emma first met Harriet and immediately became obsessed with plans for her future, but not too obsessed to look after her guests and to recommend 'the minced chicken and scalloped oysters, with an urgency which she knew would be acceptable to the early hours and civil scruples of her guests'.

At the fishmonger's you will find that oysters are about thirty times dearer than mussels. As, in this dish, they are not thirty times nicer, I suggest you go for mussels. They are the cheapest of delicacies, and many people may well prefer their stronger flavour for this kind of treatment.

Scrub 3½ kilos (7 lb or pint) large mussels, throwing out any damaged ones. Put in batches into a large covered pan. Set it over a high heat, and remove any open mussels after 3 minutes, then after 5. The thing is to heat them as briefly as possible. Discard any mussels that remain firmly shut, and discard the shells of the opened ones. (If you can rise to oysters, allow 6 per person, open them and bring them to just under boiling point in their own juice, then cool and drain them.)

Butter 8 scallop shells or ramekins. Scatter each with a teaspoon of fine breadcrumbs. Put in half the mussels, or oysters, pour over 1½ teaspoons each of melted butter and strained mussel or oyster liquor. Repeat with breadcrumbs and mussels or oysters, then cover with a topping of breadcrumbs and be slightly more generous with the butter. Grill for 5–7 minutes, turning the shells occasionally until the tops are golden brown and sizzling. Serve with buttered wholemeal bread and lemon quarters, and the pepper mill.

Note Chopped parsley, garlic and shallot may be added to the melted butter, though this is not really the Austen style.

FRICASSÉE OF SWEETBREAD

In *Emma* when most of the local families were at a ball, old Mrs Bates spent the evening with Mr Woodhouse to keep him company. The two of them had a pleasant evening but 'there was a little disappointment. The baked apples and biscuits, excellent in their way, you know; but there was a delicate fricassée of sweetbread and some asparagus brought in at first, and good Mr Woodhouse, not thinking the asparagus quite boiled enough, sent it all out again.' This was in May, when asparagus first comes in.

The sweetbread should be calf's; it is larger and more succulent than lamb's, but it is not always easy to find. You may have to substitute lamb's – they will cook in a shorter time, being so much smaller.

> 1 kilo (2 lb) sweetbreads
> lemon juice, salt
> 1 medium onion, chopped
> 1 large clove garlic, crushed
> 60 g (2 oz) butter
> 250 g (8 oz) mushrooms
> 2 heaped tablespoons flour
> ½ litre (17–18 fl oz) veal stock
> 150 ml (5 fl oz) each soured and whipping cream
> pepper, nutmeg, grated lemon peel
> triangles of toast
> cooked tips of a kilo (2 lb) bundle of asparagus

Soak the sweetbreads for an hour in salted water. Drain and put into a pan with a tablespoon of lemon juice and enough water to cover. Bring to simmering point and leave to cook for about 10 minutes, until the sweetbreads have lost their raw pink look; the time taken will depend on the size of the sweetbreads. Drain, run under the cold tap, and remove gristly bits and excessive skin. Put on a plate, lay another plate on top and chill. This can be done in advance, even the day before. Cut the sweetbreads into slices before reheating.

To make the sauce, cook the onion and garlic gently in the butter. When they are soft but not brown, add the mushrooms. Cook a minute or two longer, then stir in the flour, and the stock to make a sauce. Simmer 10 minutes, add the creams and simmer a further 20 minutes, reducing the sauce to a thickish consistency. Season with salt, spices and lemon peel to taste. Put in the sweetbreads and simmer a further 15–20 minutes. Correct seasoning, and add a little lemon juice if you like. If there is too much sauce – a fricassée should be lightly bound together – pour it off. Arrange in

a dish, surrounding the fricassée with asparagus tips and toast.
Serve very hot.

Note When making this dish out of the asparagus season, frozen
asparagus may be substituted for fresh; a half-kilo packet should
be enough, as the whole spear is edible. Alternatively you could
use flowering broccoli spears in winter, or small green beans in full
summer.

'ALL THE DESSERT'

When Emma caught up with Mr Elton and Harriet in the lane,
hoping to overhear a romantic conversation, she was disappointed.
Mr Elton was describing, with animation, what they had had for
dinner at a friend's house the previous evening, and Emma 'was
come in herself for the Stilton cheese, the North Wiltshire, the
butter, the celery, the beetroot and all the dessert'.

As our North Wiltshire farmhouse has a cheese-room, I feel sad
that the local cheese faded out before 1914. It was very much the
business of farmers' wives, and they sold their products at Marlborough and Devizes. Sometimes it went to Faringdon and Buscot
to be shipped down the Thames to London. Speed was especially
important with the young fresh cheeses, but most of them were
hard cheeses in the style of the Single Gloucester. Double Gloucester is the nearest available these days. In our county, we had no
Joseph Harding to modernise manufacture and save the North
Wiltshire, as he saved Cheddar cheese.

To southerners the idea of eating beetroot with cheese may seem
odd, but it is still popular in the Midlands and northern England. I
do not much care for it myself, especially when the beetroot is
awash with malt vinegar, but this is a matter of personal taste.

To this cheese course, you could add Bath Olivers. There is a
recipe for making them at home in Martha Lloyd's manuscript
receipt book, and they appear in contemporary cookery books, but
they can be very tricky.

> *375 g (¾ lb) strong plain flour*
> *1 teaspoon salt*
> *225 ml (7 fl oz) warmed milk*

1 level teaspoon dried yeast
½ teaspoon sugar
30 g (1 oz) butter

Sift the flour with the salt and warm slightly in the oven. Mix half the milk with the yeast and sugar, and leave it until frothing and creamy. Mix the rest with the butter to dissolve it. Pour these two liquids into the flour and mix to a dough – use a dough hook for this and the kneading, or knead by hand. Leave to rise for 1–1½ hours in a warm place; wrap the bowl in a plastic carrier bag, fastening the top with a metal tie. Or cover the bowl with a tight stretch of cling film.

Take some of the dough and roll it fairly thinly on a floured board. Cut rounds and prick with a fork. Bake on Bakewell paper on baking sheets at mark 2, 150° (300°) for about 20 minutes. But keep an eye on them. This is the tricky part – the biscuits should be soft when taken from the oven, and not too coloured; on the other hand, they must be baked enough to harden to the characteristic texture when cool. Repeat either until you have enough biscuits (surplus dough can be used for pizzas, after a second rising time of 20 minutes), or the dough is used up. When you are successful, you will find that the edge of the biscuits has the slight 'seam' running round it, and that the texture is crisp but mealy; home-made Bath Olivers taste better than bought ones, but as I said above they are a little tricky to get right.

Serve with salty Welsh or farm butter.

BLACK CAPS, PAR EXCELLENCE

Miss Bates, as you may remember from *Emma* always kept baked apples in her sitting-room cupboard, to offer her visitors. Even a sophisticated young man like Mr Frank Churchill had complimented her on them, and graciously eaten one – though this may have had more to do with his secret love for Jane Fairfax than with the superiority of the apples.

In small houses like the Bates's, cooking was done over the kitchen fire; apples and meat for roasting had to be sent to the village bakery to be put into the big oven after the bread. This practice died out a long time ago in Britain, but I took advantage of it in France for the Sunday joint when I was first housekeeping there sixteen years ago. In Greece, it is still common practice.

This best-of-all baked apple recipes, from Eliza Acton, reduces the apples to 'a rich confection' that will 'remain good for ten days or a fortnight', a consideration that would have appealed to Miss Bates. Norfolk readers may be able to get hold of beefings (or biffins) or winter queenings, the varieties recommended: cookers of the Bramley type will foam and collapse slightly, but this doesn't matter – you can reshape them with a spoon. A recipe worth trying with large Cox's orange pippins, too, for the particularly good flavour.

> 8 large apples, cored
> 8 curls of lemon peel, cut in strips
> 60g (2 oz) candied orange peel or marmalade
> 250 g (8 oz) soft pale brown sugar
> 300 ml (10 fl oz) muscatel or sweet white wine
> granulated sugar

Run the point of a knife round the apple skins about two-thirds of the way up, to prevent them bursting. Stuff the cavities with lemon and orange peel or marmalade (dark marmalade with plenty of peel is best). Make a bed of the brown sugar in a baking dish. Place apples on top, and pour over wine. Bake 35–45 minutes at mark 4–6, 180–200° (350–400°) as convenient. Remove when cooked, cool 5 minutes, then re-shape with a spoon if necessary. Baste with the juices, sprinkle the tops with a close layer of granulated sugar and grill until the apples acquire patchy black caps. Eat with cream immediately, or reheated later on, or when cold.

WHIPT SYLLABUB

In *Lesley Castle*, an early piece by Jane Austen, a wedding was planned. The bride's sister had cooked enough food to last through the honeymoon, when a most irritating thing occurred. 'I never remember,' she wrote to a friend, 'suffering any vexation equal to what I experienced on last Monday when my sister came running to me in the store-room with her face as White as a Whipt Syllabub, and told me that Hervey had been thrown from his Horse, had fractured his Scull, and was pronounced by his surgeon to be in the most emminent Danger. "Good God! (said I) you don't say so? Why what in the name of Heaven will become of all the Victuals! We shall never be able to eat it while it is good. However, we'll call in the Surgeon to help us. I shall be able to manage the Sirloin myself, my Mother will eat the soup, and You and the Doctor must finish the rest!" Here I was interrupted, by seeing my poor Sister fall down to all appearance Lifeless upon one of the Chests, where we keep our table linen.'

> *thinly cut peel of a lemon*
> *juice of the lemon*
> *2 tablespoons brandy*
> *125 ml (4 fl oz) white or muscatel wine*
> *3 heaped tablespoons sugar*
> *300 ml (10 fl oz) double cream*
> *extra twists of lemon peel*
> *sponge finger biscuits*

Soak the thinly cut peel of a lemon with its juice, the brandy and wine, overnight. Strain into a bowl next day, stir in the sugar and then the cream. Whisk until the mixture is very thick and soft, and holding its peaks. Divide between 8 tulip-shaped wine glasses. Decorate with twists of lemon peel, and serve with sponge finger biscuits.

You can follow the habit of the time in using a whipt syllabub for trifle. Cover the base of a glass bowl with slices of proper sponge cake or sponge finger biscuits. Soak with the same wine as you used for the syllabub. Make a custard with $\frac{1}{2}$ litre ($\frac{3}{4}$ pt) single cream and 4 large egg yolks and sweeten slightly; pour over sponge. When thick and cool, top with the syllabub. Decorate with candied peel, angelica, crystallised cumin seeds etc (*not* glacé cherries which are too brash for the taste of those days).

Thomas Jefferson (1743–1826)

'I am an Epicurean,' wrote Thomas Jefferson. 'I consider the genuine (not the imputed) doctrines of Epicurus as containing everything rational in moral philosophy which Greece and Rome have left us.

> Happiness the aim of life
> Virtue the foundation of happiness
> Utility the test of virtue
> Pleasure active and In-do-lent
> In-do-lence is the absence of pain, the true felicity
> Active, consists in agreeable motion: it is not happiness, but the means to produce it.
> Thus the absence of hunger is an article of felicity; eating the means to obtain it.'

Unlike many people in power, Jefferson felt that such felicity was for everyone. This great and attractive man, author of the Declaration of Independence, third President of the United States from 1800 to 1809, and founder and designer of the University of Virginia, saw that his new country could be an earthly paradise, if its natural wealth were to be exploited according to the best of European civilisation. As one writer has pointed out, in 1743, the year Jefferson was born, the English in America were a fringe of Europe on the seabord, focussed on London, the interior was viewed more as a barrier than a treasure house; by 1826 when Jefferson died, there was a population of ten million Americans, the hinterland was being explored and inexhaustible raw materials were being found.

Jefferson's ideas were advanced when he went as Minister Plenipotentiary of the new country to France in the 1780s. He determined to discover the most successful aspects of European

life, so that America might benefit and avoid European mistakes. He travelled to Holland (where he bought a waffle iron), Germany, Italy, England (he was ravished by our gardens, but thought the architecture wretched), with the aim of discovering how our agriculture might be adapted to American circumstances. He sent seeds, plants, trees to the States, and had American seeds, plants and trees sent to friends in Europe.

On a journey into Italy, he bribed a porter to take out rice from Piedmont; then fearing that he might not succeed, filled his own pockets with rice – the penalty, had either been caught, was death, so jealously guarded was the export of rice from the Po valley. Many people thought Italian rice superior to Carolina on account of a special machine used to husk and clean it. Jefferson discovered that although quality control was severe, the superiority lay in the variety. Later in life he said that one of his greatest benefactions to America, was the introduction of 'dry' rice that could be grown without unhealthily swamped fields. He would be pleased now, I think, to see the packets of Carolina rice on sale in every French supermarket.

At his ingeniously designed house of Monticello in Virginia, then at the White House, a French steward Petit, and two French chefs, Julien and Lemaire, were employed to supervise and train his staff. Jefferson's elder daughter, Martha, acted as hostess – her mother had died when she was a child – and in 1791 he gave her for Christmas a recent augmented edition of a cookery book published in 1746, *La Cuisinière bourgeoise*, by Menon, one of the best and most popular books of the day. Martha had accompanied Jefferson to Paris, had been educated there, so understood well what the highest standards of cookery should be.

Jefferson deplored English guzzling, just as Sydney Smith did a generation later (*q.v.*). He praised the French: 'In the pleasures of the table they are far before us, because, with good taste, they unite temperance. They do not terminate the most social meals by transforming themselves into brutes.' What would he say about American steaks these days, and 'doggy bags'? At the White House and Monticello, he banned the habit of drinking healths at dinner. The health was bound to be returned, and that set up a chain of health-drinking that had half the guests under the table before the meal was through. This prevented conversation, and conversation round a well-supplied table was Jefferson's idea of a civilised dinner.

Jefferson is sometimes criticised from hindsight by modern commentators for not being a more passionate reformer, especially in the matters of slavery and women's rights. He treated his own slaves as well and better than other people treated their white servants, and phrases indicating his concern with the lot of all poor people, whatever colour they were, thread through his letters. He well understood that improvement was not to be effected by flannel and charitable bowls of soup, but by the increase in national prosperity that the energetic and powerful could achieve for the country. He did not regard poverty as immutable, or the just reward of idleness.

From a famous passage in a letter to Lafayette, his attitude is clear: he urges Lafayette first to get to know the condition of the provinces – a matter in which French governments have not excelled – 'you must ferret the people out of their hovels as I have done, look into their kettles, eat their bread, loll on their beds under pretence of resting yourself, but in fact to find out if they are soft. You will feel a sublime pleasure in the course of this investigation, and a sublimer one hereafter, when you shall be able to apply your knowledge to the softening of their beds, or the throwing a morsel of meat into their kettle of vegetables.'

SOUPE AU RIS
RICE SOUP

When Jefferson became President, he relaxed protocol at the White House. All ambassadors were treated equally – which upset those who thought they were important, of the first rank – and instead of huge levées twice a week, he held small dinner parties, never more than fourteen people. So that conversation might be general, the table was a round one. So that his guests could feel free in their conversation, he introduced dumb waiters so that everyone could help themselves without the need for footmen. Apart from politics, there was no restraint on the conversation. Like Talleyrand, he understood that good food, good wine, intelligent talk and humour are the best background for diplomacy – and for happiness in general.

Even a Federalist opponent had to admit that the food was delicious. This is what they had: 'rice soup, round of beef, turkey, mutton, ham, loin of veal, cutlets of mutton, fried eggs, fried beef, a pie called macaroni which appeared to be a rich brown crust . . . Italian dish. Ice cream, very good, crust wholly dried, crumbled into thin flakes; a dish somewhat like a pudding – inside white as cream or curd, very porous and light, covered with a cream sauce . . . very fine' (p. 105).

> ¼ *litre (8 fl oz) Carolina rice, or Italian rice*
> *1¼ litres (2 pt) good beef stock or veal*
> *strong essence from roasted beef or veal if possible*

Wash the rice well, three or four times. Stew it in the stock gently for at least an hour. Remove any fat from the soup, taste to see if it needs salt and add the strong meat essence.

Note For this simple soup, it is essential to use a home-made stock made with shin of beef or veal knuckle bones.

EGGS WITH CAPER AND GARLIC SAUCE

When Jefferson was in the south of France, he was struck by the similarity of its climate and conditions to those of the southern states of America. Many things grown there could, he felt, be introduced with success to augment the 'natural bounty' of the place. He took careful notes about the caper, whose pickled buds – not fruits, as he wrote – added an agreeable sharpness to many dishes such as this one in the *Cuisinière bourgeoise*.

The caper is a tender plant, needing to be cherished in the winter. On average it will provide two pounds of capers, and requires little cultivation. 'The principal work is the gathering of the fruit as it forms. Every plant must be picked every other day from the last of June till the middle of October. But this is the work of women and children. This plant does well in any kind of soil which is dry, or even in walls where there is no soil, and it lasts the life of man.' He had taken his information in the neighbourhood of Toulon, but could not vouch for it entirely as 'the inhabitants speak no written language, but a medley, which I could understand but very imperfectly'.

The main object of his concern, apart from rice, was the olive, 'assuredly the richest gift of heaven, I can scarcely except bread. I see this tree in among the Alps where there is not soil enough to make bread for a single family.' He saw that Europe did not have enough oil to export it to America. If the memory of people who introduced rice to South Carolina is held in respect, 'a plant which sows life and death with almost equal hand, what obligations would be due to him who should introduce the olive tree. Were the owner of slaves to view it only as a means of bettering their condition, how much would he better that by planting one of those trees for every slave he possessed!' And so Jefferson persisted, year after year after year, but that particular glory was not to be his. Only when the West was opened up, were olives successfully introduced into America. Meanwhile he had to content himself with oil imported from France.

6–8 large eggs
1 tablespoon malt vinegar
10–12 large cloves garlic, in their skins
8–10 anchovy fillets
heaped tablespoon capers
dash of wine vinegar
salt, pepper
10–12 tablespoons olive oil approximately
parsley sprigs, tomato slices to decorate

Put the eggs in a pan of cold water to cover them – with a tablespoon of malt vinegar, which stops them cracking. Bring to the boil, and cook for 8 minutes. Drain off the water, and rinse with cold water until they are cool enough to shell. Set aside while you prepare the sauce: if you need to leave the eggs some time, store them in a bowl of cold water in the refrigerator.

Simmer the cloves of garlic in salted water for 7 minutes. Run under the cold tap, remove the skins and put them into the blender with the anchovy fillets, capers, wine vinegar a little seasoning. Whirl at top speed until reduced to a purée. Slowly add the olive oil – it will blend with the purée to make a sauce of mayonnaise -consistency. If you think it will take it, add a spoonful or two more oil. Taste and adjust the seasonings, adding more anchovy or capers if you like. The sauce will be a beautiful greyish-green colour; spread it out on a large serving dish, cut the eggs in half and arrange them, dome side up, on top. Decorate with slices of tomato and parsley sprigs. Serve with plenty of bread.

BOILED CRABS

One young American described a day with Jefferson and Madison, in 1790, as they all waited at Rock Hall on Chesapeake Bay for a 'vessel to take us over . . . We talked and dined and strolled and rowed ourselves in boats, and feasted on delicious crabs.'

When smaller crabs are about, they make a good first course. Boil them in water so strongly salted that an egg can float in it (or use sea water, if you live on the coast), allowing a crab per person. Give them 15 minutes if they weigh half a kilo (1 lb), 10 minutes for smaller crabs, once the liquor has returned to the boil.

Remove them and allow them to cool. Rub their shells over with oil to give them an appetising shine. Pull away the little flaps and the dead men's fingers. Arrange the crabs on a large serving dish with plenty of crushed ice, and seaweed if you can get it. Provide a large bowl of mayonnaise, bread and butter, plus nutcrackers and skewers for each person, finger bowls and large cloth napkins. This makes an excellent first course; one eats a modest amount slowly.

If you can only buy large boiled crabs, unfortunately you will need to prepare them yourself. This means cracking the claws and legs to extract all the meat, and poking about in the bony part inside the main shell. Press the open side of the main shell along the curved line, so that the middle shell comes away leaving an attractive shape in which the edible part can be served.

Provide other shellfish – oysters, prawns, opened mussels and so on – if you like, but crabs should be the main item.

SEAKALE

From 1806 when he obtained it from Bernard McMahon, the seedsman of Philadelphia, until the end of his life, Jefferson grew seakale enthusiastically. One year he put in 400 plants, and ordered fifty special 'earthen pots for covering plants of seakale' –

to blanch them – 'in the garden. I am told they are made at a pottery, in or near Richmond.'

Seakale was very much an English vegetable. It was in semi-cultivation in the seventeenth century, then it was taken into gardens from its wild habitat between sand and shore in the eighteenth century (on some parts of the south coast of England, especially around Hastings, during April and May you may still gather wild seakale that has been blanched beneath the banks of pebbles and sand blown up by the wind). The great French chef, Carême, was much impressed by *sikell* as he called it, when he was cooking for the Prince Regent in England. Mr McMahon specialised in receiving and acclimatising seeds from Europe, and plants, and would send American seeds and plants to Europe – a two-way business that Jefferson was keen to encourage.

In this country now, seakale is still a rare vegetable grown by people who like good things. You may buy seeds, root cuttings and plants from A. R. Paske, Regal Lodge, Kentford, Newmarket, with full instructions. From January until picking time in April, the plants need to be covered with pots to blanch them (no need for special pots from Richmond, Virginia – any plant pot will do, so long as you remember to put a tile over the hole to exclude light).

Scrub all grit from the stalks. Cut away the leaves if you like, for salad, but there is no need. Tie the stalks in bundles and cook them like asparagus. Serve them, well drained, with melted butter or hollandaise or mousseline sauce, as a first course.

MRS RANDOLPH'S OCHRA, CIMLIN OR CUSTARD MARROW, AND TOMATOES

The Virginia Housewife, written by Mary Randolph and published in 1825, was the first regional American cookery book. It contains many standard European recipes of course, but there are plenty of ways of dealing with the vegetables characteristic of Virginian gardens such as Monticello. Jefferson was unusual for his time in preferring vegetable dishes to the high protein diet that most people enjoyed (he felt that too much 'animal food' is what makes the English character so gross, rendering it 'insusceptible of civilisation'). He described himself as eating little meat, 'and that not as an aliment so much as a condiment for the vegetables which constitute my principal diet'.

Here are three of Mrs Randolph's recipes, all simple to follow, in her own words:

TO MAKE OCHRA SOUP

Get two double handfuls of young ochra, wash and slice it thin, add two onions chopped fine, put it into a gallon (4 litres – the American pint being closer the half-litre than to the Imperial pint) of water at a very early hour in an earthen pipkin, or very nice iron pot. It must be kept steadily simmering but not boiling: put in pepper and salt.

At twelve o'clock, put in a handful of lima beans; at half passed one o'clock, add three cimlins [custard marrows] cleaned and cut into small pieces, a fowl, or knuckle of veal, a bit of bacon or pork that has been boiled and six tomatoes, with skin taken off. When nearly done, thicken with a spoonful of butter, mixed with one of flour. Have rice boiled to eat with it.

Note Okra came from Africa with the slaves, but was soon valued by their masters as well for its flavour, and for the sticky juice which gives a jellied smoothness to sauces, stews and soups. It can also be cooked with onion and tomato: leave it whole, just removing the hard outer skin from the cone at the stalk end – do not pierce through, as the juices should stay in when okra is to be served as a vegetable on its own.

TO COOK SQUASH OR CIMLIN

Gather young squashes, peel and cut them in two. Take out the seeds, and boil them till tender. Put them into a colander, drain off the water, and rub them with a wooden spoon through the colander. Then put them into a stew pan, with a cup full of cream, a small piece of butter, some pepper and salt – stew them stirring very frequently until dry. This is the most delicate way of preparing squashes.

Note A recipe that can be used for every kind of squash, although it is at its best with custard marrow (cimlin). Pumpkin, cucumber, courgettes, chayote all do well, though with the more watery kinds, it is essential first to drain the purée, and then to dry it out over a moderate heat, before adding cream etc.

TO SCALLOP TOMATOES

Peel the skin from very large, full ripe tomatoes – put a layer in the bottom of a deep dish, cover it well with bread grated fine; sprinkle on pepper and salt, and lay some bits of butter over them – put another layer of each, till the dish is full – let the top be covered with crumbs and butter – bake it a nice brown.

Note Tomatoes were treated with caution by the English and northern French until modern times, but Jefferson loved them. One variety he grew, Spanish tomatoes, were especially fine and large – what the trade nowadays calls 'beefy'. Marmande and Eshkol are similar in style, firm flesh, no wateriness, and ideal for cooking as for salad. Avoid sloshy tomatoes from the supermarket; not only do they have no flavour, but they will ruin this dish with their moisture.

SWEETCORN

To the Americans, just 'corn' – with the young fresh cobs known as 'green corn' when they are at the right stage for picking, and are rushed in to the kitchen where a pan of water is ready boiling. This is not a myth – if the cobs wait around, the sugar turns to starch and the fine flavour has gone.

Jefferson liked green corn so much that he could not live without it in Paris (in France still, corn on the cob is a rare dish, maize being a field crop grown for animals, oil and the plastics industry). He had to send for seeds from America, to be sure of getting the right tender variety.

Here is the southern way of cooking corn from Evan Jones's *American Food*: pick twelve ears of corn, and remove the husks and silk. Have boiling a litre of each of milk and water ($1\frac{3}{4}$ pt), with 250 g (8 oz) butter. No salt. Put in the corn, and when the liquid returns to the boil, give the cobs eight to ten minutes. 'And some say it will keep in the milk-water mixture for at least an hour after the pot is taken from the fire, tasting as fresh as when the cooking stopped.'

Serve with cloth napkins, and melted butter. Remember, too, that Jefferson introduced finger bowls to America – after corn, they are a good idea.

CORN BREAD

One opponent – narrow minds and political smears are always with us – resented Jefferson's attempt to introduce his fellow country-men to something better than slabs of meat and hard liquor by the quart, declaring that Jefferson 'abjured his native victuals'. This was not true. Jefferson liked good food, choice and in small quan-tity, wherever it came from. When he was President, the governess came from Monticello to the White House to make sure he had his favourite 'batter cakes, fried apples and hot breads served with bacon and eggs' at breakfast.

Spoon and corn breads were often made for him. The main difference between them is that spoon bread is softer, being made with fine water-ground white cornmeal, whereas corn bread has a more cake-like consistency and a yellow colour from the coarser yellow cornmeal that is used (it is sometimes softened with wheat flour, as in the recipe below). White cornmeal is difficult to come by, but the yellow can be found in Italian shops, delicatessens and good groceries. I much prefer corn bread to polenta; it goes well with game and turkey dishes, Jefferson's favourite guineafowl, the beef terrine on p. 98, or hot boiled ham (p. 98). Here is one of many American recipes:

> 125 g (generous 4 oz) cornmeal
> 60 g (2 oz) plain flour
> heaped tablespoon sugar
> 2 level teaspoons baking powder
> ½ level teaspoon salt
> 1 large egg
> 100 g (3½ oz) melted butter, or half butter and half lard
> 150 ml (5 fl oz) milk

Mix dry ingredients, then add the remaining items, mixing

thoroughly but briefly until smooth. Put a wide strip of Bakewell paper down, across and up the long side of a loaf tin of at least ¾ litre (1½ pt) capacity. Turn the mixture into it. Bake at mark 6, 200° (400°) for three-quarters of an hour; the bread will pull slightly away from the edge of the tin when it is cooked. Ease the paper and lift out the corn bread on to a hot plate: serve with plenty of butter.

'NOUILLY A MACCARONI'

Jefferson introduced pasta into the United States. Among his papers is this recipe for home-made noodles, to be served 'like macaroni', and a drawing and description of a machine for shaping this kind of dough into proper round macaroni. He notes that in Naples, where the machine came from, they used 'a particular sort of flour called semolina' though elsewhere other kinds seemed to be quite successful. All the best Italian pasta is made from semolina flour, milled from durum, i.e. hard wheat. With home-made noodles, you get the best result by using strong plain bread flour, which is the closest thing we can buy to semolina flour. Pasta machines are on the market, too, and if you are fond of this type of food it is well worth buying one to make your own.

Here is Jefferson's recipe for the dough in half quantity – plenty for 8 people: beat two eggs with a wine glass of milk and a teaspoon of salt. Mix in enough hard flour to make a coherent dough – about 500 g (1 lb), depending on the size of the eggs and the size of the wine glass. Divide into four pieces. Roll out the first fairly thinly. Flap it over four times or so, then cut across into noodle-wide slices. Unroll the slices and you have long strips. Repeat with the rest of the dough, putting the strips to dry over a clothes horse, or on a cloth over the back of a chair. Leave for a couple of hours, longer if you like.

Put on a large pan half-full of water to boil. Add salt and a tablespoonful of oil (prevents water boiling over and noodles sticking to each other). Put in the noodles gradually, then adjust the heat to keep water at a simmer. Cook for 7–10 minutes – taste a piece to see if it is right. Drain and serve with butter and grated Parmesan. Jefferson returned to the States with a supply of Parmesan cheese, and had it sent to him later on from time to time.

Buttered noodles can also be served with meat and game instead of potatoes or corn bread.

SMITHFIELD HAMS

The best American hams are cured at Smithfield, Virginia, in much the same way as ours. The difference comes with the pigs, which are fed on peanuts. In Jefferson's day, although the Smithfield ham had not been legally defined, excellent locally cured hams were to be found on every southern table. Jefferson liked his hams glazed with sugar, cloves and white wine, in a manner that has become familiar in this country only in recent times.

If you are dealing with a huge ham, turn to p. 124 and boil it as directed, to within half an hour of the end of cooking time. Drain it, strip off the skin and place it in a baking tin. Stud with cloves in a diamond pattern, and spread with muscovado sugar. Pour round a generous half bottle of dry white wine or Champagne. Put into the oven at mark 5–6, 190–200° (375–400°) and complete the cooking; baste with the juices every five minutes or so. The ham will not suffer if it stays in the oven a little longer.

With smaller joints, say with gammon weighing from a kilo to 2½ kilos (2–5 lb), you can follow a braising method. Soak the piece for 3–4 hours. Drain it and put it into a pan or ovenproof dish. Treat with cloves, sugar and wine as above. Cover with foil and put into the oven at mark 4, 180° (350°), allowing 1¾ hours for a kilo piece up to 3 hours for 2½ kilos. Baste every 20 minutes, and remove the foil for the last 20 minutes.

Degrease the juices and serve them separately. Baked sweet potatoes go well with ham cooked in this way. Brush them with butter, stick a skewer through the centre and, if you like a soft outer skin, wrap them in foil or butter papers. Bake them for 1–1½ hours at mark 7, 220° (425°), if the ham is being boiled. Or for an appropriately longer time at the top of the oven, if the ham is being braised. Serve with butter.

TERRINE DE PAYSANNE

Jefferson 'ate heartily, and much vegetable food, preferring French cookery, because it made the meats more tender'. Here is a recipe from the *Cuisinière bourgeoise* that may seem to demand a lot of faith on the part of the cook, but take courage because the use of belly of pork does make the beef meltingly tender. The original recipe calls for a piece from the round or topside of beef, but I use aitchbone when I can as it is well marbled with fat. If you have no *quatre-épices*, follow instructions given on p. 208.

> ¾ *kilo (1½ lb) rolled aitchbone beef, or topside*
> ½ *kilo (1 lb) thinly sliced pork belly*
> *4 spring onions, chopped*
> *bunch of parsley, chopped*
> *1 heaped teaspoon* quatre-épices
> *1 rounded teaspoon salt*
> *1 bay leaf*
> *2 tablespoons brandy or other hard liquor*

Slice beef thinly – the pieces do not have to look large or beautiful, but you will manage better if the meat is chilled and firm. Do not remove the skin from the belly or pork slices. Mix the next four ingredients together. Layer the meats into a terrine, beginning with beef and ending with pork; scatter each layer with the mixed seasonings and put the bay leaf on top. Pour over the brandy or hard liquor, plus a tablespoon of water. Cover hermetically with foil and a lid, or a flour-and-water dough plus a lid (the latter is more successful unless the terrine is completely wrapped in tight-fitting foil). Put into the oven at mark 1–2, 140–150° (275–300°), for 3 hours. Remove the foil, or chip away the lid. Carefully pour off the juices, so that you can remove the fat. Taste them, taste a little bit of the meat too, and adjust the seasonings accordingly. Bring the liquid to boiling point and pour back over the meat, which will have shrunk together into an appetising concentration. Serve immediately, cutting the terrine down into thick slices. They will fall apart, but no matter, this is a country dish of rich flavour.

Potatoes or corn bread or home-made bread can be served with it, and a salad afterwards. Jefferson grew many kinds of salading, so a bowl of watercress and chicory or a crisp lettuce after this dish in the French style, would not be inappropriate.

CHICKEN MATELOTE

Jefferson did his best to act both as mother and father to Martha and Maria. From their letters, one sees that it was a successful relationship. Certainly he gives good advice, exhorts Martha to try again with Livy. He also enters into their small occupations and interests, clothes as well as books. One of his grand-daughters later wrote, 'My Bible came from him, my Shakespeare, my first writing-table, my first handsome writing desk, my first Leghorn hat, my first silk dress.' It had been the same with his daughters, and they were quite ready to make tart remarks back, if they thought he had been a little too 'improving'. When Maria was twelve and staying with her much-loved aunt, Jefferson wrote that he was delighted she could make a pudding, and hoped she had a hen and chickens of her own to look after. Had she noticed that you often hear the first whippoorwills when the first strawberries and peas come along? Back came a slightly exasperated reply, she had had such a time protecting her chickens that she had not had a chance to listen for whippoorwills.

Some people have commented that Jefferson was not interested in women's rights and education. This is partly true, but running a big house like Monticello in those days was business career enough for any woman I would have thought. An incompetent wife could easily ruin the whole enterprise. As a southern estate owner, Jefferson had a constant stream of visitors, even more after he had been President. Like Sydney Smith, he compared his house to an inn – sometimes they entertained fifty guests – which gave Martha a busy career by any standards; she could not go to the discount store or cash-and-carry either, but had to see to the provision of basic food as well as its preparation for the table.

> *12–16 small onions*
> *2 medium carrots*
> *parsnip 'the length of two fingers'*
> *125 g (4 oz) butter*
> *2 heaped teaspoons flour*
> *¼ litre (8 fl oz) each dry white wine and beef stock*
> *bouquet of parsley, chopped*
> *2–4 Welsh or spring onions, chopped*

1 clove of garlic, crushed
bay leaf, sprig thyme
¼ teaspoon dried basil
2 cloves
1 large chicken, jointed, or capon
giblets, minus liver
6 anchovy fillets
1 tablespoon capers

Top and tail the onions, then blanch them for 7 minutes in boiling salted water. Run them under the cold tap and remove their skins. Cut carrots and parsnip into large matchstick strips. Melt half the butter in a sauté pan, cook it to a golden brown noisette stage, then stir in the flour. After two minutes' cooking, add the liquids, the onion and root vegetables, the herbs, Welsh or spring onion and spice. Cover and simmer half an hour. Meanwhile brown the chicken or capon in the remaining butter. Add to the sauce with the giblets. Simmer 30 minutes, or longer until the chicken is done, turning the pieces occasionally, and removing the breast before it overcooks.

Put the chicken on a hot serving plate with the onions and vegetable strips. Keep them warm. Skim and degrease the sauce which should be well reduced (if not, boil down hard). Crush together four of the anchovy fillets with the capers, and add them to the sauce. Simmer one minute, stirring, then taste, and add the remaining anchovy fillets if you like, crushing them first. Add seasoning if necessary.

Note Guineafowl can be cooked in the same way, and were a favourite dish of Jefferson's. Unfortunately, it is not easy to find them in this country, which is odd as they are excellent eating – like chicken with something of a pheasant flavour.

STUFFED TURKEY LEGS

The twenty-five recipes for turkey in the later editions of Menon's book would have been welcome to a young American housewife like Martha Jefferson, who even after her marriage continued to live at Monticello and kept house for her father. Even if you cannot get hold of calf's sweetbreads and have to make do with lamb's, this is a delicious way of cooking turkey legs (thigh or drumstick, it doesn't matter). If sweetbreads of any kind are impossible to buy in your part of the country, substitute cooked ham of good quality.

> *6–8 turkey drumsticks or thigh joints*
> *250 g (8 oz) blanched sweetbreads, diced*
> *200 g (6–7 oz) mushrooms, chopped*
> *3 rashers green streaky bacon, chopped small*
> *1 heaped tablespoon chopped parsley*
> *1 heaped tablespoon chopped shallot*
> *½ teaspoon dried basil*
> *3 chopped Welsh or spring onions*
> *1 egg yolk*
> *salt, pepper*
> *¼ litre (8 fl oz) dry white wine and beef stock*
> *small bunch of parsley and Welsh or spring onions*
> *6–8 small sheets of pork back fat or very fat bacon*
> *large walnut of butter*
> *heaped teaspoon flour*
> *lemon juice*

Bone the turkey. Mix next eight ingredients, and season with salt and pepper. Put about a tablespoon into each piece of turkey, then sew it up with button thread. Any stuffing left over can be put into the bottom of a sauté pan with the wine, stock and bunch of herbs. Put in the turkey and place the fat on top. Cover and simmer until cooked, turning the pieces and replacing the fat on top every so often. Arrange them when tender on a hot serving dish and discard the fat, both the pork or bacon pieces and from the top of the cooking liquor.

Strain the liquor into a clean pan and boil it down hard to concentrate the flavour. Mash butter and flour, and add in dabs to thicken it slightly. Check seasoning, add lemon juice to taste and pour over the turkey: there should be just a little sauce to moisten the dish, not a sea of it.

THE DESSERT

Jefferson loved good fruit and nuts. His efforts to introduce European varieties into America and American varieties into Europe occupied a good deal of time when he was in Paris.

On his travels to the south of France, he commented on the different taste of the oranges, and was delighted by some raisins from Smyrna that he saw at Marseilles which were seedless. When he returned to the States, he asked his French steward Petit to bring a good supply of dried figs, dried peaches and plums, almonds and raisins when he followed him. Everywhere he noted the first strawberries, as if he celebrated them each year in a small private feast.

He was pleased to see that of the fruit grown and sold in Paris, only pears and apricots were better than American varieties (though the French also grew an apricot-peach that was quite unknown to him). 'Though we have some grapes as good as in France, yet we have by no means such a variety, nor so perfect a succession of them.' The melons in Paris were worse than the worst in Virginia: 'there is not sun enough to ripen them and give them flavour'.

In the garden at Monticello every possible fruit was grown, in several varieties; and another fruit grower, Judge Buel of Albany in New York State, raised a greenish-yellow skinned plum in 1825 and called it Jefferson in his honour (in his book *The Plums of England*, H. V. Taylor notes: 'One of the best plums to grow for dessert purposes. Failed to succeed as a commercial plum in the U.S.A., but is being planted in England for that purpose now' – i.e. in 1949). The last year that Jefferson himself ordered seeds for the garden was 1825, but people were still sending them to him in the year of his death – 'I transmit twelve seeds of the indigenous oranges of Florida' – and he was writing letters to his friends on gardening matters, and making plans for a botanical garden at his University of Virginia, until two months before his death, on 4 July 1826, the fiftieth anniversary of the Declaration of Independence.

Pecan nuts were a particular enthusiasm of his. When he wrote his *Notes on the State of Virginia* for a member of the French Legation in Philadelphia – it was first published in France – he comments that pecans, the 'Illinois nut', had not been described by Linnaeus, or by Philip Miller, or even by John Clayton in the *Flora Virginica*. When he arrived in France himself, he ordered pecans by the hundred from friends in America so that he could give them to gardening friends. And on his return to Monticello he planted many pecan trees himself.

Jefferson also listed black and white walnuts, hazelnuts and chestnuts. Among fruit, persimmons mulberries, cranberries, dewberries and cloudberries, quinces, pomegranates, figs, musk and water melons, as well as the more usual kinds.

Among the varieties of cherry – Bigarreau, Duke, Kentish, Morello Duke – Jefferson grew a special sour cherry for pies. I must add that the finest cherries I have ever eaten, large black skinned cherries, were imported from the United States; often with larger fruit the flavour is not so good, but these tasted as superb as they looked.

VIRGINIAN CHERRY PIE

A Morello, i.e. a sour cherry, does give the best result in cooking, whether you are making a sauce for duck or a pudding like this. You can add sugar; it's the acid flavour you need.

Stone enough cherries to fill a deep pie dish. Put them into a wide pan, cover them with a lid and stew until the juices run slightly. Shake the pan from time to time. This pre-cooking is a good idea with puff pastry pies which require short, sharp cooking to raise and colour the crust.

Line the pie dish with puff pastry. Mix the cherries and their juice with plenty of sugar – 125–175 g (4–6 oz) per half kilo or pound. Tip into the dish. Mix a tablespoon of cornflour with a tablespoon of sugar, and scatter it over the fruit. Cover the pie with puff pastry, knock up the edges, make a central hole and so on, and brush over with beaten egg. Bake for 30 minutes at mark 7, 220° (425°) – protect the crust with foil or a butter paper after 20 minutes, if it is browning too rapidly.

APPLE AND QUINCE PIES

For a single-crust pie, follow your usual apple pie recipe, but add one quince, cut up small. Boil the peel and cores of apples and quinces in water to cover, to extract all possible flavour. Use this small amount of liquid to moisten the fruit.

For a double-crust pie, cook the filling first. Simmer the quince in the flavoured liquid, and add the apple when it begins to be tender. Complete the cooking, adding sugar to taste towards the end. Cool before using.

If you wish to eat a fruit pie cold, it will be less fatty if you make it with shortcrust pastry (use lard for a rich crust, or half lard and half butter). Brush the top with water or egg white, and sprinkle it with sugar before baking for 30 minutes at mark 6, 200° (400°).

VANILLA ICE CREAM

Jefferson liked sweet dishes. He sent recipes for wine jelly, Savoy cake, macaroons, meringues, ice cream and blancmanger to his daughters, and noted the custards, creams and fruit compôtes which were popular at the French Court when he was in Paris.

He seems to have introduced Americans to vanilla, which he had sent from France when he returned home, and he must have been one of the first to acquire an apparatus for making ice cream (see p. 39), when he bought one in 1784. He would surely have been delighted with the electric ice cream machines that the Americans produce these days: they work much better than the sorbetières that have to be put into the refrigerator or deep freeze.

1 litre (1¾ pt) whipping cream
vanilla pod
6 egg yolks
pinch salt
150 g (5 oz) sugar
¼ litre (8 fl oz) double cream

Bring the whipping cream and vanilla pod slowly to the boil. Meanwhile beat the yolks, salt and sugar together in a basin. Pour on the boiling cream, whisking all the time, then return to the pan and stir over a low heat until the custard thickens – still with the vanilla pod. Taste and add extra sugar if you like. If the custard appears at all grainy, which it can do without being curdled, remove the vanilla pod and whirl it in the blender. Whip the double cream and fold it into the cold custard. Freeze in the usual way at the lowest possible temperature, or in an ice cream machine according to the instructions.

Jefferson was anxious to bring maple trees to the south, for the benefit of their sugar and syrup. It would be in order to serve maple syrup of good quality with the ice cream – but take care with this. Some maple syrup on sale has had ordinary sugar syrup added to it. Read the small print.

BLANCMANGER

A dish that started off in the Middle Ages as a mixture of chicken breasts and almonds, always a white smooth dish, always a treat until some nineteenth-century cook had the dreadful idea of thickening milk with cornflour to make the 'shape' or 'blancmange' of institutional cookery. Here is Jefferson's recipe, or rather the recipe he passed on from his French steward, which should convert anyone to the virtues of the true blancmanger.

> *60 g (2 oz) blanched almonds*
> *¼ teaspoon true almond essence,* not *so-called almond*
>   *flavouring*
> *60 g (2 oz) sugar*
> *¼ litre (8 fl oz) single cream*
> *350 ml (12 fl oz) whipping cream or* crème fraiche
> *packet (½ oz) gelatine*
> *lemon juice (*see *recipe)*
> *almond oil*

Blend first four ingredients in a liquidiser, to make them as smooth as possible. Gradually add the whipping cream or *crème fraiche* and the gelatine dissolved in 6 tablespoons of very hot water. Taste and add a little lemon juice to bring out the flavour – this will not be necessary if you have used *crème fraiche*.

Brush out a decorative mould with almond oil (from the chemist) or a tasteless oil. Pour in the blancmange mixture and leave to set. Plenty for 8, in spite of the small quantities, because it is very filling. Blancmanger can be served with a compôte of fruit, or fresh fruit salad, or just with plain thin biscuits.

Note If you do not have a mould, divide the mixture between custard cups or tulip-shaped wine glasses.

MERINGUES

It seems likely that meringues had been eaten in Paris at least for about a century when Jefferson arrived there. An English dictionary of 1706 gives it as a French word and describes what it was (and still is); the earliest printed mention in French comes from the third, 1698 edition, of Massialot's *Cuisinier Roial et Bourgeois* (in the first, 1691 edition, they were called *mellandes*). Menon mentioned them in his *Nouveau traité de la cuisine* of 1739, but not in his *Cuisinière bourgeoise* that Jefferson bought in a later edition for his daughter. One concludes from this that they remained very much the province of the professional cook, although Jefferson did not think them beyond the capability of the Monticello kitchen staff when he sent the recipe, which he had obtained from one of his French employees.

The proportions are identical with the ones we use today, and the main problem of meringues – the cooking temperature – was well understood: 'Metter les dans un four très doux, that is to say in an oven after the bread is taken out. You may leave them there as long as you please.' They would have dried out well in the dying heat – meringues need to dry out rather than cook.

Whisk 4 egg whites until they are stiff. Then add 2 heaped tablespoons of caster sugar, still whisking; the mixture will become satiny. Fold in a further 2 heaped tablespoons of caster sugar.

Line a baking sheet or board with Bakewell parchment, and drop dessertspoonfuls of the mixture on to it. Leave space between them, and go on to a second sheet or board if necessary. Put them into the lowest possible oven and leave until they are crisp; you can even use the plate-warming oven of some solid-fuel and oil-fired cookers, and leave them for 24 hours (if they are left for more than 24 hours, they colour a pale fawnish brown).

In the eighteenth century, meringues were eaten with jam very often, so that a mixture of jam and cream would not be out of place.

PÊCHES À L'EAU DE VIE
PEACHES IN BRANDY (OR VODKA)

Fruits in brandy are a preserve we have lost the habit of making in this country. A pity. They make an excellent winter dessert, usually on their own with a little of the syrup – along the lines of preserved ginger – but also added to fruit salads, or to a dish of ice cream.

The recipe Jefferson passed on from his French steward to his daughter was for making a syrupy preserve, suitable especially for the pudding course; simpler recipes involve packing the skinned fruit into jars, half-filling them with a syrup made from 2 tumblers of sugar boiled with a tumbler of water, and topping the jar up with brandy, but this more elaborate method gives a finer result:

> *2 kilos (4 lb) peaches*
> *about 1½ kilos (3 lb) sugar*
> *bottle brandy or vodka*

Rub any down from the peaches and prick them five or six times with a fork, right through to the stone. Bring half a kilo (1 lb) sugar slowly to the boil with 1¼ litres (2 pts) water, stirring so that the sugar is thoroughly dissolved before boiling point is reached. Slip in the peaches a few at a time, bring back the syrup to the boil, allow it to boil up twice, then remove the peaches. When they are cool, remove the skins if they begin to look messy. If you like, cut them in half, remove the stones; crack the stones and extract the kernels which should be put with the peach halves. Many people leave the peaches whole.

Measure out 600 ml (1 pt) of the syrup in which the peaches were blanched. Dissolve in it a kilo (2 lb) of sugar, stirring well. When boiling point is reached, slip in the peaches again and when the syrup returns to the boil, remove them. Allow the syrup to continue boiling until it reaches 230° on a thermometer. Cool. Pack the peaches into bottling jars. Complete as above with cooled syrup and alcohol.

WINES AND BEVERAGES

Jefferson did not care for the hard liquor drinking of America, nor for the English habit of serving port and sherry with meals.

For his own table he preferred white wines – Meursault, Montrachet – though he did provide himself with the light red Volnay, and enjoyed Italian Monte pulciano and Nebbiolo wines. He knew a good deal about German wines, and when he travelled down the Rhine discovered that he preferred Rüdesheim to Hocheim by far, though they were the same price. He commented on the improvement in Johannisberg since the Bishop of Fulda had taken a hand in its production.

In Burgundy he 'rambled through their most celebrated vineyards, going through the houses of the labourers, cellars of the vignerons, and mixing and conversing with them' – as he was there in March there would have been plenty of time for sociability and for tasting, too. He corresponded with 'Monsieur Diquem' for the best of the Sauternes, and noted that Barsac was the strongest. Another dessert wine he liked was Frontignan though it 'is rarely seen at a good table because it is cheap'.

Loire wines from Anjou and Touraine were good but not so good as the Bordeaux wines. He took the route from Nantes up to Orléans, visiting the châteaux and vineyards.

With his appreciation went moderate habits. 'I double, however, the doctor's glass-and-a-half of wine, and even treble it with a friend; but halve its effect by drinking the weak' – i.e. table – 'wines only. . . . Malt liquors and cider are my table drinks, and my breakfast . . . is of tea and coffee.'

PETIT'S METHOD OF MAKING COFFEE

'On one measure of the coffee ground into meal, pour three measures of boiling water. Boil it on hot ashes mixed with coal till the meal disappears from the top, when it will be precipitated. Pour it three times through a flannel strainer. It will yield $2\frac{1}{2}$ measures of clear coffee.

'An ounce of coffee meal makes $1\frac{1}{2}$ cup of clear coffee in this way.

'The flannel must be rinsed out in hot or cold water for every making.'

The Reverend Sydney Smith (1771–1845)

If ever I have the chance of arranging a dinner party under the trees of the Elysian Fields, the first person I shall invite will be the Reverend Sydney Smith (the second will be his friend, the Irish singer and composer of songs, Tom Moore). He was witty, gay and loving, adored by his family and friends, who included everyone worth knowing at the time, but principally the Hollands, the Lansdownes, and Earl Grey of the Reform Bill and his wife. His opinions reflected his generous character. He loathed the cane, and dealt firmly with fathers who claimed 'It never did *me* any harm'. He was against boys being deluged with the classics, but felt that women should be educated: 'We know women are to be compassionate: but they cannot be compassionate from eight o'clock in the morning till twelve at night.' He ridiculed the 'very general notion, that if you once suffer women to eat of the tree of knowledge, the rest of the family will very soon be reduced to the same kind of aerial and unsatisfactory diet'.

He learned to cook, loved good food, and felt that he could feed or starve a man into virtue or vice. That character, virtues and so on 'are powerfully affected by beef, mutton, pie-crust, and rich soups'. Digestion was the secret of life, the source of humour and friendliness. As a parson he decided that God is best served by a 'regular tenour of good actions . . . the luxury of false religion is to be unhappy!'

Other Whig opinions, such as his enthusiasm for Catholic Emancipation, ensured banishment to a country parish in Yorkshire, 'so out of the way that it was actually 12 miles from a lemon'. A hard fate for a popular preacher and a great diner-out. Moreover the house was in ruins. Neither predicament daunted him. He devised a lemon substitute using citric acid and essence of lemon, and rebuilt the house.

He had to do the same thing with the vicarage at Combe Florey near Taunton in Somerset, when he moved there in 1829. His house lies a distance from the church, in a little scooping valley of its own, at right angles to the road, that forms the main garden. The old kitchen garden was up on a side slope facing south, with great stone walls. On the opposite slope is the hanging wood of beech trees and oak where Sydney Smith stationed his two donkeys one day, disguised as deer with antlers tied to their heads – to the astonishment of his guests. He turned to one of them and remarked 'You said the only thing this place wanted to make it perfect was deer; what do you say now? I have, you see, ordered my gamekeeper to drive my deer to the most picturesque point of view. Excuse their long ears, a little peculiarity belonging to parsonic deer. Their voices, too, are singular; but we do our best for you, and you are too true a friend of the Church to mention our defects.'

This vicarage, which has been lovingly restored in the last few years, is everyone's ideal family house. Hall, staircase, upstairs landing are wide and friendly. The floors shine. There is a huge drawing-room with a library en suite, and an equally large room overhead, which were Sydney Smith's main scenes of entertainment. In this house, a procession of friends drank, ate and laughed. Towards the end of his life he came to a sad conclusion, that he passed on to John Murray, Byron's publisher: 'If you wish for anything like happiness in the fifth act of life, eat and drink about one-half what you could eat and drink . . . Did I ever tell you my calculation. I found that between ten and seventy years of age, I had eaten and drunk forty-four horse waggon-loads of meat and drunk more than would have preserved me in life and health . . . It occurred to me that I must, by my voracity, have starved to death fully a hundred persons.'

The reflections of a man suffering from gout, and dying. But such moments of regret were few. He had lived and enjoyed a good life. He loved the occasional journeys abroad. His wife wanted to see the sights, 'where Sigbert the Fat slew Fiddlefid the Bold, but the aujourd'hui of life' was enough for him; the bread in Holland, dinner with the King in Brussels where he ate pâté de foie gras to the sound of trumpets, dinner with the great Talleyrand who employed the best cook in Paris on the principle that diplomacy and friendship flourish best against a background of good food. On his first journey to Paris he bought a revised new edition of Menon's *Cuisinière bourgeoise*, originally published in 1746; then later, in London, he bought Beauvillier's *L'Art du Cuisinier* which he and his wife read aloud to each other on winter evenings at Combe Florey – 'I find as I suspected that garlic is power; not in its despotic shape, but exercised with the greatest discretion.'

Sometimes, quite often, this brilliant man tired of the country – 'a sort of healthy grave' – and longed for his annual three months' duty as Canon of St Paul's to come round. How thankfully he sat down once more at Lady Holland's table. How delighted she was to have him back. He was kind to new guests who were overawed by the brilliant Whig circle. He would slip in a witty remark when the conversation threatened to become dull, and set everyone off again, laughing and happy, convinced of their own wit as well as Sydney Smith's, as they ate the excellent dinner.

MACKEREL MAÎTRE D'HÔTEL

In April 1826, Sydney Smith made his first visit to Paris and stayed in the rue St Honoré, the great street for bakers and pastrycooks (St Honoré is their patron saint). He admired the inns and the manners of their staff, 'the *cookery* admirable'. Paris water was excellent, but he criticised the lack of tablecloths in the coffee-houses, 'and the want of W.C. is one of the most crying evils in Paris'. He had a sociable time, dining out and visiting, but one evening he had no invitation 'and dined by myself at a coffee-house. I dined upon a Demi Macreau à la Maître d'hôtel, Bifsteak à l'Anglaise, des harricaux blanches à la Maître d'hôtel, Fromage de Neuf Chatel, Semi-bouteille de vin de Bordeaux ordinaire – all good and well chosen. I improve in my knowledge of Paris cookery.'

Here is the recipe for *mackerel maître d'hôtel* from Beauvillier's cookery book that the Smiths read aloud to each other in the evenings a few years later.

For eight people, clean 4 large mackerel through the gills opening. You should be able to get your fingers, and a teaspoon or thin-bladed knife into the cavity and hook out the innards. Rinse well. Put back the roes if you can do so easily, otherwise set them aside. Slit the mackerel carefully down the back, snipping the backbone with scissors in two places – this will ensure that the fish stay flat, and it will make the backbone easier to remove later on.

This whole business of cleaning and splitting becomes much easier if you follow Beauvillier's suggestion that you remove the heads first. This is up to you. Some people feel strongly that fish should be left with their heads on.

Now sprinkle the mackerel with salt, and put them into a dish. Pour over 4–6 tablespoons olive oil and scatter with 2 chopped onion and 2 tablespoons of chopped parsley. Leave them for at least half an hour, turning them occasionally.

Mash together, for the maître d'hôtel butter, ¾ packet (6 oz) lightly salted butter, 3 heaped tablespoons chopped parsley, three or four sprigs of tarragon chopped, 1–2 leaves chopped lemon balm if possible, salt and lemon juice to taste. This can all be done electrically in a chopper or processor. Form into a roll, and chill slightly.

After brushing off the debris of the marinade, grill the mackerel. If the roes came out, put them into the grill pan half way through the cooking time, so that they are not overdone.

Split the cooked mackerel in halves, discarding the back bone. Top the cut sides with slices of maître d'hôtel butter and slide under the grill to melt them slightly. Serve straightaway with bread, or a few new potatoes if they are a main course.

SOLE NORMANDE

On his second visit to Paris in 1835, Sydney Smith wrote to Lady Grey: 'I shall not easily forget a Matelotte at the Rochers de Cancailles, an almond tart at Montreuil, or a Poulet à la Tartare at Grignon's' – the two latter dishes are given later on – 'These are impressions which no changes in future life can ever obliterate.'

Au Rocher de Cancale, in the rue Montorgueil, was one of the best restaurants in Paris. Literary dinners were held there, so were theatre dinners; Balzac, Dumas, Hugo, Brillat-Savarin, Talma were all regular clients. As you would expect from the name – Cancale in Brittany is still famous for oysters – the main emphasis was on fish. There in 1837, the chef Langlais simplified a recipe of Carême's given in his *Art de la cuisine française au dix-neuvième siècle,* 1833–1835, for *ragoût de matelote normande* into the dish that has ever since been known as sole normande.

It is difficult to know from Sydney Smith's letter whether he had been so impressed by a version of Carême's *matelote,* or whether he had eaten the mixed stew of fish cooked in a red wine sauce that the French call *matelote* today. With the restaurant's connections, I think the former is more likely. An interesting thing is that Carême used a sweet white wine, Sauternes, whereas Langlais appears to have preferred the dry white wine of modern fish cookery.

The recipe below is a simplified version of Langlais', omitting the extra garnish of oysters and smelts. However, if you can afford oysters and find smelts, add them to the dish with the mussels and mushrooms: first stiffen the oysters in their own liquor over a moderate heat (add the juices to the sauce), and fry the smelts in butter.

> *1 kilo (2 lb) mussels*
> *250 g (8 oz) mushrooms*
> *butter*
> *juice of a lemon*
> *1 heaped tablespoon flour*
> *8 thick slices bread*
> *2 large soles*
> *300 g (10 oz) chopped onion*
> *250 ml (8 fl oz) dry white wine*
> *salt, pepper*
> *1 large egg yolk*

Scrub and scrape the mussels, pulling away their beards. Throw out any that are broken, or that refuse to close when tapped smartly with a knife. Set them in a heavy, lidded pan over a high heat. Shake occasionally, and check after 3 minutes to see how many have opened. Remove them, and leave the rest for a little while longer. Carefully strain the liquor through muslin, and set the shelled mussels aside. Slice and cook the mushrooms in butter, squeezing the lemon juice over them once they start to bubble.

In a separate pan, make a roux with a heaped tablespoon of butter and flour. Cook for two minutes, then moisten with the mussel liquor and the juices strained from the cooked mushrooms.

The sauce will probably be very thick, but do not worry as you will be adding the sole liquor to dilute it.

Prepare the bread by cutting off the crusts, and slicing it into triangles. Butter them on both sides and set on a baking sheet. Heat the oven to mark 1, 140° (275°) and put in the bread. Check from time to time, turning the bread so that it browns nicely. If it browns too quickly, it can be removed and reheated later.

Skin the soles on the dark side. To do this, cut a nick across the skin just above the tail. Raise it slightly, salt your fingers and grip the skin, tearing it steadily away from the fish. Cut down the backbone centre division with a sharp pointed knife, and raise the fillets slightly from the bone for about a centimetre each side. Blanch the onion in boiling water for 2 minutes.

Butter a large shallow pan (or two, if you do not have one that is large enough). Put in the drained onion and lay the soles on top, cut side down. Pour in the wine then enough water barely to cover the fish. Season and simmer until the fish are cooked. Remove them to a hot serving dish, and surround with the mussels and mushrooms. Put into the oven to keep warm.

If the pan(s) were large and the juices on the copious side, boil them down vigorously before adding them to the sauce through a sieve. If the pan was a close fit, strain the liquor immediately into the sauce, and boil it down. Whichever you do, aim to have a rich sauce of concentrated flavour. Finally whisk the yolk with a little sauce in a bowl, then put it into the pan of sauce, and stir steadily for a few minutes over a heat that keeps the sauce below boiling point. Pour over the sole, return to the oven for 5 minutes, then serve, with the triangles of bread tucked round the dish.

This Normandy style of fish cookery takes quite a lot of describing, but in practice it is simple to do. The garnish of mussels and mushrooms can be prepared earlier in the day which makes life easier. If you chance to make this dish in Normandy, the bread you should use is the *pain à potage*, those hard loaves that have been baked almost to crispness so that they will sop up the evening's soup until it is almost a panada.

POTATOES OR BEANS MAÎTRE D'HÔTEL

To his wife, from Paris, 'The Pommes de Terre, and the Arricaux a la maître d'hotel were excellent. We must learn how to dress potatoes in this manner.' Certainly it is a manner worth learning.

The secret is always to have a roll or two of maître d'hôtel butter in the fridge or freezer. If you make it in an electric chopper or food processor, this is simple and practical. Use the ingredients given under mackerel maître d'hôtel, on p. 113, or the following:

> *1 packet (8 oz) slightly salted Danish butter*
> *50 g (about 1½ oz) bunch parsley*
> *4–5 spring onions, each cut in three or four*
> *about 2 tablespoons lemon juice*

The butter must be at room temperature, even on the soft side. Cut it up and put it in the chopper with the parsley leaves and the spring onion. Whizz to a mash, adding lemon juice gradually; the butter may not absorb the lot. Dollop the mixture on to a piece of foil, and turn the foil over it, rolling with both your hands to form into a long even shaped cylinder about 3 centimetres in diameter (a good inch). Wrap completely and store.

Potatoes: kidney-shaped, waxy new potatoes are best. Scrape and boil them, then cut them into slices; for eight people, allow a kilo (2 lb). If you use old potatoes, try and get Desirée as they are the firmest on general sale. Steam or boil 1½ kilos (3 lb) in their skins. Peel and cut them into cylinders (keep the debris for soup), and slice them.

Reheat the potatoes in a wide shallow pan with about half the maître d'hôtel butter, turning the slices carefully until they are coated and very hot. Do this over a very moderate heat, so that the butter does not lose its fresh flavour.

Beans: with haricot beans, soak and boil 375–500 g (¾–1 lb) in the usual way, salting them at the end. Drain and heat through in the butter just before serving. Green beans and many other vegetables – carrots, salsify, young turnips, etc – can all be finished in the same way.

SPINACH AND EGGS

'I went yesterday . . . to breakfast with the Duke de Broglie. There was no cloth upon the table . . . There was roast fowl, spinach eggs, apples, wine, and afterwards they brought tea . . . The children drank wine for their breakfast.' He went again, a week later, and obviously did not like the family very much: 'They are virtuous sensible disagreeable people and give bad breakfasts without a table-cloth.' The Duke was the great liberal statesman of France, his wife was the daughter of Madame de Stael; and I suppose that one of those wine-drinking children was the grandfather of the two great physicists of our day. Those breakfasts were perhaps the French equivalent of our 'plain living and high thinking'. They seem to have lacked the gaiety of spirit that Sydney Smith admired as an essential companion to virtue.

Nonetheless spinach and eggs are a good combination when cooked well. You could have them with roast fowl, or as a course beforehand.

> 1½ *kilo (3 lb) spinach*
> 60 g (2 oz) butter
> 125 ml (4 fl oz) double or whipping cream, or 150 ml
>   (5 fl oz) béchamel sauce
> salt, pepper
> 6–8 eggs

Wash the spinach well, removing brown bits and the thicker stalks – the easiest way to do this is to bend the spinach leaf in half down the stem, right sides facing, then to pull or cut away the stem itself.

The English way with spinach is to cook it in its own juices in a heavy, covered pan. The French way, that is I think better if you have a large enough pan, is to bring a huge pan, just over half full of salted water to the boil, and then put in the spinach. Keep the heat high, so that the water barely goes off the boil. The leaves should float round freely, and in theory they cook more quickly on account of this. Drain them well, and chop. Reheat with the butter and either cream or béchamel. Season to taste.

Boil the eggs exactly 7 minutes, then shell them carefully (the yolks will not quite be set), or poach the eggs if this is the way you prefer.

Dish the spinach, and arrange the eggs carefully on top. Serve immediately, with toast or croûtons of fried bread. Or you can serve the spinach and eggs on individual slices of toast or fried bread.

FRICANDEAU OF VEAL

On his second visit to Paris in 1835, Sydney Smith took his wife. They stayed at the Hotel de Londres, in the Place Vendôme. From there he wrote, 'Meat thoroughly subdued by human skill, is more agreeable to me than the barbarian Stonehenge masses of meat with which we feed ourselves.'

The fricandeau is a French classic which was also popular in England in Sydney Smith's day. Now it is difficult to find a good veal butcher outside London, but it is worth persisting. Ask for a 'cushion' of veal, a piece cut with and from the muscle that lies close to the leg bone; it is a beautiful long rounded shape, being cut with the grain of the meat from the topside so that the muscle lies alone and free. You need a piece of 1½ kilos (3 lb) or more.

> *1½ kilos (3 lb) veal*
> *piece of pork hard back fat*
> *125 g (4 oz) each chopped onion and carrot*
> *60 g (2 oz) salt pork belly, or green streaky bacon, diced*
> *150 ml (5 fl oz) dry white wine*
> *about 600 ml (1 pt) veal stock, barely salted*
> bouquet garni

Lard the top and sides of the veal with whisker strips cut from the chilled pork fat: take up 'stitches' with the larding needle so that you make an orderly pattern on the outside of the meat. Cut the fatty ends to the same length neatly.

Choose a deep pot that fits the meat closely. Put in the vegetables and diced pork or bacon. Put the veal on top. Put into the oven, uncovered, at mark 8, 230° (450°) for 15–20 minutes. Pour over wine and the stock which should come barely level with the top of the veal. Lay a butter paper on top, add *bouquet*, then put on the lid. Reduce the oven to mark 4, 180° (350°), and leave for 1½–2 hours until the meat is tender enough to be cut with a spoon. Baste every 15 minutes. The lid need not fit too tightly, which will give the stock a chance of slowly evaporating.

When the meat is done, remove it from the pan to a plate. Strain off the liquid into a shallow pan (discard the braising vegetables and bacon). Put the veal back into its rinsed-out pot. Boil up the liquid, skimming off the fat and scum. Reduce it to ¼ litre (9 fl oz) of rich liquid (this is why the original stock should barely be salted). Pour it over the veal, and return to a hot oven, mark 8, 230° (450°). Keep basting until the meat is beautifully glazed with a syrupy brown essence. Alternatively, you can do this on top of the stove – the method I prefer, as it is easier to control – turning the meat over and over as the liquid reduces.

Finally, put the veal on a hot serving dish, and surround it with some vegetables – a purée of spinach goes well with it, or some green beans. Cut a few slices and pour over them the last of the brown essence in the pan.

CHICKEN TARTARE

This dish of *Poulet à la tartare* that he had eaten at Grignon's, and others like it, were still on Sydney Smith's mind after he returned to England. He wrote to his friend at Tadcaster, Richard York, 'Let me beg of you a greater attention than you have hitherto paid to *Sauce à la tartare* – it opened to me a new train of ideas. How shall I be able to live upon the large raw limbs of meat to which I am destined? Where shall I find those delicious stews, that thoroughly subjugated meat which opposes no resistance to the teeth and still preserves all its gravies for the palate? It fills me with despair and remorse to think how badly I have been fed, and how my time has been misspent and wasted on bread sauce and melted butter.' After a good holiday in France, there are many travellers today who feel much the same.

> *two 1¼–1½ kilo (2½–3 lb) chickens*
> *butter*
> *2 heaped tablespoons chopped parsley*
> *2 heaped tablespoons chopped spring onion*
> *salt, pepper*
> *breadcrumbs*

SAUCE TARTARE:

3–4 chopped shallots
3 heaped tablespoons parsley
1 tablespoon chopped tarragon
1 tablespoon chopped chervil
1 heaped teaspoon Dijon mustard
3 tablespoons wine vinegar
6–8 tablespoons olive oil
salt, pepper, sugar

Split the chickens down the breast, then open them out. With the skin side uppermost, flatten them with the broad side of a cleaver or your hand. Turn them over. With a sharp knife, remove the breastbone and cut halfway through the backbone, so that the chickens are nicely flat; this is simple to do, as the flattening process will have loosened the bones. Butter a couple of roasting pans. Put a chicken in each, skin side up. Do not be put off by their rather frog-like appearance. Pour over each one 30 g (1 oz) melted butter, and sprinkle with a tablespoon each of parsley and spring onion. Season. Put butter papers over the top and roast at mark 3–4, 160–180° (325–350°) until tender. They should not brown, neither should the herbs burn.

Sprinkle them evenly with fine white crumbs, baste with the pan juices and set the pans under a moderate grill – you will have to do one at a time most likely – and leave them for about 15 minutes to brown. Serve them flat and cut each bird into four at the table.

The *sauce tartare* is easy to make. Just mix the ingredients thoroughly together, seasoning them to taste.

I suspect that Sydney Smith may have been referring to a hot version of *sauce tartare* which is not made very often these days, as there are other similar sauces to take its place. As far as this chicken recipe is concerned, the *sauce tartare* recipe above, from a contemporary nineteenth-century French cookery book, is ideal.

ROAST VENISON WITH VENISON SAUCE

Lord Lansdowne of Bowood, near Calne in Wiltshire, was a good friend both to Tom Moore, who lived not far away at Slopperton in a *cottage ornée* with ogival windows, and to Sydney Smith who often stayed at Bowood. In his journal, Moore has left a picture of himself and his wife, summoned to Bowood for dinner, but afraid of arriving too early; they stopped their carriage on the way and practised country dances in a green lane, these two tiny figures in their best clothes. No doubt Sydney Smith practised witticisms as he dressed for dinner on similar occasions: in those days conversation was taken seriously, the great talkers like Sydney Smith and Tom Moore were expected to set the style and keep things going well.

Lord Lansdowne's friendliness extended to gifts of food as well. Once when he sent a haunch of venison to the Smiths, the label had been lost so that no one knew who had made the present. When the mystery was cleared up and he was at last able to write a thank-you letter, Sydney Smith's amends were handsome: 'I received the haunch of venison . . . It struck me at the time that to send venison to the clergy without saying from whence it came was an act of profound and high-principled piety.'

Today a smaller roasting joint is more likely to come our way. Here is a good method of cooking it. The really good sweet-sour venison sauce is Carême's recipe. He was a contemporary of Sydney Smith's, and had had a great influence on the fine cookery of Paris that he admired so much. The ingredients of the sauce are in the north European style, but they are put together in a more subtle way than usual.

> *1½ kilos (3 lb) venison roasting joint*
> *piece of pork back fat, chilled*
> *butter, salt, pepper*
> *about ½ litre (¾ pt) venison or beef stock*
> *½ jar (6–8 oz) redcurrant jelly*
> *300 ml (10 fl oz) claret or other red wine*
> *2 tablespoons red wine vinegar*
> *2 dessertspoons sugar*
> *½ lemon, peeled, pipped, roughly chopped*
> *1 heaped tablespoon flour*

Lard the venison with strips of pork fat; if you can find one of the really large larding needles of the size butchers in France use for beef, you will realize how simple a job larding can be. The small easily bent larding needles on sale here, in kitchen shops, are useful only for poultry and small pieces of meat. It is always worth larding venison, however well it has been hung. The small attention can only be an improvement.

Next butter the meat as if it were toast – i.e. lavishly. Season it with much pepper and little salt. Set it on a rack in a roasting pan in the oven at mark 7, 220° (425°) for 15–20 minutes, until lightly browned. Pour the stock into the pan, and turn the oven down to mark 4, 180° (350°). Leave for an hour. This will cook the venison pink, which is the way it should be – like beef.

Meanwhile put the jelly, half the wine, the vinegar, sugar, lemon into a pan. Heat slowly, whisking lightly to help the jelly dissolve. Then boil hard to reduce to 150 ml ($\frac{1}{4}$ pt). About 20 minutes before the venison is due to come out of the oven, melt a heaped tablespoon of butter in another pan. Cook until it is a golden brown colour, then stir in the flour and cook for 2 minutes. Pour in about two-thirds of the stock from the venison pan, or a little more, leaving enough behind to create steam for the meat. Mix well into the roux, and simmer steadily for about 15 minutes, skimming off the white foam that rises and any fat. Pour in the reduced jelly and wine mixture, plus the remaining wine. Cook hard until the sauce is down to half a litre in quantity, or just under ($\frac{3}{4}$ pt). Strain into a sauceboat, and serve with the venison. Any left over can be served with other game, such as hare.

Claret is the obvious wine for this dish. When he was in France, Sydney Smith came to appreciate the table wines of Burgundy and Bordeaux with his food; in England at that time, ports and sherries were usually served at table.

A QUESTION OF HAMS

To Lady Holland, who had sent him a present from Spain, 'Many thanks for two fine Gallicia hams; but as for boiling them in wine, I am not as yet high enough in the Church for that; so they must do the best they can in water.'

To Lady Holland, from his Yorkshire parish in 1811, January 7th 'There sets off this evening an Ham weighing 30 lb by Hartley's waggon stopping next Monday at the Bull and Mouth . . . I mention the weight that it should not be changed, and the other particulars that it should not be lost. Do me the favour to accept this my quit rent . . . I meditated a Yorkshire Pye, but Robert Markham spoke so unfavourably of the forced meat Balls, and of its unworthiness in Holland House, that I changed my plan.'

Yorkshire pies were a splendid construction on the Russian doll principle. A small game bird was boned, then put inside a slightly larger boned bird, and so on through the range of poultry, ending with a turkey; the space surrounding the monster was filled with butter, small game birds or forcemeat balls. It took a bushel of flour to raise the crust, which was made very thick so that the pie did not break on coach journeys to London, where it was especially popular at Christmas time.

According to Hannah Glasse, the reason for the superior quality of York hams was the 'large clear Salt'. Mrs Glasse added that she used to have her salt 'from Malding in Essex, and that Salt will make any Ham as fine as you can desire. It is by much the best Salt, for salting of Meat.'

When you buy a first-class ham, instructions are very often provided; read them over in the shop and make sure you understand how long it is to be soaked. Cover the ham generously with fresh water, bring slowly to the boil, skimming often. Once the liquid is at a steady simmer, timing begins. The larger the ham, the less time per kilo it needs – viz a 6 kilo (12–13 lb) ham is cooked in just over 3 hours, an 8 kilo (16–17 lb) in 4 hours, and a 12 kilo (25 lb) in 5 hours. Cool to tepid in the liquid. Drain, remove skin and press toasted white breadcrumbs into it, all over.

THE POET'S SALAD

When he lived in Edinburgh as a young tutor, Sydney Smith foresaw the day when he would become 'Master Cook as well as Master parson of my village'. His grand intention was to persuade the English poor to give up starving on fine wheaten bread, in favour of the broth and oatmeal that were favoured more sensibly by the Scots. I am not sure whether Sydney Smith was the first to attempt this. Certainly he was not successful, as people are still trying to persuade us to a better diet, while the sales of chocolate, biscuits, cakes, convenience foods, sliced bread, crisps, fizzy drinks – today's equivalent to the fine white bread of those times – go up and up.

In the end Sydney Smith's culinary triumph was salad-making for his aristocratic friends (though he never gave up preaching the virtues of a sensible diet from the pulpit and on his parish rounds). He even turned the recipe into a poem, so popular did his salad become. Eliza Acton gave a version of it in her *Modern Cookery*, which is not too satisfactory as it begins 'two large potatoes, passed through kitchen sieve'; and the dressing ends up like a mud pack.

I found that 125 g (4 oz) cooked, peeled potato, with the other ingredients, produces a sauce of more mayonnaise-like consistency. Use Orléans vinegar – 'almost wine, like a lady who has just lost her character' – and do not be tempted to omit the onion which is essential for 'perfect success'. Choose vigorous greenery – watercress, Coss or Webb's lettuce, celery, chicory or endive – and you will have an ideal winter salad; one friend serves the sauce with a large dish of greenery and cold roast chicken, and finds it a great success.

For the seasonings use a teaspoon, a tablespoon for the olive oil and wine vinegar, with a scant teaspoon of anchovy.

> *To make this condiment your poet begs*
> *The pounded yellow of two hard-boiled eggs;*
> *Two boiled potatoes, passed through kitchen sieve,*
> *Smoothness and softness to the salad give.*
> *Let onion atoms lurk within the bowl,*
> *And, half-suspected, animate the whole.*
> *Of mordant mustard add a single spoon,*
> *Distrust the condiment that bites so soon;*
> *But deem it not, thou man of herbs, a fault*
> *To add a double quantity of salt;*
> *Four times the spoon with oil of Lucca crown,*
> *And twice with vinegar procur'd from town;*
> *And lastly o'er the flavour'd compound toss*
> *A magic soupçon of anchovy sauce.*
> *Oh, green and glorious! Oh, herbaceous treat!*
> *Twould tempt the dying anchorite to eat;*
> *Back to the world he'd turn his fleeting soul,*
> *And plunge his fingers in the salad-bowl!*
> *Serenely full, the epicure would say,*
> *'Fate cannot harm me, I have dined today.'*

CHEDDAR CHEESE

When Sydney Smith moved to Combe Florey in Somerset, he could no longer send a York ham as his Christmas present to London friends. But soon he discovered an excellent substitute. 'We are famous here for cheeses, called Cheddar cheeses,' he wrote to Lady Grey in 1831, 'and I have taken the liberty to send you one made by a reforming farmer' – this was in the year before the Reform Bill was eventually passed, the year, too, when he made his famous speech about Mrs Partington and the Atlantic.

I cannot vouch for the reforming zeal of the thirty farmers who still made Cheddar farmhouse cheese in the matter of politics, but in cheese-making they have introduced the latest machinery compatible with the high quality of their cheeses. From these farms, huge 60-lb cheeses go to mature in the big depot at Crump Way in Wells, losing 4 lb as they dry out. This was the kind of cheese Sydney Smith sent to the Greys: 'It was a bargain between Lord Grey and me, that if he made me a Canon I was to send him a cheese every year. It is not a cheese but an outward and visible mark of my gratitude and affection.'

He would have deplored the huge oblong blocks of Cheddar that supermarket managers find so convenient. They are supposed to be just as good, but I remain unconvinced. After all appearance has something to do with flavour, and nothing looks more unappetising on a cheese board than a perfect brick of orange, rather than a wedge with a light brown crust.

The answer for many people these days is provided by the 9-lb truckle cheese, complete with rind. It is not always realised that a good cheese will improve if kept in a cool place – not the fridge – as it dries and deepens in flavour. If you must store cheese in the fridge, wrap it tightly in foil to exclude the air; remember to bring it out several hours before it is to be served. Really the best solution, if you have a small flat with no cold larder, is to buy cheese in very small quantities at frequent intervals.

NEUFCHÂTEL CHEESE

It is difficult to know how much a cheese may have changed over the centuries. The name may be unaltered, but the process? And the result? You have only to come within eye and nose distance of a modern farmhouse Brie or Camembert, to see how far it is from the factory cheese bearing the same name. It must also be admitted, in defence of factories, that cheese was once produced by a kind of ignorant skill. No one knew about bacteria. Few understood the need for scrupulous cleanliness. For no apparent reason, a cheese might turn out to be a complete disaster, as if it had been blighted by some malign power.

Perhaps this is why the small cheeses of France have survived so well into modern times, while our large cheeses have diminished in number. If a batch of Camembert were to go wrong, it would have been bad enough for the farmer, but if a 60 lb Cheddar was spoiled, the loss of money and effort would have been disastrous.

I suspect that Neufchâtel cheeses have not changed too much since Sydney Smith's day, though perhaps they are a little less tasty which is an inevitable result of modern methods. You may still buy them in squares or *briquettes*, in hearts or in cork-shaped *bondons*. They are a cow's milk cheese, with a piquant saltiness and a crumpled white powdery crust with rivulets of brown. Neufchâtel is on a slope of one of the sweeping chalk hills of the Bray district of northern Normandy, a great area for rich cheeses, double creams and triple creams among them.

ITALIAN CREAM

Soon after moving to Combe Florey, he reported that the neighbours were 'in the common line – port and sherry for dinner, hail, rain and snow for conversation; but the best people in any place come slowly to light and lie, like macaroon cakes at the bottom of an Italian cream, last and best'.

The best macaroons to use are the small ones in packets, imported from France. The macaroons made by pastrycooks these days in this country are short on almonds, though they can be used if the others are hard to find. Put 2 or 3 small macaroons in the bottom of eight tulip wine glasses. Pour over them a tablespoon of dry white wine per glass, and leave it to soak in. For the cream:

6 tablespoons white wine
juice of a lemon
60 g (2 oz) caster sugar
300 ml (10 fl oz) double cream
2 level teaspoons gelatine
5 tablespoons milk

Stir the first three ingredients together until the sugar is dissolved. Add the cream and whip with a rotary whisk until you have a thick soft mixture. Dissolve the gelatine in the warmed milk, and add that to the cream, whisking it in. Leave to chill, then whisk again before dividing between the glasses.

This is not unlike a syllabub, except that some thick egg custard may be substituted for half the cream. If you only have sweet white wine, use this and reduce the quantity of sugar by half. Taste the mixture at the end, and if it seems not sweet enough, stir in a little extra sugar.

APRICOT TART AND ALMOND TART

Apart from the memorable almond tart he ate at Montreuil, and Italian cream, Sydney Smith did not mention sweet things with much enthusiasm. Fruit was another matter: 'What is real piety? What is true attachment to the Church? How are these fine feelings best evinced? The answer is plain: by sending strawberries to a clergyman.'

Apricot tart was a passion of the day. Lord Alvanley had one on his table every day of the year, and it was highly approved of at Holland House, where Sydney Smith dined regularly. A young boy who was spending the day there out of school, was asked what he would like for dinner, and replied, 'Duck and green peas, with an apricot tart to follow.' Lord Holland was impressed. 'My boy,' he said, 'if in all the important questions of your life you decide as wisely as you have decided now, you will be a great and good man.'

For either tart, line a 25 cm (10 inch) tin with puff pastry. Prick the base with a fork, and make up one of the fillings which follow.

ALMOND:
125 g (4 oz) lightly salted butter

2 eggs
2 egg yolks
175 g (6 oz) caster sugar
75 ml each (5 fl oz in all) double and soured cream
125 g (4 oz) ground almonds
125 g (4 oz) almonds, blanched, coarsely ground
tablespoon orange flower water or brandy
icing sugar

Cream the butter, then beat in the remaining ingredients, apart from icing sugar, in the order given. If you can use an electric beater, so long as the butter is soft, you can throw everything into the bowl and have it mixed evenly in seconds

Spread over the pastry. Bake at mark 6, 200° (400°), for 20–30 minutes, until lightly browned, then at mark 4, 180° (350°) for 10–15 minutes. The tart will puff up in the oven, then subside. Sprinkle the top with icing sugar, and place under the grill until the sugar melts to a glaze – watch it, all the time. Serve warm, with cream.

APRICOT:
¾ kg (1½ lb) apricots, stoned weight
heaped tablespoon slivered almonds (see recipe)
125 g (4 oz) lightly salted butter
175 g (6 oz) caster sugar

Crack the apricot stones and remove the kernels. If using frozen apricot halves, without stones, you will need extra almonds, or if you cannot be bothered to crack the apricot stones, though I think this is worth it.

Melt the butter in a wide shallow pan, stir in the sugar until it is melted. Put in the apricots and turn them over and over until they are coated in the buttery juices. They should not be cooked, merely warmed. Arrange them on the pastry, with the juices, sprinkle with the kernels and almonds. Bake at mark 7, 220° (425°) for about 30 minutes, but keep an eye on the tart and lower the heat if the pastry browns too rapidly. Serve hot or warm with plenty of cream.

If you like, you can use both fillings. Line the pastry with apricots, then pour over the almond cream – both in slightly reduced quantities. Follow the cooking time for almond tart.

Note When you switch on the oven to bake tarts with slightly liquid fillings, slip in a baking sheet. The tart cooks better underneath for the initial blast of heat when you put it into the oven. An eighteenth-century idea that is worth preserving.

Lord Shaftesbury (1801–1885) & Lady Shaftesbury (1810–1872)

Aristocratic poverty is unlikely, on the whole, to tug at your heart or mine. Television dukes on crumbling battlements, succoured by lions, are unappealing by comparison with the houseless poor or with struggling writers and painters such as Zola and Monet (qqv). But give sympathy to one exception, who compelled our society to a minimal decency, in spite of – or because of? – his own background of early misery and lifelong debt.

Anthony Ashley Cooper, 7th Earl of Shaftesbury, born in 1801 to appalling parents, was a deprived battered child, often so 'pinched with starvation' and cold that he could not sleep. Social life, splendid meals went on in warmth and light in the handsome rooms of the family mansion in Grosvenor Square, while Anthony Ashley Cooper and his sisters crouched in darkness upstairs wondering whether anyone would remember to give them the leftovers. Quite often they did not. As well as being neglectful, his parents were bullies, even malevolent; when they were quite grown up, the girls were too frightened to speak in the presence of their father. Luckily for the boy, this parental savagery had been masked until he was seven by the love of Mrs Willis, the housekeeper. The memory of her affection enabled him to survive, gave him an inclination towards Evangelical religion and the sort of sympathy with other unfortunates that later pushed him towards social reform.

By chance rather than intention, he tackled first the problem of lunatics who were disgracefully and cruelly treated, then he joined the campaign for the Ten-Hour Day ('A ten-hour day? What is the country coming to? Nobody wants to work any more'). His greatest and noblest efforts were on behalf of children who were enduring a life far harder and more vicious than his own had been. At least he worked from experience of cold, hunger, lovelessness, not from distant paternalism. He could imagine from his own experience how a three-year-old might feel, alone in the dark down a mine, terrified by rats. Or how a young chimney sweep might suffer from a beating, then from the pork butcher's brine rubbed into his raw skin to harden it. Or how the mill children crept into the iron webs of machinery, to emerge, if they survived, as crippled monsters of humanity.

The strange thing to me is not that children were sent down the mines or into the mills without anyone protesting – prosperous people living in pleasant suburbs could well claim to know nothing about it, just as many Germans claimed ignorance of Belsen – but chimney sweeps? How could the lady of a grand house see a child the same age as her own, pushed weeping up a chimney, sometimes unable to get down and suffocating in the soot? Later in the century, women fought for their own rights with guile and toughness. How could their mothers and grandmothers stand by and do nothing about the sufferings of children?

The person who did do something was Lord Shaftesbury. And it took him many years, much fighting. I wonder if he would have managed it without his wife, Emily?

A year or two ago I was given a manuscript receipt book kept by Emily Shaftesbury – usually known as Minny – from 1855 when she had been married twenty-five years, until her death in 1872. At the first reading, I had the impression that she was a neurotic creature, there were so many recipes for nervous draughts, headaches and beef tea. In fact the first two kinds were for her husband, who returned from his expeditions in a state of nervous misery that affected his stomach. And no wonder – 'our business is not in transparent lakes and flowing rivers, but in the gutter and in the mire'. Once I had read his report on the East End slums and Ragged Schools, in the *Quarterly Review* of December 1846, Lady Shaftesbury's apparently straightforward collection of domestic knowledge became a moving comment on their lives and partnership. Early in the book, 'sassafras shavings will prevent bugs' – her husband often returned from the slums with a 'household of vermin' on his back – but the shavings didn't work, to judge by a sentence some pages later, 'to get rid of bugs, sassafras shavings'.

Lady Shaftesbury's childhood had been different from her husband's. Her mother belonged to the happy, disreputable and intelligent Lamb family. Lord Melbourne was her uncle. Earl Cowper was her father – officially – though it seems probable that Palmerston was really the man responsible. There had been the same sort of doubt about her mother's and Melbourne's paternity. Not that anyone seemed to worry. Life in the Lamb family was gay, entertaining and bohemian in an aristocratic sort of way. Lady Granville described their London house as 'that great ocean where a person is forced to shift for himself without clue; they wander about all day and sleep about all evening; no meal is at a given hour, but drops upon them as an unexpected pleasure.' And when Emily Lamb married Earl Cowper, she carried on much as her mother had done, bringing up her own children including Minny and her sister, Fanny, in an equally insouciant atmosphere at Panshanger.

Considering the differences, it is not surprising that when handsome but serious Lord Ashley fell in love with Minny, she needed time and persuasion. Lady Granville watched the courtship with exasperation – like Minny's mother, she was half in love with him herself – admiring his perfect behaviour, deploring her giddiness. But she admitted Minny was reacting against family pressure: 'She supposes she must marry some day, and hopes that when she does she shall love her husband, because it is right, but the later the better.' On another occasion Minny said, 'Let me forget it, and then, perhaps, I shall like him better.' Lady Granville, though, was shrewd enough to make a wise judgement – Minny has been 'perseveringly spoilt, but she is natural, gay, and good-humoured. Her only chance, I think, is to marry a good sort of man whom she likes very much.'

And that is what she did. Once committed, once in love, Minny made a perfect wife. No easy matter. There is always discomfort in living with high evangelical standards, especially when they are accompanied by depressions and vermin. And as well, Lord Shaftesbury was never out of debt, for reasons that he could not help. One major blow was to inherit a badly-run estate. A man occupied so publicly with social reform had obviously to see that his tenants inhabited model cottages, rather than rural slums. Where was the money to come from? And such money as there might have been, disappeared through the hands of his agent, a man Lord Shaftesbury could not bring himself to suspect although everyone else knew what a rogue he was.

All this comes through in the receipt book, especially the need for economy with style. Although it was begun in 1855, a number of recipes were collected earlier on, and sheets of undated recipes in different hands are crammed between the pages, waiting to be copied in. Some of these are very early. Others, just a few, seem to have been slipped into the collection by Minny's descendants. When the recipes are attributed, they show a family network of contribution, often for things to delight children, and small dishes to add charm to the staples of Victorian meals. The young Shaftesburys seem to have had a passion for ginger – ginger beer ('instantaneous'), pop, ginger lemonade, ginger pudding, ginger nuts, ginger cakes, gingerbread wafers (i.e. brandy snaps). She subjected them to sluice pudding, made with tapioca, or rice, or sago, or semolina, or arrowroot, or ground rice – reminding me of the dams and ditches we made in school milk puds as we watched for a chance to convey them to the aspidistra in the middle of the table – but retrieved her reputation, for me at least, and I hope for them, by adding whipped cream at the end.

A favourite money saver for the upper classes was staying with wealthier friends. Lady Shaftesbury notes Lord Malmesbury's method of baking bread under turf ash at Auchnacarry, and the way to make some delicious rolls they ate at Rossie, Lord Kinnaird's splendid house (he shared Lord Shaftesbury's evangelical ideas, and at one time helped him over money). Another mode of economy was to live abroad for a while, and this they also had to do for the sake of their delicate children, and Lord Shaftesbury's difficult digestion. There are recipes from Ems and Baden, Cannes and Paris. Spa in Germany so restored Lady Shaftesbury to gaiety that she was moved to write down two local extravaganzas, from the pastry-cook, Caroyer, quite against her usual careful economy: one is an almond tart using twenty-eight eggs. She also noted a Sauce Incroyable, for wild boar, which is not really so incredible though it does contain the book's only truffle.

But in the main, recipes come from or through the family. Lord Shaftesbury was not much of a man for dinners, if he could avoid them. Large family meals were more his style, with the people he loved (he had great tenderness for his children). Fanny Cowper sent many recipes; she married late – apparently because she could not find anyone to match up to her sister's husband – and wrote from many different houses, passing on the good things that her hostesses might provide. There is a muddled and over-refined version of Irish stew from Lord Donegal, father of Harriet who married the Shaftesbury's eldest son, and was much disapproved of. A recipe towards the end of the book, for rusks, from Lady Mary Farquhar, is a reminder of the more satisfactory engagement of another son to Sybella Farquhar. Dishes contributed by 'Mama's cook' are souvenirs of long visits to Panshanger and Broadlands, where Lord and Lady Palmerston showered them with affection, admiration and generous presents. Doctors' names go with recipes for strengthening broths and beef tea, sadly witnessing the delicacy and early deaths of several of the children.

POTAGE D'ORGE À L'ALLEMANDE
GERMAN BARLEY SOUP

This soup – 'excellent' – came from 'Mama's cook'. Mama, Lady Cowper, was well into her second, happier marriage to her first suitor, Lord Palmerston, by the time that Minny began her receipt book, and she lived in some style, especially at Broadlands, Palmerston's family home. The marriage, which took place in 1839, had been bitterly opposed by her children – I suppose they felt that it only confirmed the gossip of many years, including the assumption that Palmerston was Minny's father. He was so kind, tactful and generous to his step-children, and Lady Palmerston was so evidently happy that they came round. One of the Shaftesbury children became his private secretary, another was given a large sum of money to start him off in life, and the girls enjoyed the sociability of the wealthy Palmerston ménage. It must have been a relief on occasion, from their father's strong evangelical faith, social conscience and debts.

> 60 g (2 oz) pearl barley
> 2¼ litres (4 pt) veal or chicken stock
> 60 g (2 oz) butter
> white part of 4 leeks, sliced
> 375 g (12 oz) celery, sliced
> nutmeg
> 150 ml (5 fl oz) cream
> 1 large egg yolk

Blanch barley in simmering, unsalted water for 5 minutes. Drain and put into 2 litres (3½ pt) stock: cook gently until barley is very soft – this can take over an hour. Meanwhile melt the butter and stew the leek and celery in it for 10–15 minutes, without browning them; put a lid on the pan. Pour in the remaining stock, cover again and simmer until the vegetables are soft enough to be sieved into the cooked barley. Flavour with nutmeg. Check the seasoning and add extra stock or some water, if you wish to dilute the soup further. Beat cream and egg in a warmed soup tureen, then stir in the boiling barley soup, slowly at first, until it is properly blended with the cream and yolk liaison. Serve immediately.

CLEAR MULLIGATAWNY SOUP

Milagu-tannīr, 'pepper water', is a Madras soup that came into the English language as mullaghee-tawny in the eighteenth century. Dr Kitchiner remarked in *The Cook's Oracle* that it was very fashionable – in 1817 – and it remained popular throughout the century. If you have made up the Doctor's curry powder (p. 74), use some of it for this soup.

> *6 large onions, chopped*
> *125 g (4 oz) butter*
> *2 large tablespoons curry powder*
> *1¾ litres (about 3 pt) good stock*
> *either ¾ kilo (1½ lb) veal, or a wild rabbit, or a boiling*
>   *fowl*

Cook the onions in the butter, slowly at first, then a little faster, so that they end up soft and a nice light brown. Sprinkle on the curry powder. Cook for 2 minutes, stirring all the time, then add the stock. Meanwhile cut up the veal, or cut the meat from rabbit or chicken and chop it; put the meat and bones into the soup. Bring slowly to the boil, and simmer for at least an hour, longer if you like. Skim from time to time. Strain through a muslin-lined sieve, add salt if need be, and serve with a bowl of boiled, dry rice.

If you have only been used to the occasional tin of mulligatawny in a domestic emergency, you will be surprised at the excellence of this soup.

TOASTED CHEESE

This recipe came from the wife of Shaftesbury's favourite brother, William – the two went about together in society when they were young and were nicknamed 'the Sublime and the Beautiful' – and it is a good version of a favourite Victorian dish. Quantities seem tiny, but they are enough for eight for a first course; if you want to make toasted cheese for a supper dish, and your family have good digestions, serve this amount for four.

90 g (3 oz) butter
250 g (8 oz) grated dry Farmhouse Cheddar
8 tablespoons cream
3 standard egg yolks
salt, pepper, Cayenne

Melt the butter in a pan over a low heat; add the remaining ingredients, stirring them vigorously together. Heat slowly until you have a thick cream. Keep under boiling point, but give the whole thing time enough to thicken. Divide between 8 small pots, and brown lightly under the grill. Serve with plenty of toast fingers, or pieces of baked bread.

PETITS POTS DE GIBIERS

LITTLE GAME CUSTARDS

Emily Eden gave this recipe to Lady Shaftesbury in 1857, a couple of years before she published her first novel, *The Semi-detached House*, which was followed by the equally successful, *The Semi-attached Couple*. She had travelled in India with her brother, Lord Auckland, who was Governor-General there from 1835 to 1842, and had written books about her experiences there.

Finding her game recipe made me think of tales about her eccentric relation, Sir William Eden, an irascible man who had the row with Whistler over his wife's portrait. He was only affable, it seems, when shooting pheasants on the family estate at Windlestone in Co Durham, although his contemptuous and uncringing relationship with the Almighty could make these occasions uncertain in their atmosphere. One day, everything was ready, guests waiting, pheasants waiting, gamekeepers and beaters waiting. And it rained. 'Oh God!' exclaimed Sir William, deeply exasperated, as he watched the weather through the window, 'Oh God. How like You!'

On another more clement day, everyone was lined up and Sir William strode to his place, clad in his specially designed Eden tartan with a carnation in his buttonhole. 'Do we shoot hens, Willie?' shouted one of the guns. 'Yes!' came the reply. 'Shoot hens! Shoot everything! Shoot the Holy Ghost if He comes out!'

For the game stock for this dish, I would rather suggest pheasants, or even pigeons. The carcasses will do perfectly well, especially from pigeons as usually only the breast fillets are eaten, which leaves the carcasses very meaty. Simmer with aromatics, a glass or two of wine, and beef stock to cover. The stock does not need to be clarified. Flavour is the thing.

For each person allow one yolk and 100 ml (3½ fl oz) skimmed strained stock. Beat together, add seasoning and pour into buttered custard cups. Put on the lids, stand in a pan of simmering water on top of the stove, and leave for half an hour. Serve with toast or with the sandwiches of the following recipe.

HAM TOAST WITH CHEESE

An English version of Welsh Rabbit and French Croque Monsieur. The toasted sandwiches may be served on their own with drinks, or as a first course – they go well, too, with soup or savoury custards (*see* previous recipe).

Sandwich slices of good ham between thin slices of bread – do not butter it – and cut away the crusts. Dip in clarified butter. Cut diagonally across into triangles. Arrange closely together on a baking sheet. Sprinkle over with a layer of grated cheese – use well dried out Cheddar or Lancashire – and bake in a hot oven until browned. Drain for a few minutes on kitchen paper, to get rid of any greasiness, and serve very hot on a hot dish.

There is no hint as the source of this recipe; but it suggests a summer party, as it comes immediately before:

CLARET CUP

Mix a bottle claret with a small bottle of soda water, a large wineglassful of sherry and a few lumps of sugar according to taste, and the kind of sherry used. Take a small handful of borage. Separate the flowers and young sprigs. Put the tough stalks and larger leaves into a cup, and pour on some boiling water. Leave to cool. Strain enough to fill a wine glass and tip into the claret mixture. Add the blue borage flowers and young leaves, to float on the top.

The recipe can be used with Chablis or any other white wine. Add some balm to the borage, and 3 or 4 slices of lemon.

'If borage is not to be procured a few slices of cucumber may be used as a substitute.'

PRINCE RADZIWILL'S POTTED SALMON

A recipe given to Lady Shaftesbury in Paris, by Prince Radziwill – but which one? Perhaps by the father of Proust's friend, Léon (p. 233).

It is unnecessary to buy top quality, sliced smoked salmon for this kind of dish. Some shops sell smoked salmon pieces that fall from the sides as they are sliced; others may be able to supply you with the skin, which has very good pickings, so rich that you should start with a smaller quantity of butter and see how it tastes before adding the rest. The sardines may seem a peculiar addition, but they work well (the original recipe mentions an alternative of salt herring, bone included, but this is too much for the quantity of salmon I find). Don't stint the peppers.

> *125 g (4 oz) smoked salmon*
> *125 g (4 oz) unsalted Normandy butter*
> *2 medium canned sardines, or 1 very large*
> *black and Cayenne peppers*

Cut salmon and butter into rough pieces, and reduce to a purée in an electric food processor, with the sardines. Add peppers to taste. Turn into a pot, cover with cling film and chill. Serve with toast, or baked bread, or wholemeal bread.

If you have no food processor, follow the original style and pound the salmon, butter and sardine in a mortar, then push it through a hair sieve.

Note When washing utensils after preparing fish, run them (and your hands) under the cold tap first. This gets rid of the smell. Then you can wash them up in the normal way.

MOUSSAKA À LA HONGROISE
HUNGARIAN MOUSSAKA

You can look at this recipe in two ways. Either you can dismiss it as a typical example of castellated grandeur (it came from Dupplin Castle, then was mistranslated, or translated and adapted at Alloa House, presumably by one of the Erskines, before being sent to Lady Shaftesbury with the original). Or you can see it as a glorious opportunity for clearing out the refrigerator after an hospitable weekend. It might also strike you as a fairly dashing inclusion in a mid-Victorian collection of dishes.

In the end, I do not think it matters much whether you use the four meats, or two of them, or even one so long as the one is either beef or lamb. You could also mix in raw meats – but chop them separately, and start them cooking first. The quantities below are enough for eight people.

> *250 g (8 oz) cooked leg of lamb, on the rare side*
> *500 g (1 lb) cooked sirloin, on the rare side*
> *500 g (1 lb) cooked veal*
> *half a cooked chicken*
> *salt, pepper, generous tablespoon paprika, sugar*
> *large onion, finely chopped*
> *olive oil or butter*
> *medium can (14 oz) of tomatoes*
> *strong meat jelly or essence from roasting, or tomato*
>   *concentrate*
> *1 kilo (2 lb) aubergines, sliced, salted*
> *¾ kilo (1½ lb) firm fresh tomatoes, sliced, peeled*
> *breadcrumbs*

Chop meats (better than mincing them). Season with salt, pepper and paprika, plus a pinch of sugar. Cook onion in a little oil or butter, slowly at first, then faster so that it browns slightly (stir to prevent burning). Put in the meat, the canned tomatoes and jelly, essence or concentrate. Cook steadily but not too fast in the open pan for about 45 minutes until the juices have evaporated to leave you with a thick meat sauce. Taste and add more seasonings if necessary.

Meanwhile fry the aubergines, then the tomatoes. Season them.

Layer half the meat into a wide gratin dish, then the aubergines, the tomatoes and the rest of the meat. Cover with crumbs, sprinkle on melted butter, and bake until bubbling and browned at mark 6–7, 200–220° (400–425°) for about 30–45 minutes, or an hour if the dish was prepared in advance and goes into the oven cold.

MADAME GEOFFREY'S IRISH STEW

Some of the last months of Lady Shaftesbury's life were spent in Cannes, for the sake not of her own health but of her daughter's (in fact Constance survived her mother by a few weeks only). At least she had zest enough, in spite of sadness and separation from her husband, to write down some good dishes. The last complete recipe but one in the book is headed *very good cutlets (called Irish Stew)*. 'Called' is, I think, her ironic comment on the French idea that they could make an Irish stew.

> *90 g (3 oz) butter*
> *rounded tablespoon flour*
> *175 g (6 oz) chopped onion*
> *8 thick lamb cutlets*
> *generous ½ litre (¾–1 pt) beef or veal stock*
> *bouquet garni, salt, pepper*
> *8 medium potatoes, quartered*

Melt butter in a wide, heavy sauté pan. Sprinkle on the flour and onion, then place cutlets on top. Raise the heat so that everything browns nicely; remember to turn the cutlets so that they are evenly coloured on both sides. Pour in the stock, add *bouquet*, salt, pepper. Cover and simmer for an hour, adding potatoes after thirty minutes. Arrange cooked meat and potatoes on a hot serving dish. Skim all fat from sauce, check seasoning, and boil it down if necessary to concentrate the flavour. Strain over the cutlets and serve.

BOEUF PRESSÉ AU CHASSEUR
HUNTSMAN'S PRESSED BEEF

Again from 'Mama's cook', and again like the barley soup a recipe from 1863, two years before Lord Palmerston's death at Brocket Hall. The original indicates a piece of brisket weighing 15 to 20 pounds, four times the quantity of the brine ingredients below and a salting time of one day per pound. With smaller joints, of the kind that we can accommodate, the brining time should be extended to a week; in any case I think the recipe is not worth doing with pieces under 5 lb boned weight.

Of course you can circumvent the business of salting the beef, by buying it already cured from the butcher. If you do this, be sure to ask whether it will need soaking before you cook it. Having made sure about this, you can go straight to paragraph two of the method.

2½–3½ kilos (5–7 lb) boned brisket

BRINE:
10 g (2 teaspoons) saltpetre
¾ kilo (1½ lb) sea salt or block cooking salt
125 g (4 oz) dark brown sugar, preferably Muscovado
6 cloves
15 g (½ oz) whole allspice, slightly crushed
heaped teaspoon black peppercorns, slightly crushed
2 bay leaves
2 large sprigs thyme
2 large sprigs parsley
600 ml (1 pt) water

If the brisket is rolled, untie it and lay it flat in a pot or plastic box that fits closely. Bring remaining ingredients slowly to the boil, stirring to dissolve sugar and salt. Cool, then strain over the beef.

Using tongs, turn the beef over once a day, and leave for a week. Keep the pot or box covered, and store in a cool place.

Drain the beef. Put into a large pan and cover with water generously. Bring to the boil, then reduce the heat so that the liquid barely simmers. Allow 1½ hours for a 2½ kilo (5 lb) piece of beef; or 2 hours for a 3–3½ kilo (6–7 lb) piece.

Cool beef for 2 hours in the cooking water. Drain and put on a board, with a board on top. Weight it down with tins. Next day trim off any unsightly bits and pieces. Put the beef on a dish, surrounding it with parsley. Serve with salads – an avocado salad is delicious with salt beef, though hardly in the Shaftesbury style – horseradish sauce, mustard, and either baked potatoes with butter, or a potato salad bound lightly with mayonnaise.

BROCKET HALL BREAD SAUCE

Brocket Hall, in Hertfordshire, with its magnificent saloon decorated by the demonic painter, J. H. Mortimer, was the childhood home of Lady Shaftesbury's mother, who inherited it in 1853. Although its most dramatic period was during the marriage of Lady Shaftesbury's uncle, Lord Melbourne, to Byron's Caroline Lamb, its great period of Whig splendour had been in the last quarter of the eighteenth and beginning of the nineteenth century, in her grandmother's day.

This energetic grandmother had also made Brocket Hall into an exceptionally happy home for her children. And her gift for enjoyable family life descended to her daughter. Recipes that Minny took down at Brocket Hall in the 1850s have an air of that earlier time, in particular this old version of bread sauce, which gains extra flavour from the use of consommé or stock.

> *2 shallots or one onion, chopped*
> *150 ml (5 fl oz) single cream*
> *150 ml (5 fl oz) consommé or stock*
> *60 g (2 oz) crumbs from day-old bread*

Simmer shallot or onion in the cream and consommé or stock for 15 minutes in a covered pan. Whisk in the crumbs with a fork, then leave for a further 10 minutes to cook very gently. Stir from time to time. Check the seasoning; I always add Cayenne pepper to bread sauce, but have to admit that this is not in Lady Shaftesbury's recipe.

SURPRISE AU CHOCOLAT
CHOCOLATE SURPRISE CAKE

The surprise is that the chocolate-covered cake cuts, not to a dark cake, but to a cream-coloured sponge, filled with white whipped cream. A light confection that will just stretch round eight people at the end of a large meal. If you feel it may not be enough, make two cakes rather than one double the size.

> *3 large eggs*
> *125 g (4 oz) caster sugar*
> *30 g (1 oz) cornflour*
> *30 g (1 oz) plain flour*
> *150 ml (5 fl oz) double cream*
> *tablespoon icing sugar*
> *250 g (8 oz) granulated sugar*
> *125 g (4 oz) plain chocolate*

Separate the eggs. Beat – electrically if possible – the yolks with the caster sugar until you have a thick creamy batter. Sift flour and cornflour together, and fold into the cake with a metal spoon. Whisk the egg whites until stiff, then fold them in even more carefully. Using Bakewell parchment, line a 15 cm (6 inch) cake tin with a removable base. Put in the mixture. Bake at mark 4, 180° (350°) for 45 minutes. Remove and leave to cool for 5 minutes. Stand on a milk bottle or tall jar, so that the tin slides down, leaving the cake and its base on top. Now you can easily lift the cake by the Bakewell paper edges – but go carefully – on to a wire tray to cool. When cold, halve the cake and remove some of the centre crumb. Whip the cream with the icing sugar and fill the cake. Replace the top. Slide a dish under the wire tray in readiness for the icing.

    To make the chocolate icing, stir the granulated sugar with 150 ml ($\frac{1}{4}$ pt) water in a saucepan. Bring to the boil and leave until the surface is covered with a lather of pearly bubbles. Meanwhile grate the chocolate and melt it with 2 tablespoons very hot water. When the syrup is ready, remove it from the heat and leave 10 minutes to cool. Beat in the chocolate with a wire whisk, to make a smooth rich glaze. Should it turn to mud at any stage, or seem too thick to use, add a spoonful or two more of very hot water. Pour some chocolate on the top of the cake, and smooth the surplus down the sides. Continue until the cake is coated. Scrape the overflowing chocolate from the dish beneath, and restore it to the pan, beating it until smooth.

Note Sponge cakes do not always bake symmetrically. Don't worry.

BAKEWELL PUDDING

I have often seen it stated that the 'authentic' recipe for Bakewell Pudding (and pudding it should be called, not tart) consists of pastry spread with jam and filled with a mixture of egg, egg yolks, butter and sugar. The kind of thing used by John Farley in his *London Art of Cookery* for a sweetmeat pudding (1783) and until modern times by the pastry cooks of Rouen for their *mirlitons*.

However the earliest dated recipe seems to be 1862 (quoted by Jane Thornton in her collection of cookery cards, *18th century Derbyshire Dishes*), and in the sixties the second recipe that included almonds and either breadcrumbs or flour was already about, too. Various cookery books of the time give both versions, but Lady Shaftesbury has yet another one. Her difference is a meringue topping, which does add an extra delight.

> *puff pastry*
> *apricot or strawberry jam*
> *125 g (4 oz) butter*
> *125 g (4 oz) caster sugar*
> *4 eggs*
> *90 g (3 oz) plain flour*
> *30 g (1 oz) ground almonds*
> *lemon juice*
> *extra heaped tablespoon sugar*

Line a tart tin of about 22 cm (9 inches) diameter with the pastry and spread it with a generous layer of jam. Cream the butter and sugar, mix in one whole egg, 3 yolks, the plain flour, ground almonds and lemon juice to taste – a little sharpness is agreeable, but do not swamp the milder flavours. Spread evenly over the jam. Bake at mark 4, 180° (350°) until nicely browned on top – 35–45 minutes.

Meanwhile whisk the three remaining egg whites stiffly, add the tablespoon of sugar and whisk again. Pile this meringue on to the pudding and return to the oven for 20–30 minutes, until browned. Eat hot or warm – when it is cold, the meringue can become leathery.

COFFEE JELLY AND CREAM

Judging by their cookery books, and the comments of foreign visitors, the Victorians were as bad with coffee as we are now with jellies. For us it is easy to produce drinkable coffee, with filter papers and fine-ground espresso roasts, but our reasonable prejudice against commercial jellies prevents us ever making a proper one at home. Sad, because a good jelly can be every bit as delicious as a sorbet.

1 litre (1¾ pt) freshly-made filter coffee
1¾ packets powdered gelatine
10 large lumps of sugar, or 10 rounded teaspoons
2 egg whites
200 ml (7 fl oz) whipping cream
caster sugar

When the coffee has dripped through, dissolve the gelatine in some of it, with the sugar, then add to the rest. When cold, tip into a pan with the egg whites and whisk over a moderate heat until the coffee boils, and the egg whites have collected all the impurities into a murky cloud on top. Pour the contents of the pan carefully, through damp double-muslin into a bowl. The coffee will run crystal clear from this clarifying process. Taste and add more sugar if you like; avoid oversweetening.

Divide between 8 wine glasses and chill until set. Whip cream with a little sugar, until thick and bulky but not stiff. Pour on top of the set jellies. Serve with sponge fingers, with one stuck into each glass at an angle.

DEVONSHIRE CREAM

In Georgina Battiscombe's life of Shaftesbury, this sentence struck me: 'To Minny, Palmerston had given unstinted love and admiration: in a typical letter' – of 13 March 1862 – 'thanking her for a present of Devonshire cream he describes the gift as "like the giver, excellent and perfect".'

I turned to Minny Shaftesbury's receipt book, and went through the loose sheets of recipes until I came to a very small envelope. On it, in pencil in her handwriting, was written Devonshire Cream. Inside was a piece of paper headed Broadlands, Romsey, Hampshire – Palmerston's home – and on the other side she had written this:

> *2 pints of milk*
> *1 pint of cream*
> *let it sit for 6 hours put in a pan of water on the stove*
> *for 4 hours until the cream cracks Then let it stand for*
> *one night when it is ready for skimming.*

The recipe for that 'excellent and perfect gift'? And if you have ever stayed on a Devon or Cornish dairy farm, or in some house on the Isles of Scilly where they make their own clotted cream as Lady Shaftesbury did, you will know how poor and imperfect commercial clotted cream is by comparison with the real thing.

If you keep cows yourself, or have a friend who does, you can try making it with unpasteurised milk and cream, by the old slow method described in her recipe.

MRS HISLOP'S APRICOT JAM ICE

If you use homemade jam, this is a successful and simple water ice.

Mix half a kilo (1 lb) apricot jam with 400 ml (12 fl oz) water – use a blender to reduce the lumps of fruit. Push through a sieve and flavour to taste with the juice of a lemon. Freeze at the lowest possible temperature, and when the sides are frozen, stir them into the middle, and freeze again until firm.

Mrs Hislop did not add two whisked egg whites at this point to lighten the texture, but you could. Or you could add cream and turn it into an apricot ice cream, in the manner of her:

STRAWBERRY CREAM ICE

2 pints of juice to 3 of cream, and 4 ounces of powdered sugar to every pint of the composition. Put the sugar to the juice before the cream.

Liquidise the strawberries, then sieve them, to make the 'juice', and use icing sugar for easy dissolving.

BURNT ALMONDS

Mrs Hislop's name occurs frequently at the start of the receipt book. She made a speciality, it seems, of delicious sweet things – fruit compôtes, fruit water and cream ices, chestnut puddings and these burnt almonds which are as Lady Shaftesbury notes at the end 'very good'.

Put 125 g (4 oz) granulated sugar in a heavy pan. Sprinkle it with water until it looks like wet sand. Bring to the boil, stirring, and add the same weight of almonds. Stir for 2 minutes. Remove the pan from the heat, and stir until cool. Heat again, and when the sugar reaches the crack stage, remove and cool. By this time, the mixture may well be difficult to stir. Add extra water, scraping down the sugary sides of the pan. Return to the heat for the third boiling, and leave until the whole thing turns golden brown, a rich toffee colour. Stir so that the almonds do not burn on the base of the pan, and again be prepared to add very small amounts of water, to prevent crystallisation. You should end up with the almonds bathed – not swimming – in the caramel. Cover a baking sheet, with Bakewell paper and turn out the almonds on to it, spreading them out into a single layer so that they cool in their toffee.

When cold and hard, you may break them up and serve them with coffee or at dessert. Or you can reduce them to praline powder in a blender, and keep the powder for flavouring cakes and ices.

LADY GRANVILLE'S ICED COFFEE

Harriet, Lady Granville, had been a friend of Lady Cowper's since they were both children, but was tart about Minny herself when she was slow to accept the charming, passionate Lord Ashley, in 1829. (The Granvilles had become fond of Lord Ashley when he had stayed with them at the Paris embassy a few years before.) Her daughter-in-law, Marie – Lady Granville in her turn – was heiress to Talleyrand's close friend, the Duke of Dalberg, and by her first marriage mother of the historian Lord Acton. Marie had a genius for elegant nest-making, and – or so I would have said from this recipe – a gift for providing delicious refreshments. Perhaps the easy, casual wording was hers, it is quite unlike the more careful instructions in the rest of the book:

> Cream, milk, and coffee, in equal parts, to make any quantity, from $\frac{1}{2}$ a pint to a Hogshead, sweeten it to your taste, bearing in mind that icing it diminishes the sweetness.

Quite the best recipe for iced coffee that I know; even if you are obliged to reduce the quantity of cream slightly – alas, we are not all heiresses – it is still delicious. But do not economise on the coffee.

PLUM CAKE

Two of Lord Shaftesbury's sisters, Charlotte Lyster and Caroline Neeld, were named contributors to the receipt book, with versions of pop (well spiked with brandy), gingerbread nuts, brandy butter (125 g butter whipped to a cream: add the same weight of sugar, and by degrees a glass of brandy) – and this plum cake. Such recipes belonging to the time before baking powder, when cakes were mainly raised with yeast, are still to be found all over the country, though there are less of them than there were, say in Tudor times. I suspect that with the convenience of dried yeast, these cakes are in for a come-back. As Elizabeth David remarked in her *English Bread and Yeast Cookery*, they are 'confections of remarkable delicacy and distinction'. She went on to say that as she experimented with the many recipes, she came to the conclusion that it was modern methods used with modern ingredients that had begun to seem crude and out of date.

A particular merit of a yeast plum cake is the small amount of sugar required; sweetness enough is provided by the dried fruit, which gives a subtler flavour.

Charlotte, whose recipe this is, had married into an old Shropshire family, the Lysters. Rowton Castle, near the Welsh border, which had been their home since the Middle Ages, was in process of romantic transformation to designs by George Wyatt. Lord Shaftesbury loved this 'dream castle', in its beautiful countryside. Easy to imagine him and the children returning after a long walk and reviving themselves with this cake.

> *2 level teaspoons dried yeast*
> *4 tablespoons water at blood heat*
> *4 teaspoons sugar*
> *175 g (6 oz) butter*
> *175 ml (6 fl oz) milk*
> *375 g (generous 12 oz) strong plain flour*
> *1 large egg*
> *125 g (4 oz) mixed raisins and currants*
>
> GLAZE
> *60 g (2 oz) sugar*
> *5 tablespoons milk*

Mix yeast with water and 1 teaspoon sugar in the bowl of an electric mixer. Leave 10 minutes. Cut butter in smallish chunks and melt them with the milk. Sift flour into the creamy yeast, add remaining sugar, then pour in the milk and butter which should be no hotter than blood heat. Add the beaten egg. Mix with electric dough hook or by hand, until you arrive at a dough that looks like a soft cake mixture, i.e. it should be thicker than a very thick batter, slightly coherent, but not coherent enough to knead like a bread dough. Beat it slightly, but not very much.

Place the bowl in a plastic carrier bag, and secure the top with a metal tie. Leave in a warm place for 1½ hours. Knock down and mix in the fruit. Put the dough into a buttered tin of 1½ litres (2½ pt) capacity, tie into the plastic bag and leave for 30 minutes.

Bake in the oven set at mark 5, 190° (375°) for 45 minutes. Protect the top with a butter paper or a piece of foil towards the end of cooking time. Test the cake with a skewer: if it comes out clean, it is cooked. Remove from the oven, take the cake from the tin and leave it to cool balanced across the top (if you used a loaf tin) or on a warm tray.

If you like a sticky top, boil the sugar and milk together (glaze ingredients) for a minute or two and brush over the cake while it is still hot. If you prefer a drier finish, just brush the cake over with milk while it is still hot. This gives a softer shine, which is – to my way of thinking, anyway – more attractive.

Alexandre Dumas (1802–1870)

A hefty, happy, extravagant man, a 'force of nature' according to Michelet the historian, Alexandre Dumas of *The Three Musketeers* and *The Count of Monte Cristo* loved food and cooking as much – perhaps even more – than he loved writing novels and plays. A friend who called one day heard laughter coming from Dumas's study. 'Oh, I'll wait until the other visitors have gone,' he said to the manservant. 'There's no one with him, sir. Monsieur often laughs when he is writing.'

He was so hospitable, so open-handed that his house at Port-Marly – called Monte Cristo – was always too full of people and he had to build himself a small house beside it – the Château d'If, in gothic style – for writing in. Every year he spent a fortune. His 'terrible improvidence', plus the spongers and hangers-on, ruined him in the end. His son, Alexandre Dumas *fils*, author of the *Dame aux Camélias*, tried to tone down the extravagance and frighten off the crowds who lived on Dumas *père*, but without success, and it was in his house at Puys, just outside Dieppe, that Dumas died, with little left of the enormous sums he had made. And with little help from those who had enjoyed themselves at his expense in the past (while he lived at Port-Marly, the railways receipts for the line from Paris, rose by twenty thousand francs – then fell again, when he left).

In himself, Dumas was a moderate man. He neither smoked, drank nor gambled. In spite of his mania for cooking, he ate little but provided generously. Often he did not know the names of all his guests. And as they arrived in relays at wherever he might be living, there was a constant trail from the kitchen to the butcher's for fresh supplies of steak and cutlets. The midday meal which began at about 11.30 rarely finished before 4.30 in the afternoon.

Dumas knew a great deal about dinners and cooking them. He

ALEX. DUMAS.

wrote about such things, not always accurately but always enter-
tainingly, in his *Grand Dictionnaire de Cuisine* (published after his
death, in 1873). Some people had believed that he was all talk, all
eat, unable to boil an egg. But that won't do, as the *Dictionnaire*
shows.

The rumour started, it seems, with a disappointed cook called
Sophie. She was employed by Dr Véron, the founder of the *Revue
de Paris*, and from 1831 director of the Opéra at its grandest
period. One day Dr Véron dined with Dumas, and came back
raving about the carp he had eaten there. Sophie was irked, and
went off to ask Dumas's cook for the recipe. She was told that
Dumas had cooked the carp, so from Dumas himself she received
the full instructions. When she made the dish at home for Dr
Véron, it was not as good as he remembered it. Sophie grew
morose. She was not illiterate, and knew enough of current literary
gossip to mutter that Dumas borrowed other people's feathers in
his culinary activities, just as he did in his books.

Meanwhile Dumas had been away. On his return he walked into
the Café de Paris where he and his friends dined regularly, and
asked Dr Véron, another habitué, how the carp had turned out.
Someone in the party unwisely said what had happened. Dumas
was furious. 'Come and dine with me tomorrow. Choose someone
to watch me cook, and send him along at three o'clock.' The choice
fell on the youngest person in Dr Véron's party, an Englishman
Albert Vandam, who became a journalist, and wrote this whole
story down thirty years later in *An Englishman in Paris*.

Next day he presented himself at Dumas's apartment in the
Chaussé d'Antin, and was taken to the kitchen. Apart from the
soupe aux choux (p. 158), which Dumas had been preparing all
morning, everything else remained to be cooked. Ingredients had
been washed and prepared, that was all. The cook and kitchen-
maid stood by to assist, but Dumas himself 'with his sleeves rolled
up to the elbows, a large apron round his waist and bare chest,
conducted the operations'. Albert Vandam had never seen anything more entertaining. Dumas became the hero of his life, and a
close friend.

Apart from the *soupe aux choux* and the German dish of carp
that had led to the trouble, the menu consisted of a *ragoût à la
hongroise* (p. 168), roast pheasant and a *salade japonaise* –

perhaps the one described by his son much later, in *Francillon*, consisting of potatoes, mussels and truffles? No recipe is given in the *Dictionnaire*.

As Vandam was born in 1843 and did not arrive in Paris until he was a boy of twelve, and as the menu included *salade japonaise*, I would assume that the dinner took place about 1860, or 1861.

Another, later witness to Dumas's skill was the painter Monet (q.v.). In 1868, the terrible year when he tried to commit suicide, and had retreated to his native town of Le Havre with Camille and their baby, an amiable ship-builder, Monsieur Gaudibert, gave him the support that his family would not, and commissioned a portrait of his wife. One day, seeing how depressed Monet was, he suggested that he went to see Courbet who had just arrived at Le Havre (the two painters had met three years earlier, and Courbet had visited Monet at Chailly when he was painting his huge forest picnic scene, p. 203, and cover).

Courbet suggested that they should visit Dumas. Monet protested that he did not know him. 'Neither do I,' said Courbet, 'but we have nearly met each other many times.'

And off they went to the draper's shop where Dumas had taken rooms. Courbet knocked. Dumas was busy. 'Tell him the Master of Ornans has come to see him,' said Courbet. And there in an instant was Dumas, ' a giant, his head covered with thick curly white hair, white hair covering his bare chest – he was cooking'. The two men fell into each other's arms like brothers, weeping. 'Stay for dinner,' said Dumas. So they did. And next day, and many days afterwards, Dumas and Courbet walked Monet over to St Jouin, to the restaurant of the fair Ernestine (p. 161). 'Dumas at table was marvellous, talking about everything, art, history, politics, love, cooking. . . . Courbet had to admire him, good talker as he was, and Monet, who stayed silent, admired him even more. When Dumas and Courbet were not talking, they would sing or cook together; Courbet made dishes from his native Franche-Comté, Dumas dishes from the whole world.'*

From these two young man, both impeccable sources, we may safely conclude that Dumas could cook. And if you read the *Dictionnaire*, you will find it full of tips that only an experienced

---

* From Gustave Geffroy's life, *Claude Monet* (1922): he was a close friend, and recounts many episodes that Monet had told him about directly.

cook would think of passing on. My own feeling is that for anyone who loves food and all about it, a facsimile edition of the *Dictionnaire*, an early edition if you can find one, is well worth acquiring. But there is also a good new selection translated from it by Jane and Alan Davidson that was published in a Folio Society edition in 1978 under the title *Dumas on Food*.*

After an introduction about Dumas and the writing of the *Dictionnaire*, the Davidsons pick out the best and most accessible recipes, the best asides and anecdotes: among them talk of how the great Boileau became a satirist rather than a love poet, turned sour by an encounter with a turkey when he was a small boy; his trousers were down and a turkey – turkeys, according to Dumas, see red, like bulls – pecked what he thought was a worm. Here, too, you can read how Dumas on his travels managed to have fresh butter every day, whether the local milking animal was cow or camel, goat or mare; how the soul of Prince Anthony of Naples took the form of a pig, and why the son of Grimod de la Reynière ordered seven turkeys for his dinner. If you want to cook shark's stomach or shrimps, to make madeleines or a matelote of herring, or a salad of truffles in the manner of the actress Mademoiselle Georges, you will find all that, too. Do you know what virtues are attached to kangaroo meat? What balachan or blachan is? How to make an apple's pudding? Or how the Chinese fatten dogs for the table? Or who promoted the growing of sugar beet for sugar? Or how to make a whole dinner in the ancient, lavish style from an ox and a few root vegetables?

My only complaint about the French editions of the *Dictionnaire* is that they lack a good index. You find a likely recipe, forget to mark it, and then wonder what entry to look up. In the end you are obliged to leaf through the whole thing. A mighty task with some editions.

SOUPE AUX CHOUX
CABBAGE SOUP

Here is Dumas's recipe for the famous soup which had been started several hours before young Vandam's arrival to check on his

* A trade edition is now published by Michael Joseph Ltd. – and has an index!

capability as cook. Most people will prefer to split the marathon process in two, making the *pot-au-feu* one day – perhaps in an electric crock pot or deep-frier – and serving the beef in the evening. The stock should be strained off and kept until the next day; any fat can then easily be lifted off, and the liquor used for the cabbage soup, for a dinner party. With the beef, serve coarse sea salt, gherkins, the vegetables from the *pot-au-feu* or freshly cooked ones, horseradish sauce: in very grand French houses, they will often put a bottle of Heinz tomato sauce on the table, standing on a beautiful saucer, with a long silver spoon. I wonder what Dumas would have thought of that?

> either *2 kilos (4 lb) rolled silverside, or top rump* or *1 kilo (2 lb) plus 1 kilo shin of beef in a piece, or ox cheek*
> *beef bones, sawn in pieces by the butcher,* or *a veal knuckle bone*
> *any remains of roast chicken, partridge, pheasant, pigeon, rabbit*
> *4 carrots, scrubbed, topped and tailed*
> *4 small turnips, peeled*
> *2 small parsnips, peeled, topped and tailed*
> *4 leeks tied in a bundle with 1 stick celery*
> *3 onions, each stuck with a clove*
> *1 large clove of garlic*
> $\frac{1}{2}$–$\frac{3}{4}$ *kilo (1–1$\frac{1}{2}$ lb) thin rashers uncooked smoked ham or gammon*
> *1 fine large cabbage – Dutch or Savoy is best*
> *salt, pepper*

Put the beef into a very large pan. Tie the bones into a cloth with the remains of chicken or game, bones, meat, giblets and all. Pour on 4 litres water (7 pt) or a little less if your pan will not accommodate it easily. Bring slowly to the boil, and remove the unpleasant looking grey scum with a perforated skimmer. Once the bubbles look white and cheerful, you can stop skimming. Put in the vegetables and garlic, with a tablespoon of salt. Half-cover and leave barely to simmer for 6 hours. As Dumas says, '*faire sourire le pot-au-feu*', adding that you will not find the phrase in any dictionary. 'But if ever I am one of the Forty, I shall see that it is put into the *Dictionnaire de l'Académie*' (alas he never was elected to the Academy – 'his sense of deportment was deficient' – but his very respectable son managed it).

Having kept the *pot-au-feu* smiling for 6 hours, you are now ready to make the cabbage soup, which will take a further 2¼ hours, including preparation time.

Line a pan with the smoked ham or gammon rashers. Quarter the cabbage, cut away the tough stalk and rinse it free of animals (their protein, as Dumas points out, not being required). Tie the cabbage back into shape and place it on the ham or gammon. Pour in enough *pot-au-feu* liquid to come to the top of the cabbage. Set the pan over a high heat, the highest you can manage, and bring the pot to the boil. Boil hard for 10 minutes. Quite a lot of the stock will have disappeared, so top it up, lower the heat and cover. Leave to simmer for an hour, then check the liquid level again and add more *pot-au-feu* liquid if necessary. Cover and leave for a further 50 minutes.

Carefully strain the cabbage liquor into a soup tureen. Add remaining liquid, or as much as you need to fill the tureen, from the *pot-au-feu*, and taste for seasoning. Carefully transfer the ham or gammon and cabbage to another dish, remove the string and serve with the soup, so that people can help themselves to a spoonful of cabbage and a piece of ham or gammon and stir it into their *bouillon*.

'And there, dear reader, you have the famous and excellent *soupe aux choux*, which you can give to all your guests, who will promptly ask you for the recipe.'

POTAGE À LA CREVETTE
SHRIMP AND TOMATO BISQUE

Whatever the attractions of travel or Paris were for Dumas, he was always drawn back to the sea (he quotes Byron: 'Oh sea, the only love to whom I have been faithful'). He wrote much of the *Diction-naire* at Roscoff in Brittany, and some in Normandy at Le Havre, where he met Courbet and Monet. He loved the shrimps and *bouquets roses* (prawns) of that coast, and invented this soup for them. In the end he died near the sea.

The entry on shrimps is delightful, with its picture of Ernestine's establishment near Étretat, at St Jouin (my copy of the *Diction-naire* says St Jouart, but I think this must be a mistake). Ernestine herself was wise and beautiful. The place was much visited by discriminating people from Le Havre, and 'by the painters and poets of Paris who left drawings and poems celebrating her virtues, in her album'.

Judging by a similar recipe in the soup section, this dish was invented by Dumas himself. It should be made with the remains of the *pot-au-feu* liquid and live shrimps. If you cannot manage this, use a good beef stock and boiled shrimps (or prawns, or mussels opened with white wine).

> *150–200 g (5–7 oz) shrimps*
> *¾ kilo (1½ lb) tomatoes, peeled, chopped*
> *½ kilo (1 lb) onions, sliced*
> *white wine*
> *salt, pepper, Cayenne*
> bouillon *from* pot-au-feu, *or beef stock*

Cook tomatoes and onions slowly in a covered pan. When the tomato juices flow, raise the heat and remove the lid. Simmer steadily for about 45 minutes, then sieve.

Meanwhile cover the shrimps generously with white wine, add salt, pepper, Cayenne. Bring to the boil, and cook briefly for a moment or two. Try one to see if it is ready. Strain off the liquid.† Peel the shrimps, setting aside the edible tail part. Put the debris back into the pan with the liquid, and simmer for 15 minutes to extract all flavour from the shells etc. Strain, pressing as much through as possible. Measure this shrimp liquid, and add an equal quantity both of the tomato purée and beef stock. Bring to the boil, taste for seasoning, and adjust the quantities if you like, adding a little more tomato or stock, or both. A pinch of sugar will help bring out the flavour, if the tomatoes were not particularly good.

Put in the shrimp meats, and heat for a moment, then serve. Do not keep the soup waiting, as this will toughen the shrimp tails.

Note If you use cooked shrimps or prawns, start their preparation at †, covering the debris very generously with white wine.

OEUFS BROUILLÉS AUX QUEUES DE CREVETTES

SCRAMBLED EGGS WITH SHRIMPS

As I have already said, French editions of the *Dictionnaire* sorely need an index. Versions of the tomato and shrimp soup on p. 161, occur in three places, under *potage*, under *crevettes* and under *homard* together with such unlikely items as a salad, chicken on a string, scrambled eggs of two kinds and octopus – the reason being that Dumas wanted at this point to tell us about a dinner he cooked more or less single-handed at a friend's house in Fécamp, and one of the dishes was *homard à l'américaine*.

Readers who live within reach of Morecambe Bay, will understand Dumas's enthusiasm for shrimps, and will feel like me that a dinner in his honour should have either the shrimp soup, or this scrambled egg dish, on the menu:

200–250 g (6–8 oz) boiled shrimps
200 ml (6–7 fl oz) dry white wine, preferably Chablis
8 whole eggs
4 egg yolks
chopped parsley and chives
100 g (3 oz) butter
salt, pepper

Pick the shrimps and make an essence with the debris, the wine and enough water to cover the bits and pieces, as in the soup recipe. Beat the eggs and yolks together, adding herbs to taste. Season and strain in the shrimp essence. Stir in the shrimps. Set aside while you prepare 6–8 slices of buttered toast, or little bun cases (remove lid, hollow out, brush with butter and crisp in a hot oven).

Just before the meal, melt the butter and stir in the egg mixture. Keep stirring until it is scrambled to the creamy stage. As Dumas says, scrambled eggs should never be cooked firm, as they will continue to cook a little in their own heat, and taste nicest when they are creamy.

Tip on to the toast, or into the cases, and serve.

Eggs scrambled this way can be poured into a serving dish, and put on the table cold, with thin toast, as a first course, or part of a first course.

SOLE À LA MODE DE TROUVILLE
SOLE IN THE STYLE OF TROUVILLE

A dish that seems startling for the quantity of onion, just as *sole au Chambertin* sounds odd for its combination of delicate fish with red Burgundy. But try it, first if you like with large plaice, Torbay sole or lemon sole.

> *2–3 fine large sole (1½ kilos – 3 lb or more, altogether)*
> *200 g (7 oz) unsalted Normandy butter*
> *2 heaped tablespoons finely chopped onion*
> *dry cider*
> *salt, pepper, parsley*

Trim the sole and remove the black skin – or ask the fishmonger to do it for you. Cut the fish into six pieces across. Spread a flame-proof shallow pan with a quarter of the butter. Place the sole on top, sprinkle the onion over the pieces and cover them with cider. Quickly bring the whole thing to the boil, then transfer to the oven preheated to mark 5, 190° (375°) for 10 minutes. Remove the sole to a hot serving dish, turn off the oven and put the sole in it to keep warm, leaving the door slightly ajar. Boil down the cooking juices and onion vigorously for at least 2 minutes, so that you end up with a concentrated liquor. Meanwhile cut the remaining butter into chunks. Off the heat, whisk the butter into the juices to bind the sauce: taste for seasoning, and add salt and pepper. Season the fish, too, then pour over the sauce. Scatter with a very little parsley and serve.

ARTICHAUTS À LA GRIMOD DE LA REYNIÈRE
ARTICHOKES IN THE MANNER OF GRIMOD DE LA REYNIÈRE

Alexandre-Balthazar-Laurent Grimod de la Reynière, the 'father

of French gastronomy' and a strange, sad man with webbed hands
like goose feet, cheered himself up with food. Loving, as he felt,
denied him, he took to eating and writing about it. His *Almanach
des Gourmands* appeared for eight years, from 1803 to 1812;
in 1808 his *Manuel des Amphitryons* was published. In the
Almanachs, he wrote articles on the andouilles de Vire, songs and
poems about food, gourmet discoveries of the year, the state of the
Paris markets, the sardines of Nantes, chocolate, wedding breakfasts, butter, the progress of cookery in the eighteenth century and
so on.

With many recipes. Dumas often mentions him and quotes from
him – so does every other French writer on food – and gives this
simple but delicious recipe that he invented.

> *8 medium onions, chopped*
> *125 g (4 oz) butter*
> *salt, pepper, nutmeg*
> *8 fine artichokes, boiled*
> *breadcrumbs*
> *grated cheese, preferably Parmesan, or a mixture of*
> *Parmesan and very dry Cheddar*

Sweat the onions in butter in a covered pan. As they soften and
turn gold, raise the heat, remove the lid and stir them about until
they are a pale brown. Season with salt, pepper and nutmeg, and
turn on to a plate to cool. Remove the leaves from the artichokes
(keep them for a first course at another meal). Scrape away the
chokes. Fill the bottoms with the onion mixture. Sprinkle with
breadcrumbs mixed with cheese. Colour and reheat them in a very
hot oven, or under the grill.

If the bottoms are a very shallow shape, you may have too much
onion to go into them. Spread it out on the serving dish, sprinkle
with a few breadcrumbs and cheese and brown under the grill.
Place the baked or grilled artichokes on top.

HARICOTS VERTS EN SALADE*
GREEN BEAN SALAD

For eight people, cook ¾ kilo (1½ lb) green beans. Use the tiny ones for preference, that are very tender and need no stringing. Bake 8 small onions in their skins, then squeeze out the cooked part and chop. Dice 3 or 4 small beetroot.

Put the cool drained beans into a salad bowl. Arrange a lattice of anchovy fillets on top, and in the lattice gaps, put some cooked onion and a little beetroot. Scatter with parsley and chives. Pour on a vinaigrette made with olive oil – do this carefully so as not to spoil the nice arrangement. Serve this salad cold, rather than chilled.

POTIRON À LA PARMESAN*
PUMPKIN WITH PARMESAN CHEESE

Peel a 1½ kilo (3 lb) section of pumpkin, and discard the seeds with the loose cotton surrounding them. Cut the firm part into square pieces and parboil them in salted water. Do not cook them completely, or they will start to disintegrate. Fry them in clarified butter on both sides, scattering them with salt, nutmeg and cinnamon. As they become lightly coloured, remove the squares to a serving dish, piling them up in the centre. Cover them with grated Parmesan cheese, and bake in a hot oven until the cheese is nicely golden.

Note Parmesan can be eked out with dry Cheddar.

QUEUE DE BOEUF À LA SAINTE MÉNÉHOULD*
OX TAIL SAINTE MÉNÉHOULD

Ste Ménéhould a small town, not far from Verdun, is famous for its pigs' trotters. They are cooked so long that you can even eat the bones, and they are finished with a coating of melted butter and crumbs, before being reheated under the grill. When the name is applied to other meats, it means melted butter, breadcrumbs and grilling, as in this recipe of Dumas's from the *Dictionnaire*, and sometimes a piquant sauce as well.

* These recipes come from Dumas's *Dictionnaire*.

3 fine oxtails, cut across into pieces
lard
2 chopped onions
2 diced carrots
1 chopped stalk celery
bouquet garni
3 cloves garlic in their skins
beef stock to cover
salt, pepper
melted butter
breadcrumbs

For six to eight people, you will need three fine ox tails. Trim them of surplus fat. Brown them in a little lard, and put the pieces into a casserole. Brown also onions, carrots, celery. Add them to the casserole plus *bouquet garni*, and garlic. Pour in enough stock just to cover them. Put on the lid of the casserole and stew for 4–5 hours in a slow oven, mark 1–2, 140–150° (275–300°). When the ox tail parts from the bones, it is cooked. Cool the whole thing, and leave until next day.

Take off the fat from the top of the stew. Drain the pieces of meat. Season them with salt and pepper, and dip them in melted butter, then in breadcrumbs. Dip them a second time in melted butter, and again in breadcrumbs. Now the pieces can be grilled or put into a hot oven. They are ready when they are a nice brown.

Serve them with red cabbage, or a purée of dried haricot beans, or with a soubise sauce, or with a piquant sauce such as the *charcutière* sauce on p. 188.

CANETONS À L'ORANGE
DUCKLING WITH ORANGE

Dumas was often criticised for using collaborators in writing his novels and plays. It is said he did not acknowledge their work adequately, and that sometimes they were almost responsible for the whole thing. This is a travesty. He did rely on other people – in the case of the *Dictionnaire*, he replied particularly on his friend, the chef Denis Joseph Vuillemot and he gives him plenty of credit – but it should be noticed that when his collaborators struck out on their own, their writings were boring and lifeless. Dumas added the genius.

Here is one of Vuillemot's dishes. Dumas said that he must confess his great partiality for the dish 'particularly when confected by the skilful operator from whom I have the recipe'.

> *butter*
> *2 large carrots, chopped*
> *2 large onions, chopped*
> *large stalk celery, chopped*
> *3 shallots, chopped*
> *2 duckling*
> *½ bottle champagne or dry white wine*
> *250 ml (8 fl oz) consommé or beef stock*
> *3 oranges*
> *2 egg whites*
> *pepper, lemon juice*
> *a nut of meat jelly from underneath beef dripping*
> *   (optional)*

Butter a large fireproof pan and put in the chopped vegetables, mixed together, in a single layer. Add the duck giblets, apart from the livers, and put the duckling on top. Sweat slowly for 10 minutes. Pour in the champagne or wine and the consommé or stock. Cover and simmer until the duckling are cooked – about 1½–2 hours, depending on size.

Cut the zest from two of the oranges, slice it into strips and blanch them in boiling water for 2–3 minutes. Drain. Cut the orange segments from their skins, and simmer them in a very little water when the duckling are just about ready: keep them hot.

Put the cooked duckling on a serving dish, cut them into quarters if you like (makes for easier serving). Surround them with the orange segments, and keep warm.

Pour the fat from the cooking juices, then strain them into a wide shallow pan. Spoon or blot away any fat that remains. Taste the juices and boil them down if they need concentrating; should they look murky, whisk in the egg whites, bring to the boil and boil for a moment or two until the egg whites accumulate on top in a dirty foamy mass. Strain off the clear liquid into another pan. Check the seasoning, add pepper, a squeeze of lemon juice to bring out the flavour, and the nut of meat jelly, if used. Squeeze the juice of the third orange over the duckling. Arrange the blanched strips of peel decoratively on top. Pour a little of the sauce round them, and serve the rest in a sauce boat. A good clear version of duck with orange.

Note In the spring, you could substitute Seville orange juice for lemon juice and the third orange juice. The sauce might then need a hint of sugar. Be guided by the taste.

AGNEAU À LA HONGROISE
LAMB HUNGARIAN STYLE

Another dish from the meal Dumas prepared to prove to Dr Véron that he did indeed know how to cook.

One of the most entertaining features of the *Dictionnaire* is Dumas' open mind. Unlike many of his fellow countrymen, he enjoyed good food wherever he found it, and he included far more than the classic proportion of tamed foreign dishes. At one point, he concludes that lamb cooked desert style by Arabs – complete with fleece, which was stripped off just before the feast began – tasted better than any roast gigot he had eaten at home. Of this economical recipe he says, 'one of the best dishes which I have eaten in Hungary'.

The quantity of onions seems enormous, but they collapse and reduce considerably. I use more paprika than Dumas suggests, though perhaps a pinch from those large fingers was close to a tablespoonful. For 6–8 people buy 1½–2 kilos (3–4 lb) of the meatiest breast of lamb you can find. Ask the butcher to cut it into oblong pieces, 'the size of tablets of chocolate' – 50 g size. Other things you will need are:

> *1½ kilos (3 lb) Spanish onions*
> *butter*
> *sugar, salt, pepper, Cayenne*
> *1 heaped tablespoon flour*
> *1 rounded tablespoon Hungarian paprika*

bouquet garni
up to a litre (1¾ pt) consommé or beef stock

In a large heavy pan, cook the onions in 3 tablespoons of butter, slowly at first, until they soften. Sprinkle on a level tablespoon of sugar, raise the heat and stir until the onions are lightly caramelized to an appetising brown. In another pan, at the same time, brown the pieces of lamb in butter. Season with salt, pepper and Cayenne. When the onion is right, stir in the flour, paprika and *bouquet*. Cook a couple of minutes, then add enough consommé or stock to make a creamy sauce. Put in the meat, and cover.

Simmer for at least 1¼ hours, or until the meat begins to fall from the bones. Every quarter of an hour check on the liquid and thickness, adding a tumbler more of stock when necessary. This way of cooking means you have a good strong flavour; it helps if you remove the lid of the pan after half an hour, so that the sauce reduces and you have to keep topping it up. Check the seasoning, adding a little more Cayenne if you like. Skim or blot away the surface fat. Serve with noodles.

SAUCE AU RAISIN*
RAISIN SAUCE

A good sauce for hot tongue, and for pigeons or ham.

> *150 ml (5 fl oz) wine vinegar*
> bouquet garni
> *teaspoonful black peppercorns*
> *4 cloves*
> *300 ml (10 fl oz) beef stock, or pigeon stock*
> *tablespoon* fécule *(potato flour) or cornflour*
> *2 tablespoons redcurrant jelly*
> *2 handfuls of currants and sultanas mixed*

Put vinegar, *bouquet*, peppercorns and cloves into a pan, and boil hard until the vinegar is reduced by half. Add the stock and bring to the boil. Simmer a moment or two, then mix in the *fécule* or cornflour slaked with a little water. Simmer steadily for 5 minutes,

* ibid.

then strain into a clean pan. Add the jelly, and stir or whisk until it has dissolved. Then put in the dried fruit and give it another 5 minutes for the sauce to blend and the dried fruit to swell.

Pour some over the sliced tongue in its serving dish, and put the rest into a sauceboat.

THE DESSERT

Entries on fruit bring out some of Dumas's best stories. He tells us that the Emperor Claudius Albinus one day at lunch ate 500 figs, 100 peaches, ten melons and a large number of grapes.

Another entry mentions the yearly tribute he received from Cavaillon, down in the south near Avignon. The council of the town wrote to him one day, to say they were starting a library and would he donate two or three of his best novels. 'Now I have a daughter and a son, whom I think I love equally; and I am the author of five or six hundred volumes and believe myself to be just about equally fond of them all.' He replied to the town that an author could not judge the merits of his books, but that he found Cavaillon melons excellent. He would therefore send them a complete set of his works, if the council would grant him a life annuity of twelve of their melons. This was agreed and, as he was writing, twelve years later, the town had never failed. Dumas hoped the people of Cavaillon have found his books as charming as he has found their melons.

Another good tale concerns peaches, the famous Montreuil peaches from the east of Paris. A musketeer named Girardot, in the seventeenth century, had been wounded badly several times, and had retired to a small house he had at Malassis, between Montreuil and Bagnolet. He was a friend of de la Quintinie's (p. 17), and frequently visited him at Versailles. Now Girardot wanted to ask Louis XIV a favour, so de la Quintinie said he would persuade the king in the direction of Malassis when he was staying at Chantilly for the hunting.

Next day, a dozen splendid peaches arrived for the king's dessert – no name. Everyone thought them delicious. A few days later, the king came to visit Girardot, – presumably de la Quintinie had guessed where the peaches came from – and see the espalier trees that had produced such magnificent fruit. And Girardot, all dressed up in his uniform, made his request, which was granted, plus a pension, on condition that he supplied a basketful of peaches every year, 'for the dessert of the king'.

And so the variety of peaches developed at Montreuil became famous, especially as the Girardot family and other local growers supplied a basket of their best fruit every year to the royal family until the Revolution. Although Paris has swallowed up Montreuil and Bagnolet, and Malassis has disappeared with them, I believe that a few espaliers of peaches are still grown there.

Under the entry on pomegranates, Dumas quotes a delightful piece: 'There are no beautiful fruit baskets without pomegranates; likewise there are none without oranges. A pomegranate which has been cut open, looking like a rich treasure of rubies or sparkling garnets, is one of the most beautiful jewels of our majestic fruit baskets. Nothing else can equal the effect of a few half-open pomegranates on the side of a pyramid of fruit. . . . But we must equally admit that, aside from playing this splendid role in the decoration of the tables at a buffet, the pomegranate is a fruit which does not even match the currant in quality.'

Of oranges, Dumas liked best the mandarin, from China. 'There are some mandarins the size of a walnut, which are yellow, verging on red, in colour, have a thin peel, and a smell approaching that of the lemon. The flesh of the fruit is very sweet, and contains little juice.'

Another essential fruit was the fig, the fruit which caused the Romans to destroy Carthage. In a debate at the Senate, Cato held up a fresh ripe fig, in prime condition. 'When do you think this fig was picked? . . . Only three days ago this fig was hanging from the tree, and it comes from Carthage. Judge from this how close the enemy is to us!'

Dumas noting the excellence of ripe, *fresh* dates, observed that they were rarely seen on French tables. These days we import them all the year round from Israel; they make a good addition to a Dumas feast. So, too, would candied glacé fruit and marrons glacés.

Nuts should be included in autumn and winter desserts, almonds, fresh walnuts if possible, and hazelnuts. Dumas thought the best hazelnuts came from Avellino near Naples (their virtue is commemorated both in the botanical name *Corylus avellana* and in the French *aveline* for hazelnut). 'Hazelnuts grow wild in the ravines and ruins that surround Avellino' – nowadays there are miles and miles of plantations, too. 'As a child Victor Hugo nearly killed himself by falling into one of these ravines as he was picking hazelnuts.'

Under the brief entry for walnuts, Dumas hands on a good tip. When using dry walnuts for cooking, rather than the fresh ones of the autumn, pour hot milk over them and leave to cool. This restores something of their flavour.

CRÈME AU CAFÉ BLANC
WHITE COFFEE CREAM

The use of whole coffee beans to flavour an ice – as in Elizabeth David's *French Provincial Cooking* – or a cream as in this recipe of Dumas', gives the best of all coffee flavours.

> 4 heaped tablespoons continental or after-dinner roast
>   coffee beans
> 2 strips lemon peel
> 600 ml (1 pt) whipping cream
> 2 tablespoons white or golden brown sugar
> packet (½ oz) gelatine

Bruise the coffee beans slightly in a mortar, to crack them. Put them in a pan with the lemon peel, cream and sugar. Stirring all the time, bring slowly to a thorough boil. Remove from the heat and leave to cool down, stirring frequently. Taste from time to time and when the cream is adequately infused with coffee and a hint of lemon-sharpness, strain it on to a packet of gelatine that you have dissolved in 6 tablespoons of very hot water. Taste again when cold, and add a little extra sugar if you like, but be discreet – this is not a dessert for children.

Divide between 6–8 custard cups and chill until set. Serve with thin crisp biscuits, such as the *cigarettes dentelles* imported from France. You will find the small quantities perfectly adequate for 6 or 8 people, as the mixture is rich and satisfying.

CRÈME RENVERSÉE

I always avoid this cliché of French eating when I am in France, but love making it in England out of nostalgia. Dumas obviously cooked it many times; he knew all about the trick of adding a little water to the caramel to prevent it sticking to the dish in a glassy unmoveable sheet.

1 litre (1¾ pt) milk
vanilla pod
6 large eggs
300 g (10 oz) sugar

Bring milk and vanilla to the boil, then pour on to the eggs that you have beaten up with half the sugar. Beat as you pour. Leave to cool, then extract the pod.

Bring remaining sugar to a golden brown caramel colour, with just enough water in the bottom of the pan to prevent the sugar burning as it comes to the boil. When you have achieved a good rich colour, pour in 4 tablespoons of hot water gradually – it will spit, so take the pan off the heat first, and wrap your hand in a cloth before you take hold of the handle again. Stir well, putting the pan back on the heat if necessary, so that you have a smooth liquid. Pour this into a soufflé or glass ovenproof dish of 1½ litres (2½ pt) capacity, and swill it round the sides. Gently pour in the custard. Stand in a pan of boiling water and bake for 45 minutes at mark 4, 180° (350°), then slide a knife into the centre. If it comes out clean, the custard is done. If the knife is splashed with custard, leave it for another 15, then 30 minutes, testing again. Time taken depends on the depth of the dish.

Remove from the oven. Lift the dish from the water bath, and leave it to cool. Chill well. Serve by turning it out on to a plate that is deep enough to accommodate the caramel sauce which will flow round it.

Note For a richer custard, use 4 large eggs, and 4 large egg yolks. Escoffier's proportions are 4 whole standard eggs and 6 egg yolks to a litre of milk, which makes a very good crème caramel or renversée indeed.

TOURTE FOURRÉE D'ABRICOTS À LA BONNE FEMME

HOUSEWIFE'S APRICOT TART

A simple recipe of Dumas's from the *Dictionnaire*, for a tart that can quite well be made with bought puff pastry.

> *12–16 large apricots*
> *300 g (10 oz) sugar*
> *24–32 large cherries*
> *¾ kilo (1½ lb) puff pastry*
> *beaten egg to glaze*

Halve, stone and poach the apricots in a syrup made by boiling together the sugar and 500 ml (16 fl oz) water. When they are just tender, remove the apricots to a dish to cool; remove the skins if they seem tough or obtrusive. While they cool, stone the cherries.

Roll out just under half the pastry to a large oblong, and cut it in two lengthways. Brush a good centimetre rim round each oblong with beaten egg. Arrange the apricot halves, two by two, with a cherry in each cavity.

Roll out the rest of the pastry, and cut it into two slightly larger oblongs. Use to cover the fruit, pressing the edges on to the rim of the pastry below. Knock up the edges. Make some neat slashes in the centre of each long tart, and score decorative lines over the top. Brush over with egg.

Slip on to a rinsed baking sheet, and put into the oven at mark 8, 230° (450°). After 15 minutes, see how the pastry looks. If it seems well browned, lower the heat to mark 6, 200° (400°). Otherwise leave it. Another 10 minutes should be enough, but be guided entirely by the look of the pastry. It should be well puffed and a good glossy golden brown.

Serve warm with cream.

Émile Zola (1840–1902)

Of all the people in this book, Zola had the strongest, most sensual attitude towards food. No wonder. He is the only one who had starved. As a young man he had come to Paris from Aix in Provence, and lived in a garret on bread and olive oil, and such sparrows as he could catch from the window. This state of hopeless poverty is the background to *Le Ventre de Paris*, published in 1873, his novel about the dark greedy maw of the central market of Les Halles. The new iron and glass buildings had been finished in 1866, and Zola wandered there for hours at night, day after day, sometimes with friends, always with the antagonism of the people there who thought he was spying out their business secrets. He opens the novel in the first hours of the morning, as vegetable carts trundle in from the market gardens ringing Paris. Drivers doze over the reins, leaning on carrots and cauliflowers. The horses plod over familiar cobbles. War between the Fats – the people of Les Halles – and the Thins, who include the hero Florent: an uneven war which develops against voluptuous displays of fruit, fish, cheese, charcuterie. It is only another episode in the war between fat Cain and thin Abel: 'Since the first murder, it has been a continual feast, the huge hungry ones' – the strong – 'have sucked the blood of the small eaters.'

In *L'Assommoir*, of 1877, one of his greatest novels, Zola uses the background of meals for some of the main scenes. No one who has experienced French life will be surprised at this, because it is so often round a table that families and friends come together. In the dishes at Gervaise's marriage and name-day feast, as in the dinner party given by her daughter Nana in the later novel, every dish chosen, its success, its serving, makes some comment on the plot and characters, or gives a hint – not always a subtle one – of what is to come.

When he became rich and famous – or rich and notorious – Zola seemed to epitomise the bourgeois aspects of the Belle Époque he professed to loathe. He became fat (and it must be admitted that when he decided to lose weight and succeeded, his literary powers declined, though this may have had more to do with his love for Jeanne Rozerot and their two children, which at last satisfied a different hunger). No one else has caught so well the revolting gluttony of the day, yet he himself would rush round the best shops to make sure of the first spring vegetables, and to buy exotic delicacies.

Daudet the novelist and a fellow Provençal, compared a hazel hen he had eaten at Zola's with the 'scented flesh of an old tart marinaded in a bidet' – a gratuitous remark until one learns that hazel hens, imported frozen from Russia to Paris, taste strongly of the pine cones on which they feed.

Such a dish, like the smoked reindeer tongues, may have been ordered as a compliment to Turgenev, who was often Zola's guest, along with Daudet, Flaubert, Maupassant. Cézanne, the friend of his childhood at Aix, he saw less of as they grew older. Cézanne felt that Zola had betrayed him, especially in *L'Oeuvre* of 1886; so did Monet and other painter friends who he had defended so sensationally in the early battles of Impressionism. He seemed to despise them for not being successful, now that he was a success. The large, heavily furnished apartments in Paris, the ever-increasing country house at Médan were oppressive by comparison with Monet's Giverny or Cézanne's Jas de Bouffan.

Resentment of a different kind runs through the long and splendid journal of Edmond and Jules de Goncourt. From their first meeting with Zola, when he was a starving admirer of their novels, they mark his progress from the Thins to the Fats. After Jules's death, Edmond continues fascinated but catty, the aesthete in him not quite admitting the unaesthetic depths of his anger. Naturalism, minute details of observation worked up into a novel, had been the Goncourts' idea. They had to watch the disciple overtake them, and express apparent pleasure at the success of a dear friend.

In the journal, Edmond could be more outspoken. Zola has the air of a parvenu come into an unexpected fortune; he is neither gay nor lovable; his wife's pretty face begins to look spiteful. Edmond went down to Médan on Sundays, enjoyed the Zolas' good food and generosity, yet wrote snobbishly that Zola loved the little dishes that his wife cooked for him, and rustic food of a provincial kind. Neither was he above going into the kitchen and stirring a pot if something seemed to be sticking. Once when he was given a dish of *palourdes* or carpet-shells, his fingers trembled so much with excitement that he had to wait a few moments before he could pick them up.

In fact Zola, like many people who had a hard time in their youth, was reduced to a despairing misery if he could not look forward to a good meal during the day. Even if they had wanted to, this is something the always comfortable Goncourts could not have appreciated, however keen their observation. 'I can understand,' wrote Edmond, 'the whim of gastronomic imagination that leads one occasionally to order a fine and delicate and unusual dinner, but to eat well every day is unsupportable.' And he concludes in the tone of any sophisticate who feels threatened when a more gifted provincial succeeds, that people from the south – which I take to include Daudet, who also loved his food – are always greedy and gourmand. And moreover, they aren't bad cooks.

As a footnote, one may add that when Zola took refuge in England after the Dreyfus affair and his own trial for *J'Accuse*, his sufferings where compounded by the appalling cooking of the hotel he lived in near the Crystal Palace. No sauces, not enough salt, watery vegetables, poor spongy bread, bad puddings. He took refuge in roast meat – that was all right – ham, eggs, salad, and managed to survive the disagreeable experience of biting on a clove embedded in a cake.

NANA'S DINNER PARTY

Zola's fascination and disgust drive through the orgiastic party Nana gives to celebrate her début as an 'actress'. She has no talent, only a beautiful body to show. The same might be said about her ordering of dinner – truffles with everything. She thought it smarter to have it at home. Down to napkins, flowers and foot-stools, it all came from Brébant's, a restaurant popular with writers and the Bohemian night society of Paris, because the amiable proprietor chalked up the bills. Edmond de Goncourt dined there regularly, although he was too superior to need credit, as Zola had done in his early years in Paris.

Nana's apartment is not large. The guests arrive, too many of them, gatecrashers as well. The courses come on, and on. Everyone gets red in the face, quarrelsome, jealous, bored, muddled, crowded, and fed up with food. Waiters grow careless, spilling fat on the floor and chattering loudly in the corridor as if they were back in the restaurant. Nana alternates between rage and despair. She shows off, uncertain whether to be the grand dame, or a giggling good sport. At dawn people go. The evening was a disaster. Nothing worked out. Nana looks to the opposite side of the Boulevard Haussmann (where Proust and his family lived a few years later), sees Paris waking grimly in the dawn, and demands to be taken to the Bois de Boulogne by her new lover, to drink milk fresh from the cow.

Menu

asparagus soup à la comtesse: recipe, p. 181.

consommé Deslignac: game or chicken clear soup, with a royale of egg yolks and chicken or game stock.

rissoles of young rabbit, stuffed with truffles: creamy rabbit croquettes, truffles inside, enclosed in puff pastry.

gnocchi with grated cheese: recipe, p. 183.

Rhine carp à la Chambord: a grand set piece – poached carp, with a square of pork fat studded on to its belly with truffle pieces. Garnished with mushrooms, oysters, crayfish quenelles and tails, all sauced, and two large oval quenelles, also studded with truffles. (There is a magnificent engraving of *carpe à la Chambord* in Urbain Dubois's *Cuisine Classique*.)

saddle of venison à l'anglaise: another set piece – the meat stuffed English-style, and served with a redcurrant jelly sauce, or Cumberland sauce.

chicken à la maréchale: and another – chicken stuffed with sweetbreads, brains, mushrooms bound in a *suprême* sauce, then poached and garnished with truffles and asparagus tips.

fillets of sole with ravigote sauce: recipe, p. 184.

escalopes of pâté de foie gras from Strasbourg

orange sorbet

fillet of beef with truffles

galantine of roast guineafowl in jelly.

ceps à l'italienne: *Boletus edulis* in a white wine and espagnole sauce, flavoured with herbs, shallots, finished with chopped ham.

pineapple fritters à la Pompadour with an apricot sauce, p. 198.
ices and desserts

wines: Meursault, Chambertin, Léoville.

ASPARAGUS SOUP À LA COMTESSE

At least there was a delicate beginning to Nana's overloaded meal.

375 g (12 oz) trimmed asparagus
125 g (4 oz) butter
60 g (2 oz) flour
600 ml (1 pt) chicken stock
salt, pepper
2 egg yolks
2 tablespoons double cream
pinch sugar
extra knob butter

Parboil the asparagus, then cut off the tips – which will be just tender – and set them aside. Cut the stalks into centimetre lengths. Stew them in half the butter in a covered pan until they are completely cooked. Meanwhile in another pan, melt the remaining butter, stir in the flour and then the chicken stock. Simmer, then moisten the asparagus in butter with some of the stock and liquidise. Pour through a strainer (to catch the last few stringy parts of the asparagus stalk, should there be any). Reheat gently and season.

Beat the yolks with the cream. Pour in a little of the soup, stirring vigorously, then return to the pan. Stir over a moderate heat, without boiling the soup, for 5 minutes; add a pinch of sugar to bring out the flavour, any extra seasoning required, and finally the asparagus tips which should be given time to heat through in the hot soup, and the extra knob of butter.

Note Thawed frozen asparagus can be used instead of fresh. It will not need parboiling. Add the tips to the soup before thickening it with yolks and cream, so that they have a chance of becoming thoroughly tender.

BRETON CRAB SOUP

One evening in 1884, Edmond de Goncourt and Zola were invited to dinner by their publisher, Charpentier. It was so delicious that de Goncourt wondered if Charpentier was about to abscond with the cash, and became slightly nervous about the money owing on his novel *Chérie*. The star turn was crab soup, a Breton dish little known in Paris at that time. It was like a shellfish bisque, but 'with something finer to it, something tastier, something more of the ocean'.

> *2 medium-sized cooked crabs*
> *sliced carrot*
> *onion stuck with 3 cloves*
> bouquet garni
> *250 ml (8 fl oz) dry white wine, preferably Muscadet*
> *fish or veal or chicken stock*
> *150 g (5 oz) rice*
> *up to 150 ml (5 fl oz) cream*
> *large knob of butter*
> *salt, pepper and Cayenne*

Remove the meat from the cooked crabs and set it aside. Put all the debris into a pan with the carrot, onion, *bouquet*, wine and enough stock to cover everything generously. Simmer 30 minutes. Extract the toughest pieces of claw shell, then whizz the rest in a liquidiser to extract every hint of flavour into the liquid. Pour through a sieve into the rinsed out pan – do not press too hard, just enough to extract the softer part.

In a separate pan meanwhile, cook the rice in some more stock, or water. When very tender, put it into the liquidiser with most of the crab meat (keep enough for the garnish). Blend to a purée and add to the crab shell stock. Taste and dilute further if necessary with more stock or water. Add cream to taste and reheat to just under boiling point. Put in extra seasoning, with a good pinch of Cayenne, and the crab pieces you kept for the garnish. Leave for another 5 minutes, still without boiling, then serve with croûtons or bread fried in butter.

GNOCCHI WITH GRATED CHEESE

Gnocco – gnocchi is the plural – means a dumpling in Italian, or a fool, as in 'diddle-diddle-dumpling, my son John'. Most unfair to this excellently piquant dish. Nowadays in France the name is given to small tarts filled with a potato-flour mixture topped with shreds of Gruyère and a knob of butter. At Nana's party, it seems to have been the Italian version that was served – the use of grainy semolina rather than smooth potato-flour prevents the *gnocchi* being dull and heavy, which the French version sometimes is.

> *600 ml (1 pt) milk*
> *salt, pepper, nutmeg*
> *150 g (5 oz) semolina, as coarse as you can find, or*
> *   175 g (6 oz) fine semolina*
> *2 large egg yolks*
> *60–90 g (2–3 oz) Parmesan or pecorino cheese*
> *90 g (3 oz) butter*

Bring milk and seasonings to the boil. Tip in the semolina, stirring it with a wooden spoon, and cook until the mixture holds the spoon more or less upright. The time this takes will depend on the semolina, 5–10 minutes according to the brand used. Remove the pan from the stove. Beat in the yolks, then half the cheese, and a good tablespoon of butter. This last addition makes the dough slightly shiny and more coherent; as you scrape it together from the sides of the pan, they will become remarkably clean, whereas before the dough was sticking to them.

Wet a baking tray and your hands. Pat out the dough on the tray until it is a little less than a centimetre thick. Cool in the refrigerator. Then cut it into circles or diamond lozenges. Any trimmings should be squeezed together and patted out again.

Arrange the pieces in a well-buttered ovenproof dish, piling them up in the centre. Scatter with the remaining cheese. Melt the last of the butter and pour evenly over the whole thing. Bake 30 minutes at mark 5, 190° (375°), or until the *gnocchi* are caught with

golden brown, and sizzling in the butter. Serve with extra grated
Parmesan, or with a tomato sauce (*see* p. 186).

FILLETS OF SOLE WITH SAUCE RAVIGOTE CHAUDE

In Zola, gluttony – according to the fastidious and jealous Edmond
de Goncourt – was 'doubled by a knowledge of the science of
cookery that enabled him to say what was wrong with a dish; or
whether a particular seasoning had been omitted, or how many
minutes more it should have been simmered. By examining the
shell of a boiled egg, he could tell you how old it was, how many
days, how many hours.'

Some of his knowledge, experience apart, had surely come from
Urbain Dubois's *Cuisine Classique* (first of many editions, 1856),
judging by the menu of Nana's dinner. Dubois was a great chef of
the day, who worked at one time for the Emperor and Empress of
Germany. One subtitle of his book (written in collaboration with
Émile Bernard, a fellow chef) is *L'école française appliquée au
service à la russe*, and he starts with a long comparison between the
old French service and the new Russian style.

The argument was not new. Carême outlined it in the eighteen-
thirties. He had experienced the Russian service in Russia, and
seen the advantage for the diners of a succession of courses rapidly
served, the meat or game already cut up in the kitchen, so that
everything was eaten hot and at its best. He felt obliged to come
down in favour of the host's and chef's desire to make a show,
according to the old French style: the doors of the dining-room
were thrown open, the guests came in to the spectacular sight of a
table loaded with food and luxurious set pieces, they sat down –
and waited. Waited for the elegant gentlemen to carve the meat,
poultry or game and show off their good manners. Waited for a
dish to be passed from the other end of the table.

Nana's dinner was right up to the minute, in Russian style. But in
her case, the overcrowded table and room impeded the waiters.
Conversation was perpetually interrupted by a murmur in the ear,
'Thick or clear soup?', 'Chambertin or Léoville, Madame, Monsieur?' This kind of problem was resolved by Escoffier and Ritz
(p. 229) who realised that the new order of things required a

roomy and elegant setting, with unobtrusive almost invisible service that interrupted nothing. Today, over a hundred years later, this is a lesson that many restaurateurs have not learned. Or refuse to learn on account of profits and the difficulty of training waiters.

Like the previous asparagus soup, this recipe comes from Urbain Dubois, and makes a simple contrast to such fineries as *carpe à la Chambord* and other dishes of the grande cuisine that were still served in all their majesty, but one at a time.

> *3–4 large sole*
> *fish stock (see recipe)*
> *handful of mixed greenery: tarragon, parsley, chives,*
>   *chervil, salad burnet, spinach*
> *100 g (3½ oz) butter*
> *1 heaped tablespoon chopped shallots*
> *teaspoon peppercorns*
> *teaspoon chopped tarragon leaves*
> *5 tablespoons white wine vinegar*
> *1 heaped tablespoon flour*
> *extra knob of butter*

Ask the fishmonger to fillet the sole and give you all the trimmings, with any extra whiting bones and skin he may happen to have. Use them to make a fish stock by simmering them with half water–half white wine to cover (or a little less wine if you like), and aromatics; strain after 20–30 minutes; there should be about 400 ml (generous ¾ pt). Correct the seasoning, and poach the fillets of sole in it from 4 to 6 minutes according to thickness. Transfer them when cooked to a warm dish, and keep them warm while you complete the sauce.

While the stock and fish are cooking, prepare a purée of greenery by boiling it in salted water until the leaves flop. Drain and liquidise with half the butter. Simmer shallot, peppercorns, tarragon leaves and vinegar, until reduced by half. Melt the rest of the butter, stir in the flour. Cook two minutes, then moisten with the cooking liquor from the sole; boil down vigorously to a good consistency. Strain into a clean pan, stir in the shallot mixture and herb purée. Finally – off the heat – whisk in the extra knob of butter.

SURMULETS A LA PROVENÇALE
RED MULLET PROVENÇALE

On 9 March 1882 Zola invited Turgenev and Edmond de Goncourt to an especially fine dinner – 'A gourmet's dinner, seasoned with an original conversation on good things to eat and the stomach's imagination.' At times the conversation and the meal were interrupted with complaints about their *chien de métier*, their bitch of a trade – how little contentment their good luck brought them, how indifferent they felt to success when it came, yet how upset they were by the annoyances of life and hostile criticism. In other words, they had an excellent evening, of the kind that writers enjoy.

This is what they had to eat: first, a soup made from green kern – wheat picked just as the ears begin to form or kern, and then dried (it was quite common in Europe in the past, and is still used in North African cooking); it was then cooked in stock with aromatics, much like a barley soup. Then came smoked reindeer tongue from Lapland, probably imported from Russia where it was a common sight in winter in the St Petersburg markets, frozen solid in the cold air. A truffled guineafowl followed the mullet:

> *6–8 red mullet*
> *seasoned flour*
> *olive oil*
> *125 g (4 oz) chopped onion*
> *heaped tablespoon flour*
> *175 ml (6 fl oz) dry white wine*
> *½ kilo (1 lb) chopped, skinned tomatoes*
> *3 cloves garlic*
> bouquet garni
> *salt, pepper, sugar*
> *triangles of bread, rubbed with garlic, fried in oil*

Scale and clean the mullet, but be sure to leave the livers in place. Season inside and out. Flour and fry in olive oil.

Have ready a hot tomato sauce – brown the onion in a little oil. Stir in the flour, and cook two or three minutes. Add the wine and an equal quantity of water, then the tomatoes. Put in garlic whole, *bouquet* and seasoning. Cook down to a good thick consistency. Remove the *bouquet*; fish out the garlic, and press it through a sieve back into the sauce.

Pour the sauce across the centre of the mullet, and around them. Tuck in the bread triangles, and serve very hot.

CÔTES DE PORC À LA CHARCUTIÈRE
PORK CHOPS CHARCUTIÈRE

The superb charcuterie in *Le Ventre de Paris* belongs to the hero's brother and his wife, Lisa. She is queen of the shop, the *charcutière*; her chignon and smooth passionless breasts are reflected a thousand times in the mirrors on the wall, as if she were a nightmare caricature of the girl at the Folies Bergères painted by Zola's friend Manet. The shop itself was 'a laughing place and full of light, with a liveliness of colours that sang out from the pure whiteness of the marble slabs. The sign, on which the name *Quenu-Gradelle* shone brightly in huge letters of gold, was framed with leaves and branches drawn on a delicate background. . . . The twin side panels of the shop front . . . represented little Cupids at play among the animal heads, the pork chops and garlands of sausages; and these still lifes, adorned with scrolls and rosettes, were designed in so pretty and tender a style that the raw meat lying there assumed the reddish tints of various jams. . . . This was a world of good things, things that melted in the mouth, things of great succulence.' Rillettes, jambonneaux, pots of mustard, red stuffed Strasbourg tongues, prepared trotters, black pudding rolled up like tidy snakes, bursting andouilles, pâtés, hams, tins of truffles, terrines of foie gras, canned tunny and sardines, stuffed snails, hanging loops of sausage, lacy strips of caul fat, and an aquarium with two gold fish – a scene unchanged today.

As the Goncourts remarked, Zola often uses a key adjective in his novels. With *Le Ventre de Paris*, the word is *gras*, fat. Loving and hating that shop, Zola takes us to the kitchen behind. Spotless of course, but stifling. The kitchen walls are impregnated with fat;

it rises in a sort of steam obscuring the gaslight. Lard bubbling in heavy pots. Lisa is fat and white, a decent shining spotless woman, inside and out. She betrays her brother-in-law, Florent, who will be returned to Devil's Island. And there was no need. Everyone else in the *quartier* had betrayed him too, or nearly everyone. Why? Because he would not succumb to comfort and 'live as everyone else does'.

Zola may conclude, 'What crooks these decent people are!', but he cannot help admiring Lisa, being fascinated by her skill – for instance, as she cuts and flattens with three sharp blows three pork chops for a customer, who also wants some gherkins. Presumably to make this dish.

> *6–8 thick pork chops*
> *salt, pepper*
> *1 kilo (2 lb) potatoes*
> *milk, butter*
>
> CHARCUTIÈRE SAUCE:
> *4 chopped shallots, or 4 tablespoons chopped onion*
> *1 generous tablespoon butter*
> *heaped tablespoon flour*
> *4 tablespoons each dry white wine and white wine*
>   *vinegar*
> *½ litre (15 fl oz) beef or veal stock*
> *250 g (8 oz) skinned, chopped tomatoes*
> *1 teaspoon sugar*
> *4–8 sliced gherkins according to size*
> *chopped parsley*

Season the chops and set them aside, overnight if you like. Scrub, boil, peel and mash the potatoes with milk and butter. Then make the sauce before brushing the chops over with melted butter, and cooking them under the grill.

Soften the shallot or onion in the butter and, when limp and golden, stir in the flour. Cook 2 minutes, then add the wine, vinegar and stock gradually. Leave to cook down, so that the flavour becomes strong and piquant. In another pan, reduce the tomato to a purée with the sugar. Sieve into the sauce. Correct seasoning. Add sliced gherkins last of all and parsley.

Make a mound of the potato, stand the chops against it, broad ends down. Pour a little sauce round, if you like, and serve the rest separately.

BLANQUETTE

In *L'Assommoir*, happiness ends for Gervaise, her husband and their daughter Nana, with the return of Lantier. He was Gervaise's first lover, the father of her two sons. Happiness ends not because the husband resents his return, but because the two men become friends. Gradually they bleed Gervaise of all self-respect and prosperity. Her weak and loving nature cannot withstand them.

Lantier comes back on 19 June, which is the day of Sainte-Gervaise. In other words the name-day, when 'a real blow-out' had been planned in celebration. The menu had been discussed for a month in the laundry. The main dish was to be roast goose. An immense bird with a rough skin, plump with yellow fat, was bought in good time, so that every one could admire it. What else were they going to have? *Pot-au-feu*, certainly, to provide broth for a soup with vermicelli, followed by boiled beef. Fish? No – nobody liked fish. The next thing Gervaise thought of was a chine of pork, with potatoes, and 'we shall need something with a sauce'. One of her assistants suggested blanquette of veal, as nothing makes a better effect.

Much of the cooking could be done in advance, although plenty was left for the day itself. Gervaise and her mother-in-law set to work in white aprons, filling the room 'as they bustled about, picking over the parsley, running round looking for the pepper and salt, turning the meat over with a wooden spoon'. Gervaise was just running out for some caramelised onions to finish the *pot-au-feu*, when she heard that Lantier had again been seen in the street. What would her husband say? And while the poor girl and her friends were caught up in the drama, 'Ma Coupeau took the lid off the blanquette and the pork; they were bubbling with a discreet little sound; the *pot-au-feu* was still snoring like a singer asleep with his belly in the sun.'

1½–2 kilos (3–4 lb) boned shoulder of veal
150 g (5 oz) butter
generous litre (2 pt) veal stock
2 carrots, diced
white part of a leek, or bunch spring onions
unpeeled onion stuck with 3 cloves
10 cm (4 inches) piece celery stalk
bouquet garni
18–24 pickling onions
175–250 g (6–8 oz) button mushrooms
lemon juice
30 g (1 oz) flour
1 large egg yolk
100 ml (3–4 fl oz) double cream
parsley, salt, pepper

Cut meat into large cubes, and seal them without allowing them to brown, in half the butter. Pour in the stock. Add carrot, leek or spring onions, the onion stuck with cloves, celery and *bouquet*. Cover and simmer until meat is tender. Melt a tablespoon of the remaining butter and turn the pickling onions in it. Add a good ladle of stock from the veal and leave to stew until tender (cover the pan). Cook the mushrooms in another tablespoon of butter, with a little lemon juice to keep them white. When meat is done, remove it to a deep dish – Gervaise used a china salad bowl – and keep it warm.

Make a roux with the last of the butter and the flour, then add the strained cooking liquor to make a sauce. Boil it down hard to concentrate the flavour. Tip in onions and mushrooms with their juices. Simmer 5 minutes. Beat yolk and cream together with a little of the sauce, then pour back into the pan of sauce, stirring well, and keeping the whole thing under boiling point while it thickens. It should end up the consistency of double cream. The colour should be a rich ivory, verging on yellow – another egg yolk can always be added. Check the seasoning, adding extra lemon juice if you like. Pour over the meat, sprinkle on a very little parsley, and serve hot with hot plates.

'What a hole they made in the blanquette! If no one talked much, they were chewing steadily. The salad-bowl was emptying and a spoon stayed upright in the thick sauce, a good yellow sauce which shook like jelly. They fished about for bits of veal – there was still some there, and the bowl passed from hand to hand, faces peering into it and looking for mushrooms.'

PETITS POIS AU LARD
PEAS AND BACON

When Gervaise first hears that Lantier has been seen in the neighbourhood, she tries to prevent her relations and employees hearing the news by discussing vegetables for the party. One of the girls, Virginie, says, 'Why not peas and bacon? . . . I could live on that.' And everyone agrees.

2–2½ kilos (4–5 lb) peas
150 g (5 oz) piece smoked streaky bacon, geräuchter
    bauchspeck *if you can get it*
small bunch parsley
1 large spring onion
125 g (4 oz) butter
dessertspoon flour

Shell the peas. Dice the bacon and pour boiling water over it. Leave 5 minutes, then drain – this is to remove the saltiness. If you have to use a very mild cured bacon, this is not necessary; indeed it would be disastrous, as the small flavour it has would be floated out.

Tie the parsley and onion together. Melt butter in a heavy pan, put in the bacon, and as it begins to heat through, pour in the peas and tuck in the parsley *bouquet*. Add enough water almost to cover the peas. Season. Cook half-covered, so that the liquid has reduced by the time the peas are tender. Strain off a little and mix with the flour to form a paste; stir the paste back into the pan and keep stirring. You should end up with peas bathed in a small amount of creamy, buttery sauce. Should it be too thick, add a little water and drain off the surplus; should it be too thin, boil vigorously for a moment or two.

Note You can use a kilo (2 lb) of frozen peas, but only put in enough water to come halfway up the contents of the pan, and take care the peas do not overcook.

ROAST GOOSE

Gervaise's goose, a bird weighing 12½ pounds, was roasted on a spit, and served without stuffing or sauce. Everyone was happy to enjoy so magnificent a creature on its own. Indeed this is more the French way, though usually some small embellishment does accompany roast meat, if not the overwhelming collection of items that many of us expect.

A goose has become a rare sight at the butcher's in this country. It seems to have fallen victim to our fat-phobia and to our meanness about paying for good food. It is true that a 5 kilo bird is required for 8–10 people depending on the rest of the menu, though you might get away with a smaller one as many people these days prefer to eat less meat when it tastes so satisfyingly good as goose.

To make the bird easier to carve, remove the wishbone; turn back the neck skin, feel where the bone is and use a small sharp pointed knife to cut it away until you can hook your finger in it and pull it out.

Next, fill the cavity loosely with soaked, stoned prunes, and peeled pieces of Cox's orange pippin; or a mixture of mealy puddings from Scotland, spiked with prunes and stuffed olives. Prick the skin all over. Set the bird on its side in a roasting pan and pour in a large tumbler of water.

Put into the oven set at mark 7, 220° (425°) for 45 minutes – turning it on to the other side after 25 minutes. Then turn the goose on to its back and lower the heat to mark 3, 160° (325°) until it is cooked (a further 1¾–2 hours for birds up to 5 kilos; 2–2½ hours for birds over that weight).

Transfer to a hot dish. Pour the fat from the pan (keep it for frying potatoes, making Gascony butter etc). Heat up the juices with a little giblet stock, and serve separately. Surround the goose with watercress, or extra cooked prunes and lightly fried apple, before taking it to the table.

Follow with a salad of Cos lettuce, or Webb's Wonder or Iceberg lettuce.

CHEESE AND FRUIT COURSES

Zola had a remarkable memory for smells, the sharp nose of a hound. It would quiver at a new smell, as if it had been tickled by a passing fly, and carry the recollection of it sometimes for as long as a month. In *Le Ventre de Paris*, he uses the different smells of Les Halles like colours in a painting, or notes in music. At one point the enmity of the market women against Florent, the long-suffering hero, rises with the smell of cheese into a malevolent symphony.

Mademoiselle Saget, the old maid who runs a dairy stall, has discovered that Florent is an escaped prisoner. As her cronies gather to absorb the news, 'it was the Camembert above all that they could smell. The Camembert with its gamy scent of venison had conquered the more muffled tones of Marolles and Limbourg. . . . Into the middle of this vigorous phrase, the Parmesan threw its thin note of a country flute; while the Bries added the dull gentleness of damp tambourines. Then came the suffocating reprise of a Livarot. And the symphony was held for a moment on the high, sharp note of an aniseed Géromé, prolonged like the note of an organ.'

Almost every cheese mentioned in this cruel and stinking scene, can now be bought in England. It is true that factory Camembert and Brie are insipid; and you will find it worth while hunting down farmhouse versions of Brie at Paxton's in Jermyn Street. Only two brothers produce a true Camembert, one of them in the parish of Camembert itself, but they do not have enough for export to shops. Cheese of this type was the normal thing in Zola's day; dairy mechanisation was only beginning.

Zola describes Gruyère as 'a wheel fallen from some barbaric chariot'; Roquefort with its blue and yellow marbling looks diseased, like rich people who have eaten too many truffles. He mentions 'bung-shaped' Neufchâtel and Gournay, Cantal, 'cheshire', red Dutch cheese, Port-Salut, Mont d'Or, Pont-l'Évêque, Olivet in chesnut leaves. The goat cheeses he says, are hard and greyish, 'pebbles which roll from under the rams' feet as they lead the flock round the elbow of stony paths'.

If you read this virtuoso display for yourself, you may not feel much like eating cheese for a day or two (I have left out such details as seemed offputting in a book about the pleasures of food). We complain about refrigeration, and it does nothing for cheese, but one can see it has its uses. If you have to store cheese in the cold, wrap it tightly in foil, and bring it into room temperature several hours before the meal. The best plan is to buy cheese in small quantities, when you need it, but if you do not live or work near a good cheese shop, this is impossible.

Remember, too, that in France cheese comes after the main course and salad, to go with the last of the wine. It is always eaten with bread, never with biscuits or butter. Fruit and pudding are served afterwards with sweet white wine, making a logical progression to coffee, brandy and liqueurs.

If Zola were about today, he would deplore our deodorised world, at least in matters of food. Only fruit and vegetable departments are now permitted to be natural. The best ones I know are at Fauchon's in Paris. As you go towards the greengrocery, you move into a globe of perfumed delight; it's mainly passionfruit, melon, guava and pineapple, but pears, mango, carambola and Chinese gooseberries can all be detected. You see people standing around, delaying their requests as their noses twitch in Zola style. For these smells at least, Zola had mercy. To the pretty girl in charge of the fruit, he gave the name of La Sarriette which is French for the herb savory. The skin of her neck had the freshness of peach and cherry. Her mouth was stained with red currants. A smell of plums rose from her skirts, and her carelessly knotted fichu smelled of strawberries.

THE SAVOY TEMPLE

'The dessert was now put on the table. In the middle there was a Savoy cake, in the shape of a temple with a melon-sectioned dome; and on the dome there was an artificial rose with a silver paper butterfly on a wire beside it. Two drops of gum in the heart of the flower imitated two drops of dew. Then, on the left a cream cheese swam in a shallow bowl, and in another bowl on the right a pile of huge strawberries lightly crushed were running with juice.'

While they polished off the cake and sang, Gervaise's husband went out and brought in Lantier. Gervaise 'stared at them stupidly, gently. At first, when her husband had pushed her lover into the shop, she had taken her head between her hands, with the same instinctive movement that she did in storms, at each roll of thunder. It didn't seem possible; surely the walls must fall down and crush the world. Then seeing the two men sitting down, without the net curtains stirring, she suddenly found it all quite natural.' The tragedy was now inevitable. Lantier finished off the Savoy cake, dipping it into his wine.

To make a Savoy temple you need a kugelhupf mould, preferably in red terracotta, though a metal one will do. This gives the right shape, with the sectioned dome, when the cake is turned out. Butter it and sprinkle evenly with caster sugar.

> *7 large egg yolks*
> *250 g (8 oz) caster sugar*
> *1 tablespoon orange-flower water, or water*
> *90 g (3 oz) plain flour*
> *90 g (3 oz) fécule (potato flour) or cornflour*
> *7 egg whites*
> *¼ teaspoon salt*

Whip yolks, sugar and orange-flower water or water electrically until foamy and thick. Or whisk over heat, as when making a sponge cake. Sift together flour and *fécule* or cornflour and fold it into the egg yolks. Whip the whites until stiff with the salt and fold them in, too. Turn into the mould and bake at mark 4, 180° (350°) for about 45 minutes, or until cooked – test with a larding needle.

For the cream cheese, *see* p. 241.

OEUFS À LA NEIGE

The dessert at Gervaise's squalid wedding meal – an 'extra' which caused argument when the bill was presented – was *oeufs à la neige*, eggs in the snow. Being considered rather grand, it was greeted with a respectful pause, though as it turned out the egg whites had been overcooked (take warning).

There is some argument in France as to whether you should

poach the egg whites in the milk destined for the custard. Or whether you should first make the custard and then poach the whites in water. I think the second method is easier, and it seems to make no difference to the flavour.

> *8 large eggs*
> *400 ml (14 fl oz) milk*
> *200 ml (6 fl oz) cream*
> *half a vanilla pod*
> *vanilla sugar*

Separate the eggs into two basins. Bring milk, cream vanilla pod and 125 g (4 oz) sugar slowly to the boil. Whisk it into the beaten egg yolks, then pour the mixture back into the pan and cook over a low heat until the custard thickens, coating the back of the spoon. Taste and add more sugar if you like. Strain into a large shallow dish, leave to cool, then chill in the refrigerator.

Whisk the whites until stiff, then put in 450 g (15 oz) vanilla sugar, bit by bit, as if you were making meringue. Put on a wide pan of water to boil. Adjust to simmering point. Poach 'eggs' of the meringue, shaping them with two tablespoons and slipping them into the water. Turn with a skimmer. Place them, well drained, in a pile in the middle of the custard. Try out an experimental 'egg' first, to see how you go: do not despair if the final pile looks a little raggy. Cook some sugar with a little water to a golden brown caramel and dribble it down the 'eggs' – this turns the dessert into *île flottante*, or floating island.

PLOMBIÈRE MARGUÉRITE
PINEAPPLE ICE CREAM

Pineapples were very much part of grand dinner parties in Zola's day. So were ices – they were a treat, because making them at home was a laborious nuisance in the days before domestic refrigerators. I notice that in France people still buy such items for special occasions, even when they want something as simple as oranges or lemons *givrés*. In the best pastrycook's shops, the most splendid creations are on display in a special glass-fronted cabinet freezer.

They look as if they had come directly from the more complex illustrations to Urbain Dubois's or Carême's books. And this in quite small towns. The price is high, though not so high once you reflect on the quality of the ingredients and the skill involved.

However *Plombière Marguérite* can easily be made at home. Its one grandeur – a plume of spun sugar – can be omitted, as it is purely decorative. Do not omit the other special detail, the tiny sweet shortcrust pastry cases filled with sugared raspberries, strawberries or very ripe redcurrants; they can be ordered from your local confectioner (or you could make them yourself in advance), and filled just before the meal – a pleasant change from the conventional biscuits and wafers.

> 250 g (8 oz) drained canned pineapple
> 150 ml (5 fl oz) canned pineapple syrup
> 100 ml (3½ fl oz or 7 tablespoons) Maraschino or Kirsch
> 1 litre (1¾ pt) egg custard, made with milk or milk and
>   single cream, egg yolks, vanilla pod, sugar
> ½ litre (generous 15 fl oz) double cream
> icing sugar
> 12–16 tiny sweet pastry cases, baked blind
> 12–16 huge strawberries to fit them exactly, or 36–48
>   fine raspberries, or 12–16 teaspoons redcurrants
>   stripped of stalks

Chop the pineapple, set the syrup aside for the moment, and add the alcohol to the pineapple. Freeze the custard until the sides are firm and the centre slightly creamy. Turn out and beat, electrically if possible, to an even texture. Add the pineapple syrup, and the chopped pineapple with any juice. Whip the cream with a little icing sugar and fold it in. Taste and add more icing sugar if necessary. Turn into a decorative metal mould and freeze until required. Obviously this can be done well in advance of the date of the dinner party, but not too long – say, not more than a fortnight – as I have the feeling that ices lose their finest flavour if stored too long: admittedly I have not tried this out scientifically, so it may be no more than speculation.

If your pastry cases have also been made in advance, heat them through in the oven and then allow them to cool. This restores crispness. Fill them with the fruit just before the meal – in the case of strawberries and raspberries, pointed ends up; sugar the fruit in advance and drain it – icing sugar does best. An alternative is to glaze the fruit with a little redcurrant jelly boiled with the drained juices (especially successful with raspberries), once you have positioned it.

Turn out the ice – remove it from the freezer an hour and a half before it will be required, and turn it out with the aid of hot water and hot cloths wrung out in water. To me this is the trickiest part of the whole recipe, as the fine edges of the moulded ice can so easily become blurred. If this happens to you, too, smooth them out as best you can with a knife. In any case, it is prudent to choose a fairly simple decorative mould, unless you are good at this kind of thing. I am not. I end up thinking that a French pastrycook deserves every franc he charges.

Plombière Marguérite is essentially a summer pudding; in winter time, when fresh pineapples are at their best very often, you would do better with the following recipe.

BEIGNETS D'ANANAS À LA POMPADOUR
PINEAPPLE FRITTERS WITH APRICOT SAUCE

I do not know why the Pompadour became associated with apricots, except that their colour reminds one of the paintings of her by Boucher, especially the painting in the Wallace Collection.

The problem with sweet fritters is that they come at the end of the meal and unless you are eating in the kitchen, it is impossible to serve them crisp from the pan. One solution is now provided by electric deep-friers. You can prepare everything before dinner, switch on the frier which is thermostatically controlled, perhaps when you serve the salad, and quickly cook the fritters while the cheese is cleared. At this stage of the meal, people like a longer pause.

Beforehand, cut the peeled pineapple slices in half, and sandwich them together with apricot jam. Prepare a normal fritter batter. Cook the fritters in the usual way, sprinkling them lightly, before they are served, with icing sugar.

The sauce, very simple, can also be prepared beforehand, and kept hot in a double saucepan. Stir 8 tablespoons of apricot jam, generous ones, into 300 ml ($\frac{1}{2}$ pt) tepid water. Heat to just below boiling point, then sieve into the top of a double boiler, or into a bowl set over a pan of simmering water. Add a piece of vanilla pod, cover and leave to infuse gently. Just before serving, remove the vanilla pod, and stir in half a glass – about 2 tablespoons or a little more – of Madeira or Kirsch.

When I cannot lay my hands on either of these desirable liquors, I make do with gin and a drop or two of pure almond essence. Nobody has complained so far.

MARQUISE AU CHOCOLAT

Zola and his friends, like everyone of sensibility in Europe in the second part of the nineteenth century, were much affected by Far Eastern art and objects. Monet (*q.v.*) seems to have been the first painter to be delighted by Japanese prints which he saw as a boy in Le Havre. He painted Camille in Japanese clothes, as Whistler had painted Jo (fans, kimonos, porcelain came from Madame Soye's in the rue de Rivoli in the sixties: from 1875 in London they could be bought at Liberty's). When Manet painted Zola he included two of the writer's Japanese prints, one by Utamaro (*see* p. 176).

Soon the craze extended to food – *pâtissiers* sold little *japonais* cakes, Dumas fils described a 'Japanese' salad in his play *Francillon*, perhaps the same salad as his father had served years before to Dr Véron when he wanted to convince him that he really knew how to cook (p. 156). Just into the new century, about the time of Puccini's *Madame Butterfly*, Escoffier delighted a visiting Japanese delegation with his 'Japanese' layers of pineapple, orange, tomato piled on lettuce leaves and dressed with cream and lemon juice.

Edmond de Goncourt was one of the most passionate enthusiasts (and the first to write a book on Utamaro). He was revisiting the Japanese exhibition of 1878 one day in March, when he caught sight of the chocolate-maker, Marquis, who was so amazed at the marvellous things around him that he reeled about as if he were drunk.

250 g (8 oz) good plain or bitter chocolate
2 tablespoons water
3 large egg yolks
125 g (4 oz) caster sugar
200 g (7 oz) softened lightly salted or unsalted butter
4 egg whites
100 g (3–4 oz) toasted slivered almonds or chopped
   hazelnuts

Break up or grate the chocolate coarsely into the bowl of an electric mixer. Add the water. Set the whole thing over a pan of barely simmering water, and stir until it melts. Mix in the yolks one by one. Now remove the bowl from the pan. The mixture will look very black. Beating electrically add the sugar, then the butter bit by bit. Continue beating until you have a pale-coloured mixture of an opaque creaminess. Whisk the whites stiff, add to the chocolate carefully, with half the nuts. Turn into a Bakewell lined charlotte or loaf tin of 1¼ litres (2 pt) capacity, and smooth down the top. Chill overnight, turn out and decorate with remaining nuts. Cut with a knife.

As a marquise is so filling, you should find this quantity enough for 10. Serve plain biscuits with it.

Claude Monet (1840–1926)

The American writer of a recent book on Monet reproves him for following 'the overindulgent pattern of French middle-class life', adding that he ate enough for four. I wonder whether Monet would have done better or longer – he died at the age of eighty-six – on hamburgers and ketchup?

The truth is that Monet, like most people brought up in Normandy, flourished on good things. He might have replied to the criticism in the words of another Norman, André Gide, 'Hunger . . . no moralities can put an end to it, and I have never fed anything but my soul on privations.' Privations in early life only hindered the work, and affected his family's health, in the end taking his young wife Camille from him.

Like his fellow Impressionists, Monet thrived on the strength and friendship of shared meals, whether in a Paris café where the cutlery was chained to the table and the dishes were largely concocted from stale bits of cheese, or at home sharing a meal with his wife, small son and a visitor, in the dining-room or garden. See his paintings on such occasions, if you do not believe me, with their atmosphere of quiet peace and contentment.

His first and most joyful painting of a meal was the famous *Déjeuner sur l'Herbe*, the great picnic in the forest of Fontainebleau, with Camille and his close, generous friend Bazille providing the models for most of the people in the painting. There on the cloth, in the dappled light, are a pâté in a pastry crust, a roast chicken, bottles of wine, a big loaf of bread, glasses and a pile of plates. Only a sketch remains of the whole scheme, and fragments rescued from the rotting canvas with its huge life-size figures that Monet had to abandon uncompleted, because he had no money to continue (see the cover of this book).

If you know Monet's paintings from galleries and reproductions, and recall the times that they show fruit or vegetables or meals with friends, you would never guess how difficult the first half of his life had been. He seems to have been able to switch off his distress completely once he was painting at his easel in the bright day. Certainly he was never reduced to Zola's poverty, the poverty of absolute deprivation – his drink bills, the paintings of houses he lived in, show that – but he sank low.

His paintings were rejected outside his own circle of friends. His family disapproved both of the painting and of Camille. In 1886 he was obliged to accept an aunt's offer of food and lodging – no money – at Le Havre, leaving Camille on her own in Paris to have their first baby. His family wanted him to abandon her completely, and he could not even raise the money for a train ticket to Paris to see his own son, Jean. Later on Camille was able to join him in Normandy, but the troubles had reduced Monet, who had a sturdy character both physically and mentally, to despair and attempted suicide.

A shipowner of Le Havre came to his rescue, with a commission to paint his wife. Hard to imagine anything more serene that her quiet-toned portrait, with its touches of bright colour in the shawl. Hard also to imagine a more comfortable atmosphere of well-fed harmony in another painting he did at the same time, of Camille and the baby with a friend, just about to start a meal – tilted away from the table a chair waits for Monet to put down his brush and join them (see p. 202). There are toys on the floor, and knitting. Shortly afterwards came *The Evening Meal*, a lamplit scene – unusual for Monet – at Sisley's house, with the baby in a high chair, everyone bent over their soup. Five years later the breezy light of the garden at Argenteuil, after a meal out of doors, with the coffee cups and the fruit still on the table, gave Monet one of his best subjects. The hat hooked on the tree with its blowing black ribbons, the child playing on the ground, the women looking at the flowers in the background, are relaxed in the pleasant atmosphere of a shared meal. Such conviviality was very much an Impressionist theme, but none of the other painters pursued it with such joy as Monet.

By 1883, the public was turning to face Monet's way. He was in his forties, had recovered from Camille's death in 1879. With his two young sons, he was sharing his life with Madame Hoschedé, the widow of an earlier patron, who was to become his second wife, and her children.

They found Giverny that year. Monet set about transforming the small property into both refuge and paradise. He himself mixed the two tones of yellow for the dining-room, spreading the colour over the furniture – small tables and chairs and sideboards with simple openwork panels that came from the Fécamp district of Normandy. On the wall, he hung Japanese prints.

Next door was the blue-and-white tiled kitchen, with its handsome Briffaut stove, and blue cupboards with brass handles. At a time when many kitchens were underground or in the black hindparts of the house, Monet's cook had only to glance up from her work for glimpses of light and brilliant flowers. She could look past the flower-covered terrace, through the two yew trees and down garden paths – wide paths, arched over with wide iron hoops that took the roses from one side to the other. She could not see into the water-lily garden beyond the road and railway, but she worked against a setting of lush and vigorous colour.

Her ingredients, too, were first class; truffles from Périgord, foie gras from Alsace, poultry from the yard – guineafowl still pick their careful path in a small enclosure by the water-lily studio – and mushrooms from the cellar. Monet liked to dress salads, and was an enthusiast for pepper. When they had roast duck, he would cut off the wings, season them with pepper, salt and nutmeg, and send them back to the kitchen to be grilled as a special titbit.

Monet got up at four or five in the morning, ate a huge breakfast and set out to paint. He came back to the house at eleven o'clock, ready for lunch promptly at midday. This was the time for greeting friends such as Georges Clemenceau, and distinguished visitors, more and more of them as the years went by. After the meal, which might take place on the wooden terrace in front of the house when the weather was right, everyone would walk round the garden, and over to the water-lilies. Six gardeners were employed. I am sure they were necessary, even though the garden is not so enormous, to keep growth to the exact degree of abundance that Monet required. He demanded a delicate fullness of colour and delight as much in the garden as on the table.

When Monet had been living at Giverny for ten years, Jacques-Émile Blanche, the painter, commented on the gay atmosphere of the house. He described the 'cretonnes, Japanese fans, kimonos, bamboo and turkey-red cottons', noticed the prettily set table and the delicate cookery, concluding that it was the house of 'a peaceable highly sensitive human being, a man who delighted in his comfortable home'.

We visited the garden in winter. It was being restored after long neglect. The rose hoops were newly and vividly green. The house walls were pink, though not I suspect quite the pink that Monet had chosen which came from crushed bricks mixed into the plaster. The lily pond and its Japanese bridge had been newly defined, the island restored. Soon both house and gardens will be open to visitors, though the flowers will not be at their best until the mid-1980s, or so I would say. The house was locked. And the yellow dining-room was shuttered tight. But at least we could peer into the kitchen and reflect on the dishes prepared in it. Monet expected that the superb food produced by his excellent cook would be a main point of conversation. Art was rarely discussed. Food was the major topic. Apparently anyone at table who did not enjoy and talk about the meal was regarded as a barbarian.

ASPARAGUS AT ARGENTEUIL

Some of the happiest, most brilliant Impressionist paintings were done by, or on, the Seine, when Monet and Camille were living at Argenteuil. It was there that Renoir painted Monet at his easel both indoors and outside in the garden, a square, curly-haired, bearded Monet wearing a round shallow hat with a turned-up brim. Once Manet came to stay and painted the bundle of asparagus with a withy tie that is now in the Louvre. Argenteuil was famous for its asparagus, and has given its name to classic dishes of French cookery that include it as a main garnish – chicken Argenteuil, lamb Argenteuil and so on. In France, asparagus is not just for the rich. Anyone with a garden and the right kind of soil grows it. In asparagus districts it can be bought cheaply in the markets, too.

You are unlikely to find Manet's asparagus, stippled cream, mauve and brown to a yellowish-green tip. In England we tend to prefer the green variety. Both kinds are prepared and cooked in the same way. Quantities depend on what you can afford – a kilo or 2 lb bundle is just enough for four. You can make it go further by boiling new potatoes in with the asparagus, and serving the two together with vinaigrette or hollandaise sauce. Or you can sprinkle the asparagus tips, when they are laid on the serving dish, with a little hard-boiled egg mixed with parsley. Even if you do not want to serve potatoes with your asparagus, it is sensible to cook them together. Potatoes absorb a delicious flavour from the liquid, and can be served with the main course, or kept as a basis for the evening's soup.

When you get the asparagus home, check on your pans. If it is much taller than the tallest pan you have two alternatives. Either cut it down to the right height (cook the chopped-off stalks along with the asparagus and potatoes – extra body for the soup) or cut a piece of foil and have it ready to shape, balloon fashion, over the top of the asparagus and round the rim of the pan.

Peel the stalks, tie them in bundles, and put them into the pan, half-full of boiling salted water. Cover. Cook for 20–45 minutes (they can vary a good deal). The principle is that the lower, tougher stalks boil and the tender heads steam. Once they are cooked at half-height, they are ready to come out. Drain them well.

RILLETTES

At Giverny, meals often started as they do in much of northern France, with local charcuterie. It might be a duck pâté, or a country pâté. Or rillettes.

To make rillettes, buy a large piece of belly of pork, weighing about 1½ kilos (3 lb). If you can manage to buy thick pork, with plenty of fat, so much the better. Our modern skinny pigs are not nearly so good for pâtés and rillettes and pies as the kind with a good layer of fat. Ask the butcher to skin it, but be sure to take home the skin: it can be added in small rolls to beef stews to give them a good texture.

Cut the meat into 5 cm (2 inch) cubes. Put them into a heavy pan with a ladle of water and a *bouquet garni.* Stew over a very low heat, covered, on top of the stove, or in the oven for about 4 hours, until the pieces are meltingly tender. This process can hardly be slow enough. Ideal for solid-fuel and oil-fired stoves, or for an electric casserole.

Drain and bone the pieces. Put them into the bowl of an electric beater, and switch on to a lowish speed. The beater should smash the pork against the sides of the bowl, reducing it to a thready mass. Fork it through – a fork in each hand – to lighten the texture.

Taste for seasoning, and mix in a very little of the fat – not the meaty juice – from the cooking pan. Put into pots or bottling jars (in France, they make special stoneware mugs for rillettes, which can sometimes be bought in cookery shops over here). Cool, then cover with a thin layer of lard; then when that has cooled, press over plastic film or foil. It stores well in fridge or freezer. Serve with plenty of bread.

The characteristic flavour of rillettes comes from the French spice blend, *quatre-épices*. It can be bought in any grocery over there, and is worth bringing back. If you want to make it, grind – electrically if possible – pepper or allspice, nutmeg, cloves and cinnamon, in the proportions of 7:1:1:1. Ginger may be used instead of cinnamon. When making rillettes, put some in with the pork first of all. Add extra at the end, if you like.

CEPS BAKED WITH GARLIC AND OLIVE OIL

In recent years, in our part of France, at least, ceps have become so difficult to find, that one can rarely pick enough to give to guests. Around Giverny in Monet's time, in the woods that crest the chalk cliffs of the Seine, they must have been abundant, because ceps baked with garlic and oil was a dish that appeared at his hospitable luncheon table in the late summer and autumn.

Ceps – in French *cèpe* – is the name given to various kinds of edible Boletus. The finest, the *cèpe de Bordeaux*, is *Boletus edulis*. Two other kinds are yellowish brown, *Boletus luteus*, and reddish brown, *Boletus granulatus*; they grow under conifers. But whatever the colour, all the ceps are easy to identify from their gills, which are clustered tightly together in tubes, so that they look like a sponge rather than a circle of pleated cloth. These spongy gills need not be removed in small ceps, or in larger ones for that matter unless they happen to be wet and bruised looking. The plump stalks of *Boletus edulis* should always be treasured: peel off the outer layer if it looks tough, and cut away any damaged earthy parts.

Sometimes in France you can buy ceps (at a price), but in this country you have to find them yourself, so it would be foolish of me to specify quantities. You have to share them round as best you can. The recipe can also be made with cultivated mushrooms – allow half a kilo or 1 lb for four – but the flavour is quite different and far less delicious; you may well have to add a very little stock as bought mushrooms are so much less juicy than the wild kinds from field and forest.

To prepare the ceps for this dish, slice off the stalks level with the caps. Peel and trim them, then chop them with 2–3 cloves of garlic and several sprigs of parsley. The quantity of these two items depend on taste: if the cloves of garlic are small, I would use four to a half-kilo of mushrooms.

Sprinkle the caps with salt on the gill side. Turn them upside down on a rack and leave for upwards of an hour to drain. Dry them with kitchen paper.

Choose a deep ovenproof baking dish – an oval pâté terrine is ideal – and pour in a thin layer of olive oil. Fit the ceps, stalk side up, in layers into the dish, sprinkling each layer with the stalk mixture and a little olive oil. Plenty of pepper, too. Add no salt at this stage.

Cover the dish and put into the oven at mark 4–5, 180–190° (350–375°). Leave until tender – time will depend on the size and age of the mushrooms. Check after half an hour, then every ten minutes. If the juices become copious, remove the lid and raise the oven temperature; a certain amount of liquid is essential, and delicious, but too much will flood the ceps to insipidity. The quantity of juice that wild mushrooms exude can be surprising, especially if the season has been a wet one. You may even need to pour some off, rather than overcook the ceps. In other seasons, dry seasons, you may get very little. Ceps can be very meaty and substantial.

Towards the end of cooking time, taste the juices and a little bit of cep. Add salt at this stage if necessary, and more pepper.

Serve with plenty of bread, either as a course on its own, or with meat and poultry.

HARICOTS AU VIN DE CHANTURGUES
HARICOT BEANS IN RED WINE

Beans cooked in red wine was another dish of the Monet household. Apparently Monet was not a wine connoisseur, but he very

much liked the light wines of the Loire, such as Sancerre, and this
red wine from Chanturgues on the outskirts of Clermont Ferrand.
You may find it if you spend a holiday in the Auvergne, among the
Côtes d'Auvergne. It's a delicate red Gamay wine, so whatever
you choose to take its place should not be hefty.

This seems the place to point out that in cooking you rarely get
out of a dish more than you put in. For instance, it is foolish to cook
with a wine that you cannot bear to drink (on the other hand, do
not use the finest claret either, because such wines are never for
boiling). Choose a modest wine by all means, but a respectable
one.

250 g (8 oz) dried haricot beans
150 g (5 oz) unsmoked streaky bacon, in a piece
200–250 ml (6–8 fl oz) red wine
75–90 g (2–3 oz) butter
level tablespoon flour (optional)
salt, pepper, chopped parsley

Soak the beans overnight. Or, if you are in a hurry, pour plenty of
boiling water over them and leave them for 2 hours. Drain and
rinse the beans well. If you are in doubt as to whether they have
been adequately soaked, weigh them. They should roughly have
doubled.

Put the beans into a pan or pot with two-thirds of the piece of
bacon (cut the rest into strips and remove the rind). Pour on half
the wine, then enough water to top the beans by a good centimetre.
Bring to simmering point after covering, and cook either in a low
oven or on top of the stove until the beans are tender – at least 40
minutes, though old withered beans from the back of the cupboard
may required 1½ hours. Keep an eye on the liquid level, adding
water if necessary to keep the beans covered – boiling water, not
cold. When the beans are cooked, add salt and leave another
5 minutes.

At this point the beans can be removed from the heat, and left
until required.

To finish the beans, pour off their cooking liquor into a sauté
pan, and add the remaining wine. Boil the whole thing vigorously
to reduce it to about 150–175 ml (5–6 fl oz). Meanwhile heat up

half the butter, and in it cook the strips of bacon gently. When they are almost done and lightly browned, put in the beans and turn them over and over to reheat. Do not allow the butter to blacken. The piece of bacon that was in with the beans will probably have lost all its virtue – especially if it had been lightly cured in the modern style. Taste it and see what you think. If it still has some worth, cut it up and add it to the beans.

In the unlikely event of your being able to get hold of some old-fashioned bacon, or a piece of German *geräuchter bauchspeck* which is of course smoked, use that. Then there is no need for the freshly cooked strips of bacon at the end: just put in the whole piece and cut it up to heat through at the end with the beans. Naturally the flavour will be different, rather heavier from the smoking.

To finish the red wine sauce, in the classic style, mash the last of the butter with the flour, and add it to the reduced red wine to thicken it. Keep the sauce below boiling point and stir all the time. Pour it over the beans, mix them well together and serve, with a little parsley on top.

To finish the sauce in the lighter modern style, just whisk the last of the butter into the reduced red wine and pour it over the beans. There should not be a lot of liquid in either case, just enough to moisten the dish nicely. If you over-reduced the wine, it does not matter, because you can always add a little water if absolutely necessary.

BEURRE BLANC

Monet loved fish. Naturally so, having been brought up on the Normandy coast. One day somebody was describing *beurre blanc*, the eggless hollandaise sauce invented – to serve with the shad, pike and salmon of the Loire – either around Nantes, or further upstream on the Anjou stretch of the river. The idea of this cream of butter flavoured with wine vinegar and shallots appealed to Monet. He turned to his step-daughter who was housekeeping for him, and said, 'Blanche, we must try it.'

Beurre blanc may also be served with white sea fish, from sole to turbot, brill, whiting and so on. Apart from a couple of advance

preparations, the sauce should be made when the poached fish is
lying ready to serve on a hot plate, keeping warm in the oven.

> *1 packet (8 oz) unsalted butter*
> *4 shallots, chopped to a purée*
> *4 tablespoons white wine vinegar*
> *4 tablespoons white wine or fish stock*
> *salt, pepper*

Cut the butter into ten or a dozen pieces and chill them in the
refrigerator until required. Cook the next three ingredients in a
small pan – not too fast – until the liquid is reduced by just over half
and the shallots are soft. Leave to cool.

When you are ready to complete the sauce, take the precaution
of preparing a bowl of water with plenty of ice-cubes. Unless you
are very familiar with the French technique of *monter au beurre*, a
technique which is popular with *nouvelle cuisine* chefs these days,
this prudence gives you a better chance of success as you will see.

Replace the pan of shallots over a moderate heat. When tepid,
start whisking in the butter bit by bit (use a balloon whisk or fork),
raising the pan up and down from the heat, so that the butter
creams with the shallots to an opaque sauce. Should it begin to oil
at the edges, rapidly place the pan in the ice-cube bowl, adding
another piece of cold butter at the same time. This should bring the
sauce back to the right consistency. Above all, do not panic. If the
whole thing goes completely wrong, you can mix it with a little
béchamel. Or you can turn it into a blender *hollandaise* – put a
couple of egg yolks into the blender, and add the *beurre blanc*,
slowly at first, then more rapidly, until you have a thick cream,
rather thicker than *beurre blanc*, but very good. Season the sauce
before pouring some over the fish and putting the rest into a
sauceboat or jug.

With all these kinds of sauces, there are little tricks of recovery
should they go wrong. If you keep calm, and say nothing, no one
will know – or care – that the original intention was not carried
through. All the same, persist with *beurre blanc* until you get the
hang of it. It is an ideal sauce for fish, and very quick and easy to
make with the kind of ingredients that are to hand all the time.
Unsalted butter is not strictly necessary. I often use Danish Lur-

pak, for instance, as it is always in the house for cakes and potted meat and fish. French, Dutch and Danish butters are made from ripened cream, rather than the sweet cream of English butters, and this seems to give them a better consistency for butter sauces.

SOLE MARGUERY

Monet sometimes took his family to the Restaurant Marguery in the Boulevard de Bonne-Nouvelle, in Paris. Eventually he persuaded Monsieur Marguery to give them this recipe so that they could try it at home. It's a dish very much in the Normandy style (p. 114). The dining-rooms of the restaurant, which became fashionable in the 1860s, 'were oddly picturesque, some Oriental, others medieval, yet others recalling Potsdam, and as often as not they would be thronged with a very motley company, celebrating a wedding or some festive occasion with more noise than manners'.*

> *3 or 4 large sole*
> *1 kilo (2 lb) mussels*
> *600 ml (1 pt) prawns in their shells*
> *60 g (2 oz) sliced onion*
> *30 g (1 oz) parsley sprigs*
> *100 ml (3–4 fl oz) dry white wine*
> *juice of ½ lemon*
> *2 tablespoons butter*
> *1 heaped tablespoon flour*
> *60 g (2 oz) mushrooms, chopped*
> *extra 100 g (3–4 oz) butter*
> *salt, pepper*

Ask the fishmonger to fillet the sole, and to make up the weight of the bones to at least ½ kilo (1 lb) with whiting bones, heads and skin.

Scrub, scrape and open the mussels (see p. 80). Discard shells, set mussels aside, and strain the liquor carefully through double-muslin. Shell the prawns and set the prawn meats aside. Put the

* Quoted from *Fine Bouche*, by Pierre Andrieu, 1956, translated by Arthur L. Hayward. Cassell & Co.

prawn debris into a pan which you have greased with a butter paper, and add the sole and whiting bones, onion, parsley, wine, lemon juice and mussel liquor. Add a litre (1¾ pt) water. Bring to the boil. Skim, then simmer 25–30 minutes. Strain into a measuring jug – there should be about 800 ml (1½ pt approximately).

Melt the tablespoons of butter, stir in the flour and cook 2 minutes. Add two-thirds of the fish stock and the mushrooms. Cook down steadily until very thick; season and set aside. All this can be done in advance.

Poach the fillets of sole in the remaining stock, with seasoning. When cooked, arrange them on a hot serving dish and surround with the mussels and prawns. Cover with butter papers and keep warm in a low oven while you finish the sauce.

Heat the sauce to boiling point, and add the cooking liquor. If it is on the liquid side, boil very hard for a few moments until the consistency has improved and check the seasoning again. Meanwhile cut the butter into bits. Remove the sauce from the heat and quickly whisk in the butter, bit by bit. Strain over the sole, and slide the whole thing under a fierce grill to glaze the dish slightly – it should not brown at all. Serve straight away.

VEAL RISOTTO WITH SPINACH

One visitor noted a veal risotto with spinach at a summer lunch party at Giverny. And afterwards some fruit was put on the table 'as beautiful as flowers'. How many Impressionist paintings does that remind one of?

375–500 g (¾–1 lb) roasting veal
generous 60 g (2 oz) butter
100 g (3–4 oz) chopped onion
60 g (2 oz) chopped celery
60 g (2 oz) chopped carrot
150 ml (5 fl oz) dry white wine, or half quantity Marsala
*   or Madeira*
1½–2 kilos (3–4 lb) spinach
extra butter
grated Parmesan, or mixed Parmesan and dry Cheddar

RISOTTO:
60 g (2 oz) butter
125 g (4 oz) chopped onion
500 g (1 lb) Italian rice
150 ml (5 fl oz) dry white wine, or half quantity Marsala
  or Madeira
salt, pepper

Cut the veal into neat strips or small pieces. In the butter, cook the vegetables (apart from the spinach) slowly until they begin to soften (cover the pan), then raise the heat and put in the veal. Stir it about to brown it evenly. Pour in the wine; if you use fortified wine, add an equal amount of water. Cover the pan and leave the veal to stew until tender. Make sure it doesn't dry out or overcook – water can always be added to keep the mixture juicy, but do not overdo it. Season to taste.

At the same time, cook the spinach in plenty of salted, fast-boiling water. Drain it well, and put it into a pan with a large knob of butter to reheat when the risotto is more or less completed.

To make the risotto, melt the butter and cook the onion slowly until it is soft. Stir in the rice, and when it looks transparent, pour in the wine. As the rice absorbs the wine, start adding water by the breakfast–cupful, adding successive cups as the rice absorbs the moisture. Stir occasionally, then more towards the end to prevent sticking.

When the rice is cooked, stir in the veal. Correct the seasoning. Turn on to a hot serving dish. Make a well in the centre and put in the spinach. Sprinkle with a little melted butter, and serve with a bowl of grated cheese.

POULET AUX OLIVES
CHICKEN WITH OLIVES

Monet first visited the Mediterranean during his national service in Algeria. There he experienced that 'drunkenness of vegetation and light' which often overwhelms visitors from the north. Even if the hard life ruined his health for a time, his experience of Algeria gave him conviction enough to stand out finally for painting – his kind of painting – against his parents' anger.

His second visit to the Mediterranean was to Antibes, twenty years later, with Renoir, in the same year he bought Giverny. When he returned home he soon had the gardeners growing southern herbs and vegetables to liven the staid Normandy repertoire. One visitor at lunch noticed that the roast chicken was left untouched, because a second chicken cooked in provençal style with black olives tasted so good. No doubt the tomatoes, basil and garlic had come from the famous garden.

> 2–2½ kilo (4–5 lb) farm chickn, jointed
> 1 large onion, chopped
> 6–8 small whole onions, skinned only
> 4–6 tablespoons olive oil
> salt, pepper, pinch of saffron
> 175 ml (6 fl oz) white wine or beef stock
> ½ kilo (1 lb) tomatoes, skinned, chopped
> 2 large cloves garlic, finely chopped
> ¼ teaspoon each oregano and savory
> 1 small bay leaf
> 24 small Nice olives, or 18 stoned black Greek olives
> bunch basil or parsley

Brown chicken and onions, chopped and whole, lightly in the oil. Pour off any surplus fat. Add seasonings with wine or stock and boil nard to deglaze the pan. Add tomatoes, garlic, dried herbs and bay leaf. Cover and cook gently until chicken is tender. Turn the pieces occasionally. If at the end the juices are swilling about the pan, remove the lid and raise the heat – the dish should be lightly sauced, in no way a stew. Five minutes before serving, add the olives and half the basil, chopped, or parsley. Serve with Italian rice, or triangles of fried bread, and scatter over the remaining basil or parsley, also chopped

An incomparable summer dish, if you have your own or French tomatoes, and your own basil in quantity. Still good, if you have to make do with second-best.

TURKEY STUFFED WITH APPLES AND CHESTNUTS

One of Monet's paintings in the Jeu de Paume shows a flock of white turkeys feeding on a green slope. His dabs of pinkish-red paint exactly catch the wrinkled texture, the crêpey feel of turkey neck and wattles. The sunlight shines through the displayed tail feathers of one magnificent bird. The rest strut and feed and look. An extraordinary painting of joy and gaiety, although it was done in 1877 when Monet was too hard-up to pay his wife's doctors – (she died the next year).

Here is a Normandy recipe for turkey, which in France is usually roasted as we roast ours. The difference comes with the stuffing and accompaniment, and with the lack of heavy and liquid sauces. The French prefer roast meat served with a small quantity of its juice, which helps keep the appetising lightness of the dish.

> ½ *kilo (1 lb) chestnuts, or 40 dried chestnuts*
> *turkey giblet stock*
> *6–8 eating apples, preferably Reinettes, or large Cox's*
>   *Orange Pippins*
> ½ *kilo (1 lb) boned, skinned pork shoulder*
> *150–175 g (5–6 oz) hard back pork fat, or fat belly*
> *1 large rasher smoked bacon*
> *30 g (1 oz) breadcrumbs*
> *salt, pepper*
> quatre-épices *(see p. 208)*
> *butter*
> *dry white wine (optional:* see *recipe)*

Nick, boil and peel the chestnuts. Or pour boiling water over the dried chestnuts and leave them 24 hours, renewing the boiling water once; dried chestnuts will need to be stewed in a little stock for quite a long time before they are soft enough to be compared with newly shelled chestnuts. Set aside the best chestnuts for the garnish – up to half the quantity.

Next peel, core and quarter two of the apples. Cut each quarter into thick chunks and fry them briefly in butter until they are lightly browned, but not completely cooked.

Mince the pork meats together. Soak the breadcrumbs to a paste in a few spoonfuls of stock; drain off any surplus liquid.

Mix together the least good chestnuts, the fried apple pieces and the minced pork with the breadcrumbs. Do this gently with your hands, so as not to break up the apple and chestnut pieces too much. Season with salt, pepper, and if possible *quatre-épices*, or a mixture of the spices involved.

Stuff the turkey cavities loosely. Butter it all over and roast in your usual way.

Towards the end of cooking time, finish the remaining chestnuts and apples for the garnish. Stew the chestnuts in a little giblet stock, allowing it to reduce to a glaze – add a knob of butter during the final stages, so that the chestnuts have a glossy, juicy look. Peel, core and slice the apples thickly and neatly; fry them carefully in butter until browned and tender. Arrange the apples on a serving dish, with the chestnuts in the middle, and keep warm.

Transfer the cooked turkey to a hot dish. Leave it for 15 minutes to firm up before you attempt the carving, either in a very low oven, or just in a warm place in the kitchen. This gives time for a first course.

By way of sauce, skim excess fat from the turkey cooking juices – but leave a little behind as the flavour is so good – and pour them round the bird. If they are on the short side, boil them hard with a little turkey stock and a glass of dry white wine. Or use a fortified wine. Or Calvados and a little water.

Serve a salad afterwards. To me this seems a far better way of cooking the Christmas turkey than the overloaded English style which results in piled plates crammed with turkey, stuffing (two kinds), sprouts, roast potatoes, sausages, bacon rolls, cranberry sauce, bread sauce and thick gravy.

GALETTE DES ROIS

As we drove into Giverny one winter day, past the church and churchyard where Monet and his family are buried, we saw a baker's van ahead. Bright blue. We were hungry and suddenly had a desire for the childish treat of a *pain au chocolat* – a bar of chocolate baked inside a roll. So we chased the van. Down the village street, sharp right, down a lane, sharp right again to a sudden stop by a farmyard gate. Yes, the baker did have *pains au chocolat*. He also had two round puff pastry discs, nicely browned and puffed. What can that be? 'Galettes des rois, Madame,' and I remembered that it was after all only January 12th, within the octave – just – of the feast of the Epiphany.

We continued our day's programme, visiting Monet's garden and so on, and ended up at the house of a young Monet scholar who showed us photographs of Giverny, when the garden was in its lush prime, photographs of many paintings never or rarely reproduced, and books on Monet.

Turning over the pages of one book, we came suddenly to a painting in the Durand-Ruel collection – and there were our two galettes of the morning. Painted by Monet, as they cooled on those round open wicker trays that everyone in the countryside in France has for drying small cheeses. We have a couple ourselves. So now I put our galettes on the trays when I make them, with a sharp knife alongside, black-handled like Monet's. It reminds me of our visit to Giverny, and recalls the day in 1882 when Monet kept his large family waiting for their treat while he made his sketches: his own little boys were fifteen and nearly four, then there were the children of Madame Hoschedé who shared his life after the death of Camille and eventually became the second Madame Monet. It was the year before they found Giverny, while they were still living at Vétheuil.

Monet's cakes had a swirling design and roundly curled edges. Sometimes the design is more like the star that led the Three Wise Men, with five points. Sometimes it is in criss-cross diamonds like a half-extended trellis, and the edges are cleanly cut so that they bake up into layers like the edge of a book. Some galettes are no more than pastry, but the better ones are filled with a sort of almond frangipane cream. Whatever the decoration and filling, all galettes have one thing in common – a *fève* or 'bean' in the middle. Long ago the 'bean' was a bean, a dried haricot. Nowadays it is a tiny faience fancy representing a motorcycle or a duck or some other bit of nonsense. The person whose teeth find the 'bean' becomes king or queen of the feast, and has luck for the year.

If you have a large party, make two or more galettes, rather than one big one. They can be made early in the day, and heated through when required. For one galette:

*about ½ kilo (1 lb) total weight, or 1 large packet frozen
    puff pastry*
egg yolk or cream to glaze

FILLING:
100 g (3–4 oz) blanched almonds, ground not too finely
100 g (3–4 oz) vanilla sugar
slightly rounded tablespoon cornflour
3 large egg yolks
pinch salt
75 g (2½ oz) butter, melted
1–2 tablespoons kirsch or rum (or whisky, if you like)
a dried haricot bean

Roll out the pastry and cut two circles 22–25 cm (9–10 inches across). Place one on a baking sheet and brush its rim with beaten egg or cream – the rim should be about 2½ cm (1 inch).

Mix the filling ingredients in the order given, and spread the mixture inside the rim of the pastry. Place the second circle of pastry on top, pressing down round the rim, and making a centre hole.

Now you can either trim off the edge with a pastry cutter, and knock up the edges, cutting parallel with the baking sheet. Or roll up the edges of the lower sheet of pastry – the top sheet should be just inside it, being raised up over the mound of filling – to make a plump, curving roll.

With the point of a sharp knife, decorate the top swirling lines out from the centre, or scoring a star or narrowed trellis. Bake at mark 7, 220° (425°) for 20–30 minutes, then lower the heat to mark 4, 180° (350°) for 10–20 minutes.

TARTE TATIN

According to Claire Joyes, in *Monet at Giverny*, the family had an argument at lunch one day in 1907, about the apple upside-down tart of the Demoiselles Tatin that they made at their hotel opposite the station in Lamotte-Beuvron, in the Sologne. So they all got into the car and set off to find out exactly what the tart was. Quite a journey from Giverny. Presumably they went through the Beauce and crossed the Loire at Orléans. In the book there's a photograph that shows Monet sitting on the porch of the Hôtel Tatin et Terminus. His sturdy step-grandchild, Lily Butler, stands on the steps in a coat with puff sleeves. Both look remarkably well fed.

The hotel is still there, with its porch. So is the stove that the tart was cooked on. A beautiful blue-and-white tiled stove, of a more old-fashioned design than the splendid stove in Monet's kitchen at Giverny, and it had no baking ovens, only holes in the top for burning charcoal, covered with metal lids. No doubt large joints of meat and game were cooked on spits in front of the fire. All baking that could not be sent out to the baker's oven, had to be contrived on top of the fierce heat of the charcoal. One way out was to place the food on a grid over a burner, and then cover the whole thing with a cone-shaped metal dome, called a country oven. If you have ever tried cooking a tart in a tin scout oven, over a fire or camping gas cooker, you will instantly understand the main snag: the heat from below burns the pastry before the filling on top is ready. This has happened to me several times with tarts, but I never arrived at the Tatin sisters' solution – they turned the snag to advantage, by putting apples, butter and sugar in the bottom of the tin, intending that they should caramelise, while the pastry on top cooked more slowly. To serve, they turned the whole thing out on to a dish, to show the rich brown syrupy apples. A simple, brilliant idea.

Nevertheless, it is difficult to understand how the tart became so famous; Lamotte-Beuvron is buried in the Sologne, a district of woods and meres. It had a canal and a fairly important main road, but I suspect the success of the tart was due to the arrival of the railway. This meant that wealthy Parisians could easily come down for a few days' shooting in the woods which are one of the richest areas of France for game. They built monstrous and showy houses, which were much occupied in the autumn and New Year. Today, acres and acres are firmly wired off from public gaze, though one may sometimes catch a glimpse of a mere, and flight a thousand wild duck from its reedy edges. Restaurants of high quality flourish in the autumn, with sociable parties from the shooting boxes, and extra guests. And the game season is also the apple season, with the *reinette d'Orléans* as the major local variety.

We went to eat at the Hôtel Tatin, watched coldly by the stuffed deer and other trophies of the chase. I was surprised by the *tarte Tatin*, by its darkly caramelised appearance, its air of rusticity; it was a completely different thing from the elegantly arranged, softly golden tarts of the smart French pâtissiers. Considering the district, considering its history, I came to see that this is what I should have expected. The only nearly similar version I have eaten, was served at Chez Ribe, near the Paris Hilton; it was fairly dark, and a note of country vigour had been added with a little vinegar (rather as we use vinegar in this country when making certain kinds of toffee).

In the end, there are no doubt as many versions as there are cooks, but I like to know how things are at the source. To be honest, we did not care so very much for the almost burnt version from Lamotte-Beuvron. I make a *tarte* that is somewhere between the two, reflecting presumably the moderated rurality in which most country-dwellers now live, whether in England or France.

The first thing to consider is the mould. It must be metal and a good 2–3 cm (1¼ inches) deep. A straight-sided *moule à manquer* is ideal. I have even used a heavy sauté pan which has a handle tough enough to withstand high oven temperatures: but the handle makes the tart difficult to turn out. You could quite well use a cake tin, so long as it was not too deep. The ingredients for a 22–25 cm (9–10 inches) tin are as follows:

> *60 g (2 oz) butter*
> *2 teaspoons vinegar (optional)*
> *5 heaped tablespoons caster sugar*
> *8 large Reinettes or Cox's Orange Pippins*
> *shortcrust made with 125 g (4 oz) flour*

Spread the butter over the base of the tin, then add the vinegar if you like and the sugar, shaking it evenly. Set the tin over a moderate heat until the mixture begins to caramelise to a pale golden brown; keep stirring. You can let the caramel turn to a toffee hardness and colour, because the juices from the apple will liquefy it to the right consistency later.

Remove the tin from the stove, and allow it to cool while you peel, core and slice the apples. It is up to you whether you arrange an elegant bottom layer of concentric circles. I don't. I just put them in evenly in a rough kind of way. At La Varenne cookery school in Paris, they peel, core and halve the apples, and then arrange these halves on their sides, as it were, with the cored side of one half pressed against the rounded outer curve of the next half. The apples at Lamotte-Beuvron were higgledy-piggledy.

It is quite wise to attend carefully to the first layer, making it more or less even. Then put in the rest of the apple as you like, aiming for a depth of roughly 2 cm ($\frac{3}{4}$ inch). Firm eating apples will not greatly subside, neither will they turn to a snowy pulp, but you will achieve a better result if you aim at an even depth without too many gaps.

Roll out the pastry, and cut a circle to fit closely *inside* the tin. Prick it if you like, but it does not much matter. Fit it in place, pressing it down lightly on the apples. Put the tart in the oven at mark 8, 230° (450°) for upwards of half an hour, according to how brown you want the final result to be.

Remove it from the oven, run a knife round the edge of the tin, and invert the whole thing on to a heavy serving dish. A certain amount of juice may flow, so do this quickly. Serve with plenty of cream.

Note When good eating apples run out, Golden Delicious may be substituted. They do not produce so rich and fragrant a result as Reinette or Cox's, but are quite satisfactory.

GLACE ALHAMBRA

This summery ice-cream was served at the November wedding breakfast of one of Monet's step-daughters, Germaine Hoschedé, when she married the Monaco lawyer Albert Salerou in 1902.

> *300 ml (10 fl oz) each double cream and milk, or 600*
> *ml (1 pt) single or whipping cream*
> *1 vanilla pod, split lengthwise*
> *5 egg yolks, beaten*
> *sugar*
> *300 g (10 oz) strawberries, frozen ones can be used*
> *3 tablespoons Kummel or gin and a teaspoon of aniseed*
> *300 ml (10 fl oz) whipping or double cream*

Bring cream and milk, or the 600 ml of single or whipping cream to the boil with the vanilla pod. Cover, remove from the heat and leave 20 minutes, or so. Heat again to boiling point, and pour on to the yolks. Add 2 heaped tablespoons of sugar and return to the heat, stirring until the custard is thick – it must not boil. The inside of the vanilla pod will fleck the mixture with tiny dark bits – do not worry. Add more sugar to taste. Cool rapidly by setting the base of the pan in a bowl of iced water.

Take a charlotte or other metal mould of 1¼ litres (generous 2 pt) capacity. Strain in the custard and freeze at as low a temperature as possible. When the sides are firm, smooth the soft centre ice up the walls of the mould so that it is completely lined with ice cream. Set a bowl in the centre if you like, to help the shape. Check on the mixture from time to time, smoothing and tidying the shape with the back of a spoon, and levelling the ice cream wall at the top.

Meanwhile mash the strawberries with the alcohol. If you are using aniseed, grind them with a little sugar in an electric mill, then use it to flavour the strawberry mash, adding more sugar to taste. Do not make this mixture too fine. Whip the remaining cream, fold in the strawberries when the lined mould is ready, and pour the strawberry cream into the cavity. Freeze a further three hours.

To turn out, dip a knife in boiling water, quickly dry it and run it round the ice, inside the mould. Invert the whole thing on to a serving plate. Lay a cloth on top, wrung out in very hot water. Within seconds you should be able to shake the ice free. If you are not successful, repeat the hot cloth treatment. Smooth over the ice, if it has melted messily.

Decorate with extra strawberries, or some toasted almonds, or piped whipped cream. Serve with almond biscuits.

The other dessert was Nelusko, a kind of *petits fours* that is extremely difficult to make successfully: it consists of a stoned cherry that has been preserved in brandy, the cavity is filled with pipped redcurrants from Bar-le-Duc redcurrant jam, then the whole thing is dipped in warmed fondant icing flavoured with some of the cherry brandy. The snag, as *Larousse Gastronomique* points out, is that neluskos always ooze a certain amount of juice – messy eating.

Marcel Proust (1871–1922)

I have always maintained a reserve towards the famous mixture of lime tea and madeleine. Proust, after all, did not claim much for it as food. It acted as a trigger precisely because he had forgotten it. As an adult he did not bother with tea, so that when he came in cold and depressed one day, and his mother offered him tea and a madeleine, he at first refused, then took it, and without thinking raised a spoonful of madeleine crumbs soaked in tea to his lips. As he tasted it, as it 'touched my palate . . . a shudder ran through my whole body, and I stopped, intent upon the extraordinary changes that were taking place. An exquisite pleasure had invaded my senses, but individual, detached, with no suggestion of its origin. . . . I put down my cup and examine my own mind. . . . What an abyss of uncertainty whenever the mind feels that some part of it has strayed beyond its own borders.' So he bullied his memory, tried a few more spoonfuls of madeleine and tea without success, fought a natural laziness to step back from the abyss and leave undisturbed 'the vast structure of recollection'.

'And suddenly the memory returns. The taste was that of the little crumb of madeleine which on Sunday mornings at Combray . . . my aunt Léonie used to give me, dipping it first in her own cup of real or of lime-flower tea.' The slow search, the painful search for time past had begun.*

Reserve seemed the proper attitude for a respectful reader. But one winter the dried flowers from our lime tree in France smelled more fragrant than usual (we sit under the tree every day in summer, looking down from the cliff to the Loir below, which is also Proust's Loir running through his family's town of Illiers, that became Combray). They tempted me to make madeleines to have with lime tea in the evening. Hoping for nothing, sceptical even, we were surprised by the gentle delicacy they made together.

We talked of a visit many years ago to the house at Illiers. It had been got up as a shrine, smelling of new paint, a shell of vacancy

* Most quotations in this chapter come from *A la recherche du temps perdu.*

and loss. 'In the empty kitchen a terrine in the shape of a rabbit might have held the meats potted by Françoise. The emptiness upstairs might have been the theatre and have known the drama of the child's going to bed; the door knob in one room or another might have taken around its slope the coloured Merovingian images from the child's magic lantern.' It might, but it was no longer the real thing. Not even the tinkle of the garden bell announcing Swann's arrival was real. In the church that smelt of rose-scented peonies – we were too late for hawthorn flowers – we felt closer to Proust.

Closer still, for a few moments, when we visited friends recently at midday, on the other side of the Loir. As we drank coffee in the *salon*, the meal over, our host said, 'Did you know that Proust sometimes sat here in this room? He came over from Courtanvaux with Robert de Montesquiou' – the chief model for Charlus – 'and wrote to my great-grandmother on mauve paper in gold ink.'

I reflect that there was nothing mauve and gold about Proust's enjoyment of food, even if in later life he savoured it only in memory. He loved the good, simple dishes that characterise the Loir valley, where the favourite summer entertainment is a meal under the trees. The photograph on p. 226 shows Proust and some of his friends behind a long table out of doors. Everyone smiles and poses. Glasses and plates have not been cleared away. Proust in a boater hands a pear, I think to his mother. His father, the distinguished doctor, Professor Adrien Proust, who had succeeded in freeing Europe from cholera, leans both hands on his stick, and looks calmly at the camera from under a black bowler hat. Louis Ganderax, of the *Revue de Paris*, stands behind him.

It might be a scene from Illiers-Combray, when the holidays of May and June were ruled by Aunt Léonie from her bed upstairs, and by her energetic deputy Françoise whose particular kingdom was the kitchen and dining-room. In her white starched bonnet, she was an awesome rather than a loveable figure, and valued for her unforgettable meals of pure and seasonal quality.

That part of France is not especially famous for its food, any more than it is for its landscape. It takes time, and – or so I like to think – a discernment that comes only from experience, to perceive the unsensational harmony of both. Everyone visits Chartres. They rush in, then away, as if the cathedral lay in a desert. Few understand that the windows keep the memory of brilliant corn weeds now banished from the plain of the Beauce by fertilisers – cornflower blue, poppy red, corn marigold, corn cockle purple. Or that the two spires are the summation of the Beauce, of its rich flatness broken elsewhere by smaller spires, a flatness that suddenly drops into small delightful valleys, before it suddenly and finally tips over into the wider valley of the Loir. Here unvisited small towns, as Illiers once was, present opportunities for fine eating in their markets, cooked pork shops, cake shops and bakeries.

From this unflashy ground, Proust was well able to appreciate the *nouvelle cuisine* of his day; if one can give a date for such changes in cookery, which in truth are made gradually, I suppose it would have to be 1883 when Auguste Escoffier and César Ritz started their partnership at Monaco at the Grand Hotel. They worked to combine luxury, simplicity and elegance of food and setting. For the first time, dining out became possible for women of the upper classes and bourgeoisie, dining out in public that is. Dishes, especially sweet ones, were named after them by Escoffier so that his *Art Culinaire* index reads like a register of the Belle Époque. Ritz saw to it that lighting, a civilised sense of ease and shine in the decor and service, flattered their appearance.

Concentration on quality rather than quantity was an inevitable result of the new service *à la russe*, that became the norm with Urbain Dubois and Escoffier (p. 184). When course succeeded course, with only a choice between two dishes at each one, any lack in the basic ingredients or the skill of the chefs was far more noticeable than it had been under the old buffet style of service.

After the success of the Savoy and Carlton Hotel restaurants in London, Escoffier and Ritz turned towards Paris. In 1896, in good time for the great exhibition planned for 1900, the Ritz Hotel opened in the Place Vendôme. Proust was at the opening gala dinner. He had written little but, since his meeting with Robert de Montesquiou three years earlier, he had become more and more part of that Parisian society of intellect, wealth and aristrocracy which he had despaired of encountering when he had first glimpsed it as a child at Illiers.

At his own dinner parties, he adopted the delightful habit of moving round the table with each course, to make sure none of his guests should feel neglected by the host. Towards the end of his life, during the last eight years when he became almost a voluntary prisoner in his cork-lined room, his last housekeeper, Céleste Albaret, has recorded how carefully he chose the wines for the single guest he occasionally invited to dinner. By that time, he was living on little more than a litre of milk a day, flavoured with coffee. Céleste knew he had been a great gourmet from his precise tastes, and from the way he talked about the food of his childhood, but by then he could only enjoy it in his memory, *'gourmand de ses souvenirs'*.

ASPARAGUS

As summer came along at Combray, shelled peas would be ranged in platoons of different sizes by the little kitchen maid, for exact cooking so that the largest should be as tender as the tiny ones. The next job for 'poor Giotto's Charity, as Swann had named her' was the asparagus which lay beside her in a basket. She sat with 'a mournful air, as though all the sorrows of the world were heaped upon her; and the light crowns of azure which capped the asparagus shoots above their pink jackets would be finely and separately outlined, star by star, as in Giotto's fresco are the flowers banded about the brows, or patterning the basket of his Virtue at Padua'.

No wonder she looked so wretched. She had an allergy to asparagus, and Françoise was making her clean it every day, and putting asparagus into every dish she could think of, hoping to get rid of her. In this she succeeded, though not until after the girl had had her baby.

All this Proust discovered later. At the time he only saw their rainbow-loveliness 'tinged with ultra-marine and rosy pink which ran from their heads, finely stipped in mauve and azure, through a series of imperceptible changes to their white feet, still stained a little by the soil of their garden-bed'.

Although asparagus in France, is, as I have said in the Monet chapter on p. 206, different from ours, both are cooked and served in the same way, with melted butter or an hollandaise or mousseline sauce. Or cold with vinaigrette.

If you are concerned to stretch a small quantity, combine them with another of Proust's favourite things, scrambled eggs. And remember Escoffier's tip – when you beat the eggs, spear a clove of garlic on the end of your knife or fork – it gives them a most delicately appetising flavour.

SOLE MEUNIÈRE AUX POIREAUX
SOLE FRIED IN BUTTER WITH LEEKS

Sole is everyone's favourite fish – or so you will conclude from this book – and the *meunière* method is one of the best ways of cooking it. This is what Proust liked. Indeed fried sole was the only dish he ever finished, during the last years of his life.

Proust: My dear Céleste, I think I could manage a fried sole. How quickly do you think I could have one, if it's not too much trouble?
Céleste: Straightaway, Monsieur.
Proust: How kind you are, Céleste.

And good, kind, patient Céleste would rush out to a fishmonger's nearby in the place Saint-Augustin, run back with the sole, cook it and present it to Proust on a clean, doubled napkin – to soak up any fat that might remain – with four lemon halves, one at each napkin corner.

Had Proust been alive today, and a young man, he would I think have appreciated a new French version of *sole meunière*, a version with lightly cooked, shredded leeks, not too many, just enough to make the fish even more appetising than usual. The two secrets are clarified butter and finely cut leek. Other fish can be substituted, obviously other flat fish, from turbot down to plaice, or small filleted whiting.

1 packet butter
1½ kilos (3 lb) skinned sole, preferably two large ones, or
*   2 kilos (4 lb) other fish*
seasoned flour
Cayenne pepper
4 medium leeks, trimmed to their white stalks
salt
lemon quarters (optional)

Cut up the butter into a small pan. Bring it slowly to the boil, stirring as it melts. When it has separated into golden oil and white crust, strain it through damp muslin into two fish pans, large enough to accommodate one sole each, with room to spare.

Turn the fish in seasoned flour, to which you have added Cayenne according to taste: I add enough just to make the flour slightly pink. Heat the pans, shake any surplus flour from the fish, and put in to cook – not too fast. After 3–4 minutes, according to the thickness of the fish, see if it is nicely browned underneath. Turn it over, if so, otherwise leave a little longer.

As it cooks, slice the leeks thinly so that they tumble into green and white shreds.

Add the leeks to the turned fish, and stir them about carefully so that they cook lightly in the butter. They should not entirely lose their crispness, neither should they brown – a few patches of light gold are all right, but no more. Salt the leeks, and leave them in the pan for a minute as you remove the sole to its warmed serving dish. Remove the leeks with a slotted spoon and put them round the sole in little piles or in a circle. Arrange the lemon quarters at intervals among the leeks. Serve immediately with bread, and a dry white wine.

Note Unfortunately the new French cookery depends for its light effect on brief cooking and prompt service. Easy to manage if you have help in the kitchen that you can trust, or if you always eat in the kitchen and do not mind leaving the table to cook between courses. If your problem is the lack of a second fish pan, remember that the sole will survive waiting around better than the leek shreds. Brown the sole in turn, using half the butter, over a slightly higher heat (golden-brown, not black-brown), and put them on their dish in the oven set at mark 2, 150° (300°) to complete their cooking while you cook the leeks in their juices, refreshed with the remaining butter. If something is served before the sole, this really must be done between courses.

BARBUE RADZIWILL
BRILL RADZIWILL

'Upon the permanent foundation of eggs, cutlets, potatoes, preserves, biscuits . . . Françoise would add as the labour of fields and orchards, the harvest of the tides, the luck of the markets, the kindness of neighbours, and her own genius might provide' – a turkey perhaps, or brill 'because the fishwoman had guaranteed its freshness.' Here is a good recipe for brill from a book published in Paris when Proust was fourteen: it can be adapted to other flat fish, chicken halibut or chicken turbot, Dover, or Torbay sole.

I do not know which Radziwill was honoured in this way (there were a lot of them, scattered across Europe). Perhaps it was Prince Constantin, who owned the château at Ermenonville with its famous eighteenth-century garden, where Rousseau was buried on an island in the lake. Much of the Prince de Guermantes was drawn from him. Léon, his son, the contemporary and friend of Proust, and one of the originals for Saint-Loup, would have been too young. So would his distant cousin, Michel, who married Proust's childhood love, Marie de Bernadaky from whom so much of Gilberte was taken.

2 kilos (4 lb) brill, trimmed
100 g (3½ oz) butter
1 heaped tablespoon finely chopped onion
bouquet garni, *salt, pepper*
300 ml (½ pt) béchamel sauce
2–3 tablespoons grated Parmesan
1 heaped tablespoon breadcrumbs

Cut down the centre of the dark-skinned side of the fish, and cut the fillets away from the bone to make a pocket. Push in a quarter of the butter. Scatter a flameproof dish with the onion, *bouquet* and seasoning. Place brill on top, cut side down. Spread a third of the remaining butter over the top. Pour a tumbler of water round the sides. Either put into the oven, mark 4–5, 180–190° (350–375°), until cooked, or cover and simmer on top of the stove. Transfer the cooked fish to a warm plate.

Reduce the cooking juices to a small amount of concentrated flavour, stir in the béchamel, then flavour to taste with 1–2 tablespoons of Parmesan, tasting as you go. Off the heat, whisk in the rest of the butter, and strain the sauce over the fish. Mix the last of the cheese with the crumbs, scatter on top of the fish and brown lightly under the grill.

ROAST CHICKEN

One morning Proust – or rather the Narrator as a child – took his usual pleasant way to the kitchen to see how lunch was coming along, and had a painful surprise. Françoise was on her own – the poor little maid, Giotto's Charity, was recovering upstairs from having a baby – and was trying to kill a chicken without much success. '"Filthy creature! Filthy creature!" she screamed with rage. It made the saintly kindness and unction of our servant rather less prominent than it would do next day at dinner when it made its appearance in a skin gold-embroidered like a chasuble, and its precious juice was poured out drop by drop as from a pyx. . . . I crept out of the kitchen and upstairs, trembling all over; I could have prayed, then, for the instant dismissal of Françoise. But who would have baked me such hot rolls, boiled me such fragrant coffee, and even – roasted me such chickens?' Well, yes.

Those chickens were undoubtedly fattened on maize, as they still are in those parts. It gives them an excellent flavour and a golden tinge. Françoise roasted them on a spit, which some people will be able to do, but one can manage a lot with our farm chickens even without a spit, to make them almost as succulent as hers.

Using a sharp knife, carefully raise the skin from the neck end of the chicken, and wriggle you fingers into the gap until the skin is free of the breast and the top of the legs. Mash about a third of a packet of butter with salt and pepper; add a shallot or tablespoon of onion and a large clove of garlic, chopped together to a pulp. Using a broad knife or your fingers, spread this butter between the skin and meat of the chicken.

Make a stuffing, by mixing the following together:

60 g (2 oz) dry white crumbs
2 tablespoons chopped parsley
pinch oregano, salt, pepper
grated rind of half a lemon
1 tablespoon lemon juice

60 g (2 oz) melted butter
1 egg

Place the stuffed bird on to a roasting rack in a pan and cook at mark 5, 190° (375°) for 15–20 minutes per half kilo or pound, plus 20 minutes. No need to baste, or turn the chicken about. Should the breast become brown too quickly, protect it with a butter paper.

Remove surplus fat from the pan juices, and boil them up with giblet stock and a glass of wine. Aim at a small quantity of concentrated juice. The French do not have our passion for jugs of gravy.

VEGETABLES

A couple might accompany the chicken – or the roast mutton and any other large pieces of meat. Cooked chicory, or spinach, and always mashed potato (though sometimes to make an exciting change, Tante Léonie would order boiled potatoes with béchamel sauce). Proust loved chips, though rather as a snack, and when he was hardly eating anything – towards the end of his life – would occasionally ask his housekeeper, Céleste, to make some for him. Like everything else, they had to be exactly to his taste, though in fact they could not compete with the way such dishes had tasted in the past. If he asked for something he remembered enjoying, he might take a couple of spoonfuls – that was all.

One vegetable of Françoise's kitchen that is no longer familiar to us is the cardoon, cardoon served with beef marrow sauce. If you grow such things, here is the recipe for the sauce, which can also be served with boiled celery or chicory:

100 g (3–4 oz) beef marrow
2 tablespoons butter
1 heaped tablespoon flour
4 tablespoons meat jelly, glaze or juice from roast meat
about ½ litre (¾ pt) beef, or other appropriate stock
· lemon juice, salt, pepper, parsley

Slice and poach the marrow for about 10 minutes in a very little water (or boil the bones, upright, as usual, and extract marrow when cooked). Make a sauce with the butter, flour, meat jelly etc, and stock. Boil down to a good consistency. Add lemon and seasonings, then the marrow to reheat, and finally the parsley. Pour over the cooked cardoon stalks.

BOEUF À LA MODE

À l'ombre de jeunes filles en fleur, the second part of Proust's novel, starts in comic irony, with dinner given by the parents to the old but still powerful ambassador, the Marquis de Norpois. The routine diplomatic charm is misunderstood, too much is hoped for – by the father anxious about his clever child's future, by the schoolboy son who longs for nothing but an invitation to Gilberte's house (and who understands to his amazement the emptiness of Monsieur de Norpois' mind). Social comedy against an excellent meal of *boeuf à la mode*, baked York ham, truffle and pineapple salad – the mother had counted greatly upon the salad, but the guest made no comment – and Nesselrode pudding (p. 246).

Françoise, in Paris now since Aunt Léonie's death, had been for two days in an 'effervescence of creation'. In honour of the distinguished visitor, she had herself gone to Les Halles 'to procure the best cuts of rumpsteak, shin of beef, calves'-feet, as Michelangelo passed eight months in the mountains of Carrara choosing the most perfect blocks of marble for the monument of Julius II'. Monsieur de Norpois was delighted with the cold beef spiced with carrots, which had 'made its appearance couched by the Michelangelo of our kitchen upon enormous crystals of jelly, like transparent blocks of quartz'. Though perhaps there was a hint that it was not quite the thing, when he added that he would like to have seen how the family Vatel would have tackled *boeuf Stroganoff*.

My own favourite piece of beef for *boeuf à la mode* is not easy to get outside Scotland, and I have to order it by special delivery post, then store it in the freezer: Charles MacSween & Son, 130 Bruntsfield Place, Edinburgh, supply it – plus superb Aberdeen Angus beef of all kinds, fruity and mealy puddings, haggises and so on. This special cut is the long lean muscle from the inside of the blade bone, known by many names, principally as the shoulder fillet, but also as the salmon cut or fish tail. I first saw it in our butcher's shop in France, and cannot understand why English butchers do not provide it. Pared of external fat, it is a beautiful looking piece of meat, which tastes especially good and carves beautifully. Alternatives are rump and silverside.

Another point to bear in mind is the weight of the meat. If you intend to serve the beef cold, then you will find that a piece weighing about 1¼–1½ kilos (2½–3 lb) trimmed weight, will do for 6–8 people depending on the rest of the meal. If you intend to eat the beef hot, you would be wise to buy from 2–3 kilos (4–6 lb), and then make a beef mould from the left-overs. The cooking time will not be much increased, as the piece of beef will be longer rather than thicker and it is thickness that decides the matter. If you possess a slow electric casserole cooker, it will produce a tender piece of beef, and you will have no worries about it cooking too fast.

> *piece shoulder fillet, rump or silverside*
> *250 g (8 oz) piece pork back fat, chilled*
> bouquet garni
> *2 chopped onions*
> *1 chopped celery stalk*
> *3 crushed cloves garlic*
> *4 tablespoons olive oil*
> *white wine*
> *2 pig's trotters or one calf's foot*
> *kilo (2 lb) carrots*
> *½ kilo (1 lb) sliced onions*
> *beef stock, barely salted*
> *250 g (8 oz) shin beef* (see *recipe*)
> *2 egg whites* (see *recipe*)

First lard the beef. Cut long strips of pork fat, push a lardoire with a u-shaped groove through the length of the piece, push a strip of fat into the groove and pull the lardoire back so that the fat is introduced into the meat. Repeat regularly. Not only will this help the tenderness, it also gives each slice an attractive appearance. I find that the small larding needles sold by kitchen shops are no good for big pieces of meat: they should only be used for poultry and small pieces of game and meat. Tie up the beef, if necessary.

Put it into a close-fitting bowl, with the *bouquet*, chopped onions and celery, garlic, oil and enough wine to cover. Put a piece of foil over the top and leave for a few hours to marinate, or in the refrigerator overnight.

Next cut the pork skin into squares about 3 cm (generous inch). Put them into a pan with the trotters or calf's foot, add enough cold water to cover and bring to the boil. Leave for 2 minutes, then drain and rinse under the cold tap.

Dice half the carrots. Put them into the base of a flame-proof casserole that is barely larger than the beef and trotters. Add the onions. Cover and put into a really hot oven, mark 7–8, 220–230° (425–450°) for half an hour; remove the lid and give them another 5 minutes. This 'pinches' the vegetables, making them slightly brown, and for a braised dish it works better than browning the vegetables in fat.

Remove the casserole and lower the oven temperature to mark 2, 160° (300°). Strain the marinade – remove the meat first – on to the carrots and onion, and scrape about with a wooden spoon to dislodge the brown bits. Place the beef, pork skin and trotters or foot into the pot. Add enough beef stock barely to cover. On top of the stove bring the whole thing to boiling point, put on the lid and transfer to the oven for about 3 hours – test with a skewer or small larding needle. Towards the end of cooking time, simmer the remaining carrots, neatly sliced, in a little extra beef stock. If you intend to serve the beef hot, you can also glaze a few onions and turnips to go with the carrots.

To serve hot: remove the beef to a dish, cut away the string, and keep it warm. Cut the meat neatly from the trotters or foot, and put with the pork skin, the freshly cooked carrots etc, around the meat. Strain the cooking liquor into a wide shallow pan. Degrease it, and boil steadily for 20–30 minutes. Remove scum and skin as they rise, until the sauce is reduced to a clear, syrupy glaze. Slice some of the meat, pour over the glaze and serve.

To serve cold: leave the beef to cool down in the pot for 3 hours. Take a little of the liquor, put it into the refrigerator and see how well it sets. If the jelly is weak, reduce the stock. If it is strong, you can proceed straightaway to clarifying it with shin of beef (not essential, but desirable to add flavour and colour) and egg whites.

Strain the liquor through a damp double muslin into a pan, and whisk in the 2 egg whites and the minced shin of beef. Continue whisking as the pan comes slowly to the boil. Boil for 10–15 minutes, until the white of egg and beef form a thick, unpleasantly grey layer with a spongy look. The scummy look comes from the impurities in the stock, which below this layer will be crystal clear. Pour it out gently through another clean piece of double muslin.

Put a thin layer of this clarified stock into the bowl or terrine in which you intend to mould the beef. Leave it to set in the refrigerator. When it is firm, arrange some of the separately cooked carrot slices on top. Gently pour a little stock round the slices, and transfer again to the fridge until the pieces are set in place. Cut away the string from the meat and put it into the bowl or basin on top of the carrots (keep the pork skin and pork trotter meat for a separate meal, heating them through and serving them with a sauce tartare, p. 120).

Arrange the rest of the sliced carrots round it and pour in the rest of the stock. Return to the refrigerator and leave to set firm – until next day if possible.

Turn out and serve with a salad. Or else follow Françoise's style, and separate the meat from the jelly when you turn the whole thing out: chop the jelly and carrots into large cubes and surround the beef with them. This is easier for carving, and easier for larger pieces of meat altogether.

Note The instructions above are based on Richard Olney's recipe for *boeuf à la mode*, in the Time-Life book *Beef and Veal*, in the Good Cook series. There are many versions, as you would expect for so classic a dish, but I find his the best.

RIZ À L'IMPÉRATRICE

As a child, Proust was already a lover of the theatre, 'a Platonic lover, of necessity, since my parents had not yet allowed me to enter one'. When they were living in a street near the Madeleine, he would study the playbills stuck on to the nearest Moriss column, imagining fantastic performances. At last his parents told him to choose between two plays. 'I had shewn myself such vivid, such compelling pictures of, on the one hand, a play of dazzling arrogance, and on the other a gentle, velvety play, that I was as little capable of deciding which play I should prefer to see as if, at the dinner-table, they had obliged me to choose between rice *à l'impératrice* and the famous cream of chocolate.' Anyone who feels an aversion to rice puddings, may be encouraged to try this one and think again.

> *125 g (4 oz) long grain rice*
> *600 ml (1 pt) milk*
> *half a vanilla pod*
> *4 egg yolks*
> *125 g (4 oz) sugar*
> *2 heaped teaspoons gelatine*
> *300 ml (½ pt) double cream*

Boil the rice in water for 3 minutes, then drain and rinse it under the cold tap. Return to the pan with half the milk, cover and simmer until very tender. Bring rest of the milk to the boil with the vanilla pod, then whisk into the yolks and the sugar. Pour back into the pan and stir over a lowish heat until the custard thickens (use a double boiler if you are not accustomed to making egg custards). Melt the gelatine in 2 tablespoons of hot water and add to the hot custard. Strain into a bowl, and add the cooked rice which will have absorbed all the milk. Cool. Whip cream and fold in. Turn into a lightly oiled mould. Chill, and serve with soft fruit or stewed pears that have been lightly poached in syrup (p. 245).

CRÈME AU CHOCOLAT
CHOCOLATE CREAM

When the main part of the meal was over, Françoise would bring in 'a work composed expressly for ourselves, but dedicated more particularly to my father, who had a fondness for such things, a cream of chocolate, inspired in the mind, created by the hand of Françoise'. It was as 'light and fleeting as an "occasional piece" of music, into which she had poured the whole of her talent. Anyone who refused to partake of it, saying: 'No, thank you, I have finished; I am not hungry' would at once have been lowered to the level of the Philistines. . . . To have left even the tiniest morsel in the dish would have shewn as much discourtesy as to rise and leave a concert hall while the "piece" was still being played, and under the composer's very eyes.'

The recipe that Françoise invented is lost for ever, but here is a light version of the favourite *mousse au chocolat*, by Édouard de Pomiane, who visited friends in that part of the world, or a little further to the west (and was often grateful for what it could still provide in the shortage of the last war).

180 g (6 oz) plain chocolate, bitter for preference
6 egg yolks
6 teaspoons sugar
125 ml (4 fl oz) double cream
6 egg whites

Break up the chocolate or grate coarsely into a pudding basin. Add 3 tablespoons water. Set over a pan of simmering water, and stir until the mixture is smooth and melted and fairly hot (though nowhere near boiling – if you overheat chocolate, it turns to mud). Remove the basin from the pan, and rapidly beat in the egg yolks and the sugar. Whisk the cream until thick, and stir it quickly into the cooled chocolate. Finally whisk the egg whites until stiff and fold them in with a metal spoon last of all. These last two operations should be done delicately, so that the cream will be as airy and light as possible. Divide between one large shallow dish, or eight glasses. Chill until set. Serve with plain or almond biscuits.

CREAM CHEESE WITH STRAWBERRIES

At Combray, the hawthorn. '"Just look at this pink one; isn't it pretty?" And it was indeed a hawthorn, but one whose flowers were pink, and lovelier even than the white . . . it was attired even more richly than the rest, for the flowers which clung to its branches, one above another, so thickly as to leave no part of the tree undecorated, like the tassels wreathed about the crook of a rococo shepherdess were every one of them "in colour" and consequently of a superior quality, by the aesthetic standards of Combray, to the "plain", if one was to judge by the scale of prices at the "stores" in the Square, or at Camus's, where the most expensive biscuits were those whose sugar was pink. And for my own part I set a higher value on cream cheese when it was pink, when I had been allowed to tinge it with crushed strawberries. And these flowers had chosen precisely the colour of some edible and delicious thing. . . .'

Even in that celebrated paean to the hawthorn – the flower of love from the porcelain shepherdesses of Chelsea or Meissen to Gilberte framed in an arch of pink hawthorn, imaging that unknown world of her existence which Proust thought never to penetrate – food has its place. I cannot think of a passage in our literature, English literature, where such a comparison is made. And so perfectly, so naturally. But then, he had Ronsard before him, another poet of the Loir, comparing the pale skin of his love's neck and breast to the cream cheese that they had brought to the meadows on its rush mat for their picnic.

And the best, richest cheese, especially the goat cheese after the kids have been born, comes in spring, at hawthorn time when you may see the pink may here and there in an otherwise creamy fall of flowers.

Proust had a passion for it, to the extent that his father warned him against eating too much, when he was grown up and not too healthy.

To get the cheese right, as close as can be to the dish that appears on every table in the Loir valley, you should buy an imported *fromage frais* (Jockey from France) or quark from Germany. English brand of curd and cream cheese are too much dried, the wrong texture. To half a kilo of this (1 lb) – assuming a family party – add a small fresh goat's cheese if possible; such things are easier to find now at a health food shop than they were even a year ago.

Whisk 150 ml (5 fl oz) of double cream, with 3 heaped tablespoons of caster or icing sugar. Fold into the cheese mixture, and add more sugar to taste. Icing sugar dissolves in more easily than caster or granulated.

If you want to make the whole thing lighter, and bulkier, whisk 1 or 2 egg whites until stiff, and fold in last of all. Turn into a large and beautiful bowl.

Serve with strawberries and sugar. Later in the year with raspberries, peaches and so on. In winter it can be eaten with homemade apricot or strawberry jam, the kind with big pieces of fruit in it.

There is always a biscuit of some kind to go with the cream cheese and fruit. *Tuiles amandes*, or tiny biscuits from the *pâtissier*, or sponge fingers of a kind superior to the normal brand of boudoir biscuits on sale, with their over-rigid shape are the most popular.

PITHIVIERS ALMOND CAKE

The other great dessert of the region is the famous almond cake from Pithiviers. Sometimes cream cheese is served with it, and well they go together. Years ago I bought one in Illiers, and a long loaf of bread shaped like an ear of corn in the *épi* style; and I have since wondered whether it was from these shops that Françoise had ordered her almond cake, or 'a fancy loaf, because it was our turn to "offer" the holy bread'. If you take a swing round from Chartres towards the east, rather than south-west to Illiers-Combray, you will find Pithiviers on the map. Its cake is unchanged after nearly two centuries at least. The town smells of honey on the Chartres side, from the factory where they make *pain d'épice*. In the centre, shops and restaurants try to rival Chartres, the capital of the great corn plain of the Beauce, with lark pâtés and pies. So expensive has a Pithiviers become, that we see it less frequently in the small Loir towns than we did when we first went to live there. Nowadays I make it at home in England. We eat it more often in Wiltshire than we can afford to do in the Loir valley.

½ kilo total weight (1 lb) puff pastry
beaten egg to glaze
icing sugar

FILLING:
125 g (4 oz) ground almonds
125 g (4 oz) caster sugar
60 g (2 oz) melted butter
2 large egg yolks
2 generous tablespoons double cream
2–3 tablespoons rum or brandy (or malt whisky)

Roll out half the pastry, and cut a circle about 25 cm (10 inches) in diameter. Place it on a moistened baking sheet. Brush a 2½ cm (1 inch) rim with beaten egg.

Mix the filling ingredients in the order given, to make a thick but not completely stiff paste. Put it on the pastry. Spread it almost to the rim. Roll out the other half of the pastry to a slightly larger circle, and place it on top, lining up the two edges and pressing gently but firmly all round the rim (the extra size of the top circle will be taken up by the mound of filling). Make a small central hole, knock up the edge so that it looks like the edge of a book with its leaves, and brush over with beaten egg. Leave 5 minutes.

Using a knife, nick the edge twelve times at regular intervals. This is easier to judge if you make the first two nicks opposite each other, then give the sheet a half turn, and make two more nicks, so that the whole thing is quartered; the other eight nicks can be judged perfectly after that. With your thumbs press in and upwards to form a petal effect at every nick, Tudor-rose style. Score light inner scallops with the point of a knife, being careful not to go right through the pastry. Then score curving lines from the central hole to the scallops to make a swirling design.

Bake for 15 minutes at mark 8, 230° (450°). Check to see how the pastry is colouring, and leave the temperature as it is unless the brown is already pronounced, for a further 15 minutes. Or else lower the temperature to mark 6, 200° (400°).

Remove the Pithiviers, raise the heat again to mark 8 if necessary. Spread out some newspaper on the table, put the baking sheet on top and dredge the cake with icing sugar. Try not to make a very thick layer, and confine it to the cake if you can (easier said than done). Return it to the oven for the sugar to melt to a rich brown shiny glaze. Open the door frequently to see how it is going. If there are runnels of white where you scored the pastry, it does not matter, as long as the main effect is dark and glassy and rich. Serve warm.

The cake can be made in advance and reheated.

POIRES BOURDALOUE

A classic dish of fine flavour and straightforward ingredients. It can look unimpressive, but to eat, it is a delight. Céleste Albaret would sometimes bring in a *poire Bourdaloue* from a restaurant nearby, hoping Proust would try to eat this favourite dish of his early days. But no, he would take a couple of spoonfuls and that was that.

Why Bourdaloue? I do not know. Bourdaloue was one of the greatest of seventeenth-century preachers, but he went on for so long that the ladies of the court became uncomfortable before he had finished. Prudently they equipped themselves, or so it is said, with flowery pots of a waisted, pear- or kidney-shaped design, that could be discreetly used. These pots became known as Bourdaloues (Madame de Sévigné had an especially pretty one; it's on show at her much loved home, Les Rochers, in Brittany).

This brings us no nearer the answer, unfortunately. Let us return to the ingredients – the choice of macaroons needs care, as often these days bought ones consist of ground rice or something of the kind and almond essence: the best solution is those tiny macaroons imported from France, under the BN label. They are in any case a useful store-cupboard item. For six to eight people, you will need:

> *6–8 fine ripe dessert pears*
> *lemon juice*
> *375 g (12 oz) sugar*
> *vanilla pod*
> *sweet shortcrust flan case, 22–25 cm (9–10 inches),*
> *   baked blind*
> *375 ml (12 fl oz) milk*
> *75 g (2½ oz) caster sugar*
> *1 large egg*
> *3 large egg yolks*
> *50 g (scant 2 oz) flour*
> *2 heaped tablespoons macaroon crumbs*
> *60 g (2 oz) lightly salted or unsalted butter*

Peel, core and halve the pears, and rub them over with lemon juice to prevent discoloration and enhance their flavour. Stir the sugar into 600 ml (1 pt) water, and when it has dissolved, allow it to boil, then simmer for 4 minutes with the vanilla pod. Slip in the pear halves, and simmer until they are tender. Remove, drain and keep warm in the oven, set at mark 2, 150° (300°); at the same time put in the pastry case to heat through.

Make a frangipan cream. Extract the vanilla pod from the pear syrup and bring it to the boil slowly with the milk. Strain on to the caster sugar, egg, yolks and flour that have been well beaten together. Whisk as you do this, to avoid lumps. Tip back into the pan, and stir over a moderate heat for the custard to thicken. It should boil very gently indeed, but only for a minute or two (the flour prevents the eggs curdling disastrously; should the mixture look slightly lumpy, blend it in the liquidiser and it will smooth out). Keep stirring. Remove from the heat and add half the macaroon crumbs and just over half the butter. Put a layer into the pastry case, arrange the pears on top, and cover with the remaining frangipan.

Scatter the last of the macaroon crumbs over the top, and sprinkle with the last of the butter which you have melted. Place under a hot grill to glaze and brown slightly. Serve at once with whipped cream.

Variations 1) Cook the pears and frangipan in advance, as well as the pastry. Assemble just before the meal, leave in the low oven to reheat and glaze at the last minute.
2) Omit the pastry case, and prepare the dish in an attractive but grill-proof shallow pot.
3) To make a more elaborate looking dish, for a larger number of people, increase the number of pears appropriately and arrange them; when cooked, on a rather thicker bed of frangipan cream; omit the top layer of cream and the glaze, but decorate by brushing the pears over with the much reduced syrup they were cooked in, and distributing angelica leaves, lightly toasted split almonds and a few glacé cherries in between them.

NESSELRODE PUDDING

An iced pudding flavoured with chestnuts and dried fruit was invented by Monsieur Mony, chef for many years to the Russian diplomat, Count Nesselrode, in Paris. He passed the recipe on to Jules Gouffé who published it in his *Livre de Cuisine* of 1867. Glacé fruit and peel were a further embellishment to the Nesselrode by the time Proust was old enough to notice such things.

1 tablespoon sugar
60 g (2 oz) mixed currants and raisins
*60 g (2 oz) mixed glacé fruits, angelica, candied orange
  peel*
Maraschino liqueur (or Madeira, Marsala etc)
300 ml (10 fl oz) single cream
vanilla pod
4 large egg yolks
*125 g (4 oz) sweetened chestnut purée, or unsweetened
  with vanilla sugar to taste*
300 ml (10 fl oz) double cream
marrons glacés and whipped cream (optional; see recipe)

Bring the sugar to the boil with 3 tablespoons of hot water and
simmer the dried fruit in this syrup for a minute. Remove from the
heat and leave to cool. Put into a basin with the chopped glacé
fruits etc, and add enough Maraschino to cover. Leave several
hours or overnight.

Bring single cream to the boil slowly with the vanilla pod, and
pour on to the beaten egg yolks, whisking. Return to the pan and
cook slowly without allowing the custard to boil, until it thickens.
Cool slightly, then strain on to the fruits, and add the chestnut
purée (it will mix in more easily if the custard is still tepid). Whip
the double cream, fold into the chestnut mixture, and freeze in the
usual way at the lowest possible temperature.

Turn out and decorate with the marrons glacés and whipped
cream, if you like: Monsieur Mony served a cream and egg custard,
chilled and flavoured with Maraschino, but the habit of serving a
custard sauce with ices is not popular any more.

Note Rhapsodizing about ice-creams in *La Prisonnière*, Albertine
mentions chocolate and lemon ices, also – see pp. 39, 105, 223 of
this book – raspberry, vanilla and strawberry.

MADELEINES AND LIME TEA

Madeleines, said to have first been made in Lorraine at Com-
mercy, are plump little cakes that look 'as though they had been
moulded in the fluted scallop of a pilgrim's shell'. Special tins are

needed, which not only shape the base of the cakes in the characteristic way, but cause the mixture to rise into a central dome. If
you use ordinary bun tins, madeleines will look as gently curved as
any other small plain cake. It also follows that you can bake a
variety of mixtures in the tin and achieve the same effect: I sometimes feel that the many brands of madeleines on sale in France in
plastic bags – some of quite good quality – have been made from an
easier pound-cake mixture (4 oz each of butter, sugar, self-raising
flour, eggs – i.e. 2 eggs). Indeed, if you flavour this with orange-
flower water, you can get a good result, although the following is
closer to the real thing:

> scant 100 g (3 oz) butter
> 125 g (4 oz) caster sugar
> 3 large eggs
> 120 g (4 oz scant) self-raising flour
> 1 tablespoon orange-flower water (or milk)

Cream butter, add sugar, and cream again. Beat in eggs one at a
time, alternating with the flour. Stir in the orange-flower water. Fill
buttered and floured tins to their rim, then bake until golden
brown at mark 7, 220° (425°). About 10–15 minutes.

Lime tea is made from dried lime blossoms. Every year people
pick the flowers on a warm day at the height of their scent, and
spread them out on newspapers in a dry place until they are brittle.
Store in plastic bags if you are confident that all the moisture is
gone, or in brown paper bags; close them well. When you want to
make the *tisane*, or lime tea, remove enough dried flowers to fill a
large stoneware jug; don't ram them in, just put in enough to fill
the jug lightly. Pour on boiling water almost to the top, and leave to
infuse for about 5 minutes. Strain this *tisane* into a warmed jug, and
serve with madeleines. A soothing end to a Proustian evening, or a
pleasant tea in winter time. Health food shops and delicatessens
often sell packages of lime tea from France. They will be labelled
tisane, with *tilleul* underneath, meaning lime, as opposed, say, to
mint or vervain.

GENERAL INDEX

INDEX OF RECIPES